WAY TO GO, SMITH!

ALSO BY BOB SMITH

Growing Up Gay

Openly Bob

WAY TO GO, SMITH!

BOB SMITH

ROB WEISBACH BOOKS
William Morrow and Company, Inc. New York

Published by Rob Weisbach Books
An Imprint of William Morrow and Company, Inc.
1350 Avenue of the Americas
New York, N.Y. 10019

Library of Congress Cataloging-in-Publication Data

Smith, Bob
Way to go, Smith! / Bob Smith.
p. cm.
ISBN 0-688-16287-8
1. Gay men. 2. Homosexuality, Male. 3. Gays—Identity. I. Title.
HQ76.S58 1999
306.76'62—dc21
99-045710

Printed in the United States of America

First Edition

1 2 3 4 5 6 7 8 9 10

BOOK DESIGN BY RICHARD ORIOLO

www.robweisbachbooks.com

For my sister, Carol

Contents

Wolf Whistling in the Dark 1

Is He Wearing Hai Karate? 60

Way to Go, Smith! 89

To Grandmother's House We Go 106

My Pen Pal 133

Our Fathers 164

I'm Just a Love Machine 196

War and Piece of Ass 238

Acknowledgments 285

WAY TO GO, SMITH!

Wolf Whistling in the Dark

The mutual actions of two bodies upon each other are always equal, and directed to contrary parts.
—*Principia Mathematica*, Laws of Motion, Sir Isaac Newton.

TOM MOVED out in December. When I made spaghetti for the first time after he left, I discovered that he had taken the large metal serving spoon and had left me with the large metal slotted serving spoon. Smiling at his attempt to be scrupulously fair, I asked myself, *Why did he split up the set?* Then my smile faded as I fruitlessly searched in the drawer for a ladle. Feeling slightly annoyed I thought, *But he took the better spoon. He took the all-purpose spoon. How am I supposed to use a slotted spoon with spaghetti sauce?*

After finding a wooden spoon, I reached for the salt, overcome by the fear that I would find it gone and the pepper shaker in tears. I envisioned Tom gathering our belongings together and then painstakingly dividing the coupled possessions as he prepared to move out. As the

TV and VCR begged us to reconsider, Tom would have ignored their cries of protest while separating the oil cruet from the vinegar cruet. When a childless couple divorces, it's always the possessions that suffer the most.

If I had called him on it, Tom would have reminded me, "Bob, I asked you about the kitchen stuff and you told me to divide everything fairly. You didn't want to be bothered—you were too busy writing. You left it all up to me." Tom was right. I hate to be bothered. At times I'm a small unfriendly nation, a principality smaller than Monaco, that takes inspiration from the early flags of the American colonists which featured a rattlesnake and the motto *Don't Tread on Me.* The national emblem of my country is a squashed mosquito and my motto is *Don't Bother Me.*

In my search for a ladle I was pleased to find that Tom had taken the spaghetti tweezer, a one-piece aluminum serving utensil with two long arms that ends in spatulate hands with stubby fingers. It looks like a prosthetic device for chefs who have lost an arm in a mincing accident. The spaghetti tweezer is just an overbred fork with the same drawbacks as an overbred dog or cat. It has a designer pedigree but is riddled with inherent flaws that made its upkeep as labor-intensive as owning an Irish setter with a leaky bladder.

Making excuses for the spaghetti tweezer as if it was a beloved pet, Tom would admit. "Bob, you just have to get the hang of it." To which I would reply, "I don't want to have to read a manual to learn how to operate a simple kitchen utensil." Whenever Tom drained pasta in the sink, it would irritate me when he opened a drawer to look for the spaghetti tweezer, especially if he already had a fork in his hand. It was almost like the spaghetti tweezer needed to be taken out of its kennel for some exercise. Primarily I resented the spaghetti tweezer because while Tom got to play with it, I was the one who had to take care of it.

Since Tom likes to cook—an assumption the lazier person in the relationship always makes about the person who's fixing his dinner—he usually prepared dinner and I usually washed the dishes. Washing the spaghetti tweezer was a chore because the prongs become clotted with gunk that has the adhesive qualities of Super Glue.

I've never believed the idea that most gay men can be neatly divided into tops and bottoms in the bedroom, but Tom was definitely a kitchen top and I was clearly a kitchen bottom. (A porn movie for couples in long-term relationships should always include this line of dialogue: "I'm going to make a big mess and you're going to clean it up! Yeah, clean up my big mess!")

When Tom moved out, he departed with the replacement spaghetti tweezer, as I had deliberately thrown out the first one. We had fought about something that day; I honestly can't remember exactly what, or why I wanted to punish him, but I can vividly recall my retaliation. There are instances of my own adult immaturity that remain as clear in my mind as if they were significant childhood memories. Hours after our quarrel, as I scrubbed the starch-encrusted tines of the spaghetti tweezer, the scouring pad kept catching again and again. Suddenly I became incensed and tossed the stupid thing in the trash can. The vehemence of my reaction surprised me, but I've found that in the limbo dance of pettiness, I'm always able to go a little bit lower.

With my rage disposed of, I promptly forgot about the spaghetti tweezer until two weeks later, when Tom was making pasta and he asked, "Bob, have you seen the spaghetti tweezer?" I felt an abrupt spasm of guilt and lied. "No, I haven't seen it." Meanwhile the devil in me (many people don't know that Bob is short for Beelzebub) wanted to add, *Did you ask the garbageman? He might've seen it.*

It was deliciously gratifying that Tom also called his pasta tongs "the spaghetti tweezer" and his adoption of my insulting nickname for his cherished kitchen utensil was one of the things that I loved about him. Doubting my honesty, Tom asked again, "You're sure you haven't seen it?" Then he figured it out. "Did you throw it away?" Tom could always tell when I was lying—his drag name should be Polly Graph—and when he confronted me with the accusation, I confessed to the crime, which started a huge argument.

When I finally sat down to eat my bowl of spaghetti, the first I had prepared for myself in a long time, I thought, *How pathetic. I'm still fighting with Tom and he's not in the apartment. He's not even in the relationship.* I saw myself becoming an old man who constantly mutters to himself in public. Now, whenever I see an old man talking to himself, I assume that he's probably still bickering with an ex who moved out years ago, taking with him a significant piece of silverware.

Other people's emotions are like your friends' mothers. They're easier to enjoy than your own mother because you don't have to deal with them all the time. One of the most difficult parts of breaking up with Tom was having to disclose the news to my mother. I kept putting it off because in some ways it felt like coming out to her all over again, as if I was resuming the conversation, after more than fifteen years, by adding a twist to my previous declaration, "Mom, about the gay thing . . . well, since the last time we spoke, I've learned that I'm not very good at it." Knowing my mother, I was afraid that her response would be, "Well, Bob, if you're not very good at it, why do you keep trying? No one's forcing you to do it."

In the end I never had to tell her. My sister, Carol, decided to give her the lowdown after it began to appear that I might never do it myself. Immediately afterward, Carol called me. She said, "Bob, I finally told Mom about you and Tom. She was talking about maybe visiting you two next month and she needed to know. I hope you're not mad."

I felt immensely relieved. "No. I'm glad you told her," I said, then, curious, added, "So what was Mom's reaction?"

Carol laughed. "The first thing she said was, 'Oh, that's terrible about Bob and Tom. What's Bob going to do without his Tom?' Then she said, 'And the neighbors were just getting used to the idea of me talking about Bob having a boyfriend. I don't think they're going to like me talking about him having several boyfriends.' "

I said, "The good news is that this will take some of the pressure off you for being divorced and remarried."

"Right. Now Mom can complain to you, 'Bob, what am I going to tell the girls in Card Club? None of *their* gay sons are divorced.' "

"Yeah, and when I tell her, 'Mom, none of the girls in Card Club *has* a gay son,' she'll say, 'Bob, that's not the point!' "

Carol had a suggestion. "We need to try to convince Mom that having more than one husband and one boyfriend isn't a bad thing. Then the next time she goes shopping with Mary Lou and she starts bragging about her kids' happy marriages, Mom can say, 'So what if my kids are divorced! At least Carol was popular enough to get another husband! And Bob will too. Mary Lou, your kids are a mess. None of *them* could get a second man.' "

Having exhausted our fantasies of our mother's behavior, Carol became serious. "How are you doing?"

"Not too good but I'm all right. I'm busy, which helps."

"Well, Mark and I are here if you need anything. You know that." Carol ended the telephone call with, "You know that Mom will be calling you right away to get the scoop. She'll want to know the whole story."

A few hours later my mother called and said straight out, "All right. What happened?" Before I could respond, she blurted, "Was it another man?"

Boy, did that piss me off. My mother still didn't think I was capable of ruining a ten-year relationship all by myself. Tom and I have never felt that we needed outside help in ruining our relationship. When I told my mother, "No, it wasn't another man," she reminded me, "Well, you were away a lot last year. You know what they say, 'When the cat's away . . .' " It hadn't occurred to me that Tom might be cheating. But my mother has an instinctive knack for thinking the worst and then, like one of the "imagineers" at Disney World, bringing it to Animatronic life for the edification of her children.

As far as I knew, the only other man Tom had been seeing was a therapist, and while I had never met the guy I was unduly confident that I was cuter than him. On second thought, maybe that assumption was wrong. The therapist was gay, and for all I knew he was a hunk with washboard abs. I imagined Tom in a session with a studly therapist who listened to him while doing crunches on his "Ab-ench," an exercise cradle that turns men into babies who rock endlessly but never become sleepy. As I daydreamed my mother began to contemplate my revenge against Tom. She must have decided that I wasn't capable of doing that by myself either.

"I wish I hadn't sent him the money for that shirt," she declared lightheartedly. "Tell him now he can smoke all he wants." The last time my mother had visited us, Tom had mentioned a shirt that he liked and my mother offered to buy it for him if he quit smoking. Taking offense as well as pleasure at her remark, I said, "Mom, that's nice. Why don't you just send him a carton of cigarettes and get him hooked again?"

"I'm sick of being nice. In this family you're either in or you're out."

She made it sound as if being nice was a bad habit that she been meaning to quit for years. Becoming a widow had been a salutary experience for my mother. Having survived my father's death, she felt supremely confident that she could handle the loss of the rest of her family and still feel chipper enough to go bowling or have lunch with her girlfriends.

For many reasons I had been hesitant to tell my mother that Tom and I were breaking up. Despite her current wish to harm his lungs, she was actually quite fond of him. Mainly, I felt an embarrassing sense of failure even though I knew that a relationship that lasted for ten years could be considered a triumph. I tried to keep in mind the oft-quoted statistic that over fifty percent of the marriages in America end in divorce. Hearing that sobering figure, I'm surprised that people don't question the institution of marriage more. If NASA had a fifty-percent rate of failure launching rockets, people would demand that the space program be seriously reconsidered or abolished. At the same time I think most Americans look at marriage as our *other* national pastime, and from a baseball fan's point of view batting .500 is phenomenal. Explaining to my mother why I struck out with the man I was living with at age thirty-eight was as difficult and humiliating as explaining why I wasn't getting along with a playmate when I had been eight. The story would have to be dragged out of me and I was never going to tell my mother everything.

I didn't immediately respond when my mother gingerly inquired, "Bob, what happened between the two of you? You and Tom seemed to always get along."

I was evasive. "This year we had a lot of problems and we couldn't work them out."

My mother snapped, "Well, something had to have happened! Your father and I had a lot of problems too. But we stuck it out." Her description of her marriage as an endurance test was unintentionally chilling. I thought, *How many happy marriages end with the husband drinking himself to death?*

I said, "Mom, a lot of things happened. I'm still trying to figure it out myself."

Impatient with my lack of frankness, she gave me my marching orders. "Well, figure it out! And when you do, let me know."

Her instantaneous change from deep concern to open hostility demonstrated my mother's emotional agility. I like to imagine that she hears voices in her head, but not diabolical or mystical ones; the voices my mother hears are theatrical. Her voices are audience participants who have been encouraged to shout out suggestions as she performs emotional improv. Every time she speaks, they yell different states of feeling and it's her job to choose one and play it to the hilt. "Impatience!" "Rage!" "Contempt!" "Compassion!" This time she chose "concern."

"Bob, are you all right? How are you doing?"

"No. I'm not all right," I admitted. In our family, complete honesty is a sign that things are bad, while white lies and evasion connote happiness and contentment.

My mother offered, "That's okay. After Dad died, I felt bad for a long time." I remembered that for months after my father's death, she called me almost every day. And I knew she was talking to my sister and my brothers almost every day, too. She'd say, "It's lonely without your dad. I miss talking to him, but I'll get through it." I'd try to comfort and reassure her then that it was all right to feel sad and tell her that she could call as often as she wanted.

She said, "Bob, it's good to talk about feeling sad. You boys don't talk about things and you should."

I agreed, "I know. So we don't go mental."

"Right. We've had enough mental in this family. We don't need any more mental." She sounded as if she were turning away a persistent salesman.

I knew that I was about to begin a long period of unhappiness and almost felt that I should write *dejection* repeatedly in my Daily Planner.

Impulsively I confessed, "I tried to figure out what Tom wanted and yet I couldn't make him happy."

"Bob, you couldn't make Tom happy. He has to make himself happy. Everyone has to make themselves happy."

"Maybe," I joked. "But what about me making Tom miserable?"

"Oh sure, you could do that," she replied cheerfully. "We can all make each other as miserable as hell. I don't know why it doesn't work the other way around, but it doesn't."

I realized that I felt comfortable whining and talking to my mother—I never worried that I was becoming repetitious or boring. My mother had been listening to me ever since I started to speak, and so far, I had been unable to find a subject that would make her lose interest. My mother was a friend I couldn't shake no matter how unbearable I became.

"Bob, you know, you're not the easiest person to live with. You don't pay attention as well as you should. You spend a lot of time in never-never land. I'll be talking to you on the phone and you'll say 'yeah' 'uh-huh,' or 'groovy' a few times and then I know for sure that you're not listening."

Hearing these words, I put down the magazine I was flipping through and pushed away a pile of the day's mail.

She continued, "And you and your sister. All you do is mock, mock, mock. Not everything is funny. Not everything is for the public. But you like having your own way and doing what you want. You're a little selfish, but in your favor, you do let other people be selfish too."

"Hey, I'm not so hard to get along with."

"No, I'll give you that. But one reason you're easy to get along with is that you're not really paying attention to other people and don't care what they do."

When I talked to my mother I expected her to make inane generalizations and hated when she hit the occasional bull's-eye.

"Bob, did you two fight a lot?" she suddenly demanded.

"No, not really. Sometimes."

"Well, everyone fights. You fight and make up. That's about it for marriage."

"That's very helpful, Mom. You should do couple counseling."

"I should! I've been through enough." She stopped

speaking for a minute as she considered the possibility of hanging out her shingle. "Are you sure you two can't work it out?"

"No, we've tried. I don't want to break up, but Tom does."

"Well, I'm really sorry to hear that. You must be really sad." Reconsidering our relationship, she offered, "Listen, you two never fought much. You two liked being with each other. At least when I saw you."

My mother wasn't well informed about homosexuality in general and she had even less knowledge about the specific homosexual relationship of her son. Only a few years before, she had seriously asked my sister, "Carol, do the gays fight? Because Bob and Tom never seem to argue." This led me to suspect that a possible source of homophobia might be heterosexuals' resentment, stemming from the secret suspicion that people in gay relationships actually *like* each other.

It wasn't that Tom and I didn't fight. We just never fought when we visited our families. Visiting our families brought peace to our relationship in a way that resembled Stalin's alliance with the West during World War II. When faced with a greater threat, we could put aside our differences in the common pursuit of surviving our families' attempts to drive us insane.

At an early age I discovered that if my mother got hold of one hard fact, she used that kernel of information to raise bumper crops of theories about what her children should do with their lives. I avoided talking about my life with my family, not out of shame, but out of the belief that knowledge is power. The power to annoy. Don't Bother Me.

Before she hung up, my my mother advised, "And Bob, now that you're going to be single again, you should try to stop biting your nails. You always have your hands up to your face. It makes you look like one of those little hamsters you used to have as pets."

I laughed.

Thinking aloud, she continued, "Well, I better check up on you regularly now. You don't like big changes and this is a big one. Jesus, why, I remember I thought you'd never get your driver's license . . ."

The strangest part of breaking up my life after ten years was discovering that my mother was, in her own inimitable way, a source of comfort and, most shockingly, insight and wisdom.

At one time I thought Tom and I had clicked, but in hindsight this might have been no more than the sound of his doubts being locked up. Over the course of ten years we had made the natural transition that every couple makes from fucking like bunnies to fucking like Easter bunnies. Every time we had sex, it felt like a holiday. But during our last year together there were no holidays. It wasn't that I didn't find Tom attractive. He's smart and funny and one of the handsomest men I know. He's tall, with light brown hair and green eyes, and he has this great set of thick, kissable lips. But the previous January Tom had unilaterally decided that he was no longer going to fully participate in our relationship. To register his dissatisfaction, Tom held a love stoppage, a "love-out." Any of the small moments of affection that we had always exchanged were no more. When I kissed Tom in passing, there was no response. When I kissed him good night, there was no response.

Suddenly I felt as if I was a British viceroy of India dating a gay Gandhi who has decided to practice civil disobedience as a way of forcing a change in our relationship. When Tom got into bed at night, it was almost like he was lying down in protest. If I wanted him to get up the next day, I'd have to call the police and have him forcibly removed.

At night, we no longer snuggled in bed like spoons—in our mutual hostility, we were two knives stuck in the headboard. We slept with our backs to each other, only occasionally touching—four cold shoulders huddling for warmth. Our bed was a beautiful mahogany sleigh bed made in Baltimore during the 1830s. It's quite plain and possibly the noisiest piece of furniture ever built. The mattress and box spring are supported by large, thick hand-hewn wooden slats, and every time one of us sat on the bed the protesting groans gave the impression that, tonight, even if we were willing, the bed had a headache. When I bought the bed I imagined it as a vehicle for romantic sleigh rides. I didn't think that it would end up being a means of escape from the howling pack of doubts and fears that chased me. There are times when I think that sex can be defined as two scared people wolf whistling in the dark. Intimacy can be terrifying: once you're with someone, you discover that you're still all alone.

I was hurt by Tom's behavior and I thought he was being incredibly unfair. He had made no announcement that he was changing his behavior because he assumed that I would simply pick up on the changes. It was a reasonable assumption on his part, but my understanding of someone's behavior has never included the presumption that I could change or influence that behavior. Most days I feel that I barely have control over my own behavior, let alone anyone else's.

I didn't say anything to Tom about our lack of intimacy because my first reaction to strange or irrational behavior is to avoid rather than confront the person. I shied away from Tom in the same manner that I would shy away from a crazy person on the street. I especially didn't want to antagonize the kook since we were sharing the same bed. I honestly thought that he would stop his love-out if I tried really hard to show that I loved him. Undue optimism, however, can be dangerous. Looking on the bright side for too long can cause blindness.

I was impressed by Tom's ability to stay angry for months at a time. In no other area in life did he show such perseverance. If he had worked on his acting career with the same determination, he would be a legend. I know that was mean to say, but Bob is short for Beelzebub. On the other hand, I can hear the Beelzebub in me sneering, "Tom has incredible perseverance. After all, he stuck with *you* for ten years."

Tom should have known that not having a dialogue with one's significant other doesn't mean there's no communication going on. He never considered that avoiding my feelings wasn't something I did just for myself. I also did it out of consideration for his feelings. I could have spoken at length about my rage, leaving no doubt about how in touch with my emotions I was. I wanted to say, "I wish you could hold a job as long as you can hold a grudge." To which Tom would have replied, "Oh yeah, well, I wish you put a fraction of the effort into our relationship that you put into writing your book."

In our daily life Tom and I were still able to go on "dates," but we had no expectations that at the end of the afternoon or evening there would be some sex. One Sunday afternoon I dragged him to see a revival of Truffaut's *Fahrenheit 451*, a film I hadn't seen in twenty years.

Of course, I had forgotten that the film tended to drag in places, and as we left the theater, I asked Tom, "You hated the movie, right?"

"Yes. I can't believe we wasted an entire Sunday afternoon."

"You didn't like the music?" (Bernard Herrmann wrote the unforgettable film score.)

"You don't go to a movie for the music. It's the soundtrack to a nervous breakdown."

"I know. That's what I love about it."

"No. The movie was terrible."

"What about that last scene? I love that."

In a world where all books are banned, the main character of the film is a fireman who burns books and then falls in love with reading. In the last scene he meets members of an underground group who have completely memorized their favorite books in order to preserve them. When the members step forward to introduce themselves, each person announces the title of the book that he or she has memorized and, in a sense, *become*. "I'm *David Copperfield*." "I'm *Wuthering Heights*." "I'm *Madame Bovary*."

"Bob, the movie was just not that good."

"Listen. I know the movie wasn't as good as I remembered."

I knew that Tom was more disappointed than angry and that going home and reading the newspaper and having dinner would soon make him forget the movie. Each of us had picked our share of duds over the years as we had also picked films or plays that turned out to be amazing.

Sounding a bit less grumpy, Tom said, "Truffaut should have included the titles of the books that would really be preserved. They wouldn't be the classics. 'Hello, I'm *Back Pain No More*.' "

I loved that idea.

I said, "He should have included a big theater queen walking up saying, 'Hello, I'm *Judy Carne: Laughing on the Outside, Crying on the Inside: The Bittersweet Saga of the "Sock-It-to-Me" Girl.*' "

"Or, 'Hello, I'm *Get Rid of Cellulite Forever!*' "

We could share a comic idea as if we were sharing a dessert, but a few moments later our mood would change again.

As we drove back from the movie theater, Tom lamented, "This week I've got so many catering jobs, I don't think I'll have time to do anything else." He had been asked to write and perform a piece at Highways, a performance-art space, and had told me that he was going to have to tell them he couldn't do it. I insisted, "Tom, you have to do it. You want to be an actor and now someone's giving you a job."

"I don't know if I can do it with my schedule." For someone who had difficulty settling upon a career, Tom had an incredibly busy work life.

I paid close attention to Tom's dreams and hopes because I always wanted to be included in them. When we talked about his work, though, I was always in danger of straying into an area that was off-limits. Tom wanted to talk about his work, but when I tried to be helpful, most often I was shot down. Perhaps I was too enthusiastic about suggesting ways he could improve his life (a trait that if left unchecked can lead to the founding of your own religion). When Tom complained about working as a waiter, I would advise, "Tom, maybe you should try to start a business, like buying antiques or collectibles and then selling them to dealers. You would like that. You could do it without a lot of overhead and you could still control your own hours and take acting jobs."

An expression of tension and panic would sweep across Tom's face. "Okay, I really can't talk about this right now," he'd say. I would persist, having become excited by my plan, but he would shut me off. "No. Really. I can't talk about this right now." I found it confusing. I was supposed to figure out when we needed to talk about us, but we could never talk about him. I guess we needed to talk about me. But I didn't know where to start.

Two basically nice guys can get into a disastrous fight just by the limitations they put on what they will say to each other. If Tom and I are ever short of money we could both teach a class: The Unsaid as a Second Language. I read in *The New York Times* recently that humanity has developed at least six thousand different languages. It's almost as if we're desperately trying to find one that really works.

I knew that we had "problems" but I was optimistic that we could solve them because in my head I kept thinking that Tom and I were "working on" our relationship. It's one of the pitiful ironies of my life that until I wrote this sentence, I never realized that my workaholic nature was one of the things that helped alienate Tom. My identity as a comedian is stronger than my sexual orientation—I've cracked a joke in bed but I've never had the desire to have sex on a stage. A telling indication of how my brain is wired is that when I read or hear the words "Sodom and Gomorrah," my first thought is that it sounds like a vaudeville team.

Throughout our last year together I was scared that I was losing Tom. Unfortunately, a comedian's response to fear is not even close to what a lover's should be. A comedian takes pride in finishing his time under the most hostile conditions. I had noticed that Tom was no longer smiling, but a comedian has to believe that he can win back the crowd. I can see now that when a relationship is bombing, the sensible thing to do is to immediately stop and inquire what's wrong. Perhaps I didn't want to know what was wrong because I suspected it was me. The injunction to "know thyself" is scary advice. What if we learn that we don't like the person? Then we're stuck with an acquaintance that we'll never be able to lose. But I pressed on and redoubled my efforts to make Tom happy. Maybe it would have been helpful if I had banged on his penis like it was a defective microphone and said, "Is this thing working?" But after ten years of trying, I think Tom felt that I had run out of material.

I loved Tom and I loved my work, but it became clear to me and to Tom that I was living my life with him the way a selfish boy divvies up a single stick of gum. I was willing to share, but I wanted to keep the biggest piece for myself. At some point I needed to grow up and learn to give the bigger piece to someone else.

"Hi, Bob."

"Hi, Mom."

"Guess what? I'm going to be on the local news tonight."

"Why? Were you arrested again?" I mocked.

"No!" she replied. "I was at the zoo, looking at the ducks, and a television reporter was interviewing people about the new zoo that they want to build downtown."

"What did you say?"

"Whatever's best for the animals."

As part of her program of recovering from my father's death, my mother had become "a joiner" and one of the groups she had attached herself to was the Buffalo Zoo, where she took regular strolls.

"What else did he ask you?"

"He asked me why I liked the zoo and I told him that I find the zoo relaxing and that I like to talk to the animals."

"Did you say that on TV?"

"Yeah."

"That's great. People will think you've gone off your rocker."

"Oh, people know what I mean."

Years of close observation had given my mother's family only a limited understanding of what she meant most of the time and I thought that her belief that strangers would be able to understand her in a two-minute news segment was being unduly optimistic.

I couldn't resist adding, "I hope you didn't tell the animals all of our business."

When I was growing up, my mother was always worrying that one of her children would tell the neighbors all of our business. She made it sound as if she was afraid that we were going to let slip our family's secret formula for unhappiness, a formula that we valued like the Coca-Cola Company did the ingredients of its soft drinks.

I never saw the zoo interview, but two friends called my sister after they saw it because they were worried about our mother. We weren't really concerned about her because I knew that when she talked to the animals, she said, "Oh, aren't you a pretty musk ox" or some other petlike endearment. I had no reason to suspect that she was asking the llamas, "Why don't I have any grandchildren yet?" Nevertheless, after she publicly announced that she was starting to take other species into her confidence, I decided that I'd better call her more often.

* * *

In contradiction to Yeats's statement that when things fall apart the center cannot hold, as things fell apart for Tom and me, parts of our relationship revealed a sturdiness that was ultimately misleading. During the months of our unraveling there were always moments when we talked during which I waited for the smile to appear on Tom's face like a Druid waiting for the sun to appear at the winter solstice.

What I found confusing was that outside of the bedroom our relationship was still capable of astonishing us. I was amazed that after ten years Tom and I could spend an entire day together without running out of subjects to talk about, while Tom was amazed that after ten years we could spend an entire day together avoiding subjects that we needed to talk about.

It's possible I've overemphasized our lack of communication. Frankly, in some ways the communication between Tom and me was extraordinary. For all the vaunted forms of electronic communication that have been developed, I still feel the fastest means of conveying information will always be a glance between two lovers. A split-second look between Tom and me could transmit bytes of information and volumes of meaning more quickly than any technology.

At the Rose Bowl Flea Market, I could indicate to Tom with a flash of my eyes to check out the guy in the red shorts. Tom would catch the look and know immediately that I was talking about the shirtless guy who had tattooed a huge portrait of Faye Dunaway on his back, and full profiles of her on his right arm and his leg. Without my having to say anything, Tom knew: (a) that I thought the guy was a kook; (b) that I loved a good kook; (c) that I especially loved kooks who were bonkers about a celebrity; (d) that I wondered, "Why Faye Dunaway?"; (e) that we had seen Faye Dunaway perform the role of Maria Callas in the play *Master Class* and had admired her performance; she conveyed diva hauteur bordering on parody and yet she had the acting chops to do a good impression of Aristotle Onassis; (f) that even with his ridiculous tattoos, I thought the guy was handsome; (g) that I wondered, since his tattoos appeared to represent the Faye Dunaway of *Chinatown*, why didn't he go the more conventional route (if you can call turning your body into an altar of fan worship conventional) and have a tattoo of the actress playing Joan Crawford in *Mommie Dearest*, thereby getting two legends for the price of one?; (h) that I wondered if, as he aged, he would have to have face-lifts done on his tattoos; (i) that the week before Tom had surprised me by talking about the possibility of getting a tattoo, and perhaps a portrait of Faye might be a way to go; (j) let's remember to talk about him later.

Tom made me laugh when he suggested, "Imagine if we saw a shirtless ninety-eight-year-old gay man who had a tattoo on his back of his favorite silent-Ofilm star, Lillian Gish. That's how weird that guy's going to look when he's old."

The great thing about the shareware between a couple is that the network is limited to the two of you. No one has ever better understood me or known me better than Tom, but recently we seemed to have forgotten each other's access code.

"Hi, Bob. It's your mother!" she greeted in a chirpy singsong voice.

"Hi, Mom."

"What are you up to?"

"I'm making dinner."

"Are you doing all right?"

"I guess so. The apartment's a little lonely and depressing now."

"Well, sure it is!" she said brightly. "But imagine living in a whole empty house like I do. Listen, if I get lonely, I go and take a walk in the park."

"Mom, I'm glad to hear that," I said encouragingly. "Are you picking up guys in the park? Good for you!"

"No!" She dismissed my suggestion as preposterous. "I go for the exercise. We all sit too much. Do you exercise?"

"Yeah. I've been going to the gym a lot."

"That's good. Take care of yourself. People think you can stop exercising. You can't. I told Bonnie that I was feeling lonely. And she said, 'Oh, Sue. Everybody's lonely.' And she's right. Even once you're married, sometimes you're lonely." Her assessment of the human condition was bleaker than my own worst thoughts, but somehow her jaunty acceptance of it almost convinced me that she was telling me a piece of good news.

At breakfast one morning in June I noticed that Tom's ring finger was bare. I asked him, "When did you stop wearing your ring?" I was surprised and angry. It seemed like he had gone on a diet to lose *me* and that each month he was cutting down more and more on our relationship. Later I reflected on how long the ring had been off before I noticed.

"I can't believe you took off your ring without saying anything!"

Tom was a little taken aback, but he replied, "I took it off in rehearsal because the character I'm playing wouldn't wear a wedding ring." Tom had been cast in a play, but I wasn't buying his explanation.

"The character you're playing is a gay man in a relationship. Why wouldn't he wear a ring?"

"They've only been together a few months and he's unsure of the relationship. *We* didn't buy our rings until we had been together for two years."

"Tom, that's bullshit."

I couldn't believe that he was trying to convince me that his decision had to do with his part in a play. We had waited for a few years before we bought our rings in Provincetown, but I wasn't buying this acting hooey. I understood that in slipping off his ring, Tom was trying on being single. While we didn't have a wedding ceremony, buying our matching gold rings was a huge commitment, as we are both repelled by men who wear too much jewelry. I thought that if Tom's commitment was weakening, he should have replaced his ring with a piece of costume jewelry to symbolize that the relationship was losing its value.

Later that day, in a useless form of retaliation, I decided to take off my own ring. I thought, *If he's not going to wear his ring, why should I wear mine?* Since I'd worn the ring for eight years, it didn't come off easily—I had to pull and yank to get it over the knuckle. I put the ring in the top drawer of the dresser and I felt a little sick doing it. For months afterward, my ring finger had a raw, "girdled" appearance, almost as if my hand was trying to remind me that we still had time to change our minds.

* * *

"Hi, Mom."

"Oh, hi, Bob. What's going on?"

"Nothing much."

It was a dismal rainy night and I had decided to call my mother because I was wallowing in self-pity and wanted to know if someone else cared to join me.

"You don't sound too happy."

"It's raining . . ." In Los Angeles the absence of sun is a universally understood explanation for unhappiness.

"Well, call some friends and get out of the house. That's what I do."

"Maybe."

"Tom's been gone two months. Maybe you're ready to start dating again."

"Mom, there's no reason you couldn't start dating someone."

"No. I had your father. That was enough." She didn't elaborate any further and I couldn't tell whether this was a statement of satisfaction or whether she had had her fill of him.

"Your father was a good-looking man and he loved me. Do you know just a few months before he died, I was wearing my red velvet dress and he said to me, 'Wow, Sue. You look great.' At sixty-five! How do you like that?"

"Mom, maybe he was drunk."

She laughed. "Maybe he was! No, he couldn't have been drunk. We were going to a dance at the Hyatt and he had to drive."

"Mom, you don't know. There might be some man your age out there that you'd like."

"I don't want a man my age. You should see them. They all look like hell. And I'll be damned if I'm going to have anyone tell me what to do! Now I make *myself* happy. Bob, you don't need a man to make you happy. You have to make yourself happy."

"Mom, that's true, but I'm too young to become a spinster like you."

"I know. That's what Bonnie said."

"Oh, have you and Bonnie been talking about my love life?"

Bonnie was my mother's new best friend. I had met her once, and before I was introduced, my mother had filled me in on her background. "She's a widow too. Her husband died of a stroke. He was a drinker too. Worse than Dad. He was mean. But Bonnie's a rip. She has high cholesterol and yet she still eats sausages and all that stuff. Well, good for her.

"Bonnie and I just talked about you for a minute because Bonnie doesn't approve of being gay. You may think it's okay to be gay, but a lot of people don't accept it." Having finished passing along the news that homophobia existed and had I heard about it, she added, "Look at that Ellen De-Jeer. People didn't watch her show."

"Mom, it's DeGeneres, not De-Jeer, and whatever her ratings were, still millions of people watched her show." I was glad that Ellen DeGeneres had made television history by coming out on her show, but the downside of having gay celebrities was that every perceived failure of one of them was now my failure too.

"Listen, Bob, she's funny, but I'm just telling you."

"Hey, Mom. Since you don't like the men your age, I know a lot of eligible lesbians if you want to try something different in your golden years. Maybe you should go lezzie the second time around."

"No! I don't want to go lezzie—you go lezzie." She paused, and, after weighing the pros and cons of sapphic love, declared, "Hmm . . . women can be even more difficult than men to get along with. I don't know how they do it. Oh shit. It doesn't matter. Men or women. We're all hard to get along with."

As my relationship with Tom fell apart, we never discussed it with our friends. But the previous September we conveniently arranged for many of them to figure out that something was wrong. Two friends of ours from New York, John and Danny, were flying to Hawaii and planned to spend a two-day layover with us. Tom and I decided to introduce them to some friends in Los Angeles—Glenn and Larry, and Robin and Margaret.

We met for dinner at a restaurant near our apartment. Miraculously, everyone immediately hit it off. Our conviviality was considerably helped by drinking two rounds of Cosmopolitans while we waited an hour at the bar for our table. The bright red candy-colored martinis made with cranberry juice are the perfect drink for adults unwilling to relinquish their youth. A Cosmopolitan looks like a kiddie cocktail all grown up—a Shirley Temple that has become Ambassador Shirley Temple Black.

During dinner I was talking to Danny and John about their dog, Mona, and Larry, who was listening, asked, "What kind of dog do you have?" Larry loved dogs and I was always touched when he went out of his way to give a dollar to a homeless man with a dog. Glenn and Larry had three large dogs named Lorna, Liza, and Joey—named after the children of Judy Garland. When the dogs came bounding up to greet guests, Glenn would yell, "Lorna! Liza! Joey! Get down!" He sounded like an attendant at a rehab center trying to prevent his patients from hurting themselves as they went through various forms of drug withdrawal. John asked, "Bob and Tom, have you guys ever considered getting a dog?"

"We've thought about it," Tom replied. "But we're not ready to do it right now." He looked over to me as if he could read my thoughts. I hadn't answered because I thought, *We can't plan anything until we know if we're going to stay together.*

At the end of the meal Larry happened to notice something that he probably wouldn't have noticed if he hadn't been a little tipsy. He had one of those moments of clarity that only come to a person whose thinking is slightly fuzzy. He suddenly exclaimed, "Bob and Tom, you're not wearing your rings!" Feeling the effects of two Cosmopolitans, Larry put his foot in his mouth as if he thought his head was a shoe. Realizing his mistake, he asked, "Uh-oh, what does that mean?"

Tom and I exchanged a look that said, "We don't want to talk about this now," which paradoxically is the easiest thing to communicate when you're not communicating. We ignored his question as the conversations around the table stopped and everyone examined our hands for the incriminating lack of evidence. Robin is an executive with a company that runs day-care centers across the country, and her skills in dealing with children came in handy here. Picking up on our wish not to talk about it, she changed the subject by saying to Danny, "So where are you guys staying in Maui?" No one mentioned the rings again, which made it seem to me that Tom's and my problems were so deep that even our friends couldn't bring themselves to talk about them.

Shedding our rings removed an important link between us, and in October, I was sitting at my desk in the office of our apartment when Tom told me that he had decided to break up. We used our second bedroom as an office and each of us had a desk that faced a different wall. Our office made it seem like we were business partners who were trying to ignore the fact that the company was in trouble and that we were in danger of going under.

Tom was in the dining room. I shouted from the office, "Tom, I need to know if you're still going to come with me to Miami. I have to confirm the plane reservations."

Months before, I had asked Tom to accompany me to a gig in South Beach. Tom had never been there and I thought we could stay on for a week and maybe reconnect with each other. Tom didn't answer my question but walked in the office and said, "I wanted to talk to you about that."

My stomach tightened. I knew that something bad was about to happen with more certainty than a man plunging from the top of the Empire State Building.

"Bob, I'm not going to go to Florida with you because I don't think I want to stay in our relationship." I was seated at my desk and Tom was standing before me and it sounded like he was giving me two weeks' notice before quitting his job. Hearing him say this, I felt strangely calm and sickeningly panicked, as if I couldn't make up my mind on how to be unhappy. I had hoped the trip might be a chance for us to reconcile. I tried to get Tom to change his mind, but as I presented reasons why I thought he should come with me to Miami, my words began to sound forced. It's a sign of desperation when you hope that room service and a tan might save your marriage.

* * *

Tom was adamant. "No. I don't want to do any more couple counseling. It hasn't worked." I insisted that we do couple counseling at least one more time to make sure that we had tried everything to save our relationship. I knew that I was beating a dead horse, but still I wanted a second opinion from another veterinarian. The one bit of wisdom that I've painfully acquired as I've grown older is that regret is a feeling that you should make every effort to avoid. I wanted to make sure that I did everything possible to keep us together.

At first Tom refused the couple-counseling session, as we had already tried every form of mediation except shuttle diplomacy. But I reminded him, "Tom, Ralph said that even if a couple decides to break up they could benefit from couple counseling." Ralph was the one therapist that we had both liked and my involving him now was a stretch, as I usually ignored his advice. I couldn't remember why Ralph thought a final session was necessary or good for couples who had decided to call it quits. During the last session, is the therapist's goal to make both parties agree that they can't stand each other? Tom eventually agreed to the session when his regular therapist told him that he couldn't find any reason not to. It was hardly a ringing endorsement, but I was willing to grasp at the straw.

A week later we were headed to the couple counselor's office located a half hour's drive from our apartment. It was a perfect Los Angeles fall day. Instead of the blinding white light of summer, everything was bathed in gold, almost as if the sun itself had mellowed.

The couple counselor's office was located in a minimall, and when we arrived at his door, we knocked and discovered that he wasn't there. Tom peeked through the mail slot and saw that the office was dark and empty. I said, "That's weird—are you sure you got the time right?"

"Yes. He's probably just running behind." The therapist's unpunctuality felt like a bad omen. Maybe it was too late for us.

A few minutes later the therapist showed up. "I'm so sorry for being late. I hope you guys weren't too worried." He was a pleasant-looking gay man in his late thirties with thinning dark hair, and I tried to read his face as if his expression was an augury of our destiny. Before we walked into his office I briefly considered building an altar out of the collected works of Freud and Jung and sacrificing a chicken on it to propitiate the gods of reconciliation, but once we were inside, my pessimism deepened. The room looked as if it was furnished with stuff that the therapist got a good deal on when two of his patients split up. As we sat down, I looked around at the random assortment of castoff furniture and wondered, *How good a couple counselor can he be if he can't even keep a pair of matching chairs together?*

Since Tom and I had done this many times before, it only took a short while for us to get started. As we recounted painfully intimate details, each of us in turn giving his side, it crossed my mind that our story had become like one of the gimmicky reversible jackets that my father used to wear. There were two very different sides, but it was ugly inside and out. It's a shame that old problems never grow on you or that bad memories never acquire a warm silvery patina of age that makes them appear endearing or nostalgic.

"Hey, do you remember the time we had that big fight on our first trip to Los Angeles?"

"Sure I do. How could I forget? You were driving the rental car and you backed up into a metal pole and then you blamed me for the dent because you said you were tired and I had made you do all the driving."

"And how about the day when after months of letting me take care of all the bills you suddenly flipped out and said that I was spending all of our money and that you didn't want to have a joint checking account anymore?"

"And what was the name of the restaurant where you told me that you felt that I was a failure?"

"I think it was Arriba! Arriba!"

"No, it didn't happen in New York. Don't you remember? We were driving to the airport. I think you said it around the corner of Third and La Cienega."

"Really? I could've sworn . . . And where were we living the first time that you told me that you had doubts about our relationship from the beginning? Was it in the studio apartment or had we already moved to the one-bedroom?"

"I think it was in the one-bedroom because I remember going to bed and shutting the door on you."

"I think you're right . . ."

After having listened to more problems than God hears in a day, the therapist suggested that I tell Tom what I wanted.

I said, "I want us to stay together and try to work things out."

Then the therapist said, "Tom, why don't you tell Bob what you want?"

Before Tom had a chance to reply, the therapist suggested, "Tom, why don't you take Bob's hand and tell him what you want." Tom didn't move. The therapist prompted him again and Tom moved in his seat but made no motion to take my hand. I felt myself starting to cry. The therapist said, "Tom, take his hand, he's crying. Tom . . ." Tom reluctantly took my hand but it was too late. I was devastated. I can understand Tom's hesitation but it was amazing that such a simple and wordless gesture could be so painful and say so much. For the first time I felt it was over. Tom said slowly and tentatively, "Bob, I think we should break up."

Afterward, with what I thought was too much haste and too little consideration, the therapist declared, "Well, I don't think that this relationship can be saved." He spoke in a dry tone. "No, you'll have to accept it. There's no chance that you two will ever get back together. You've drifted apart and there's an ocean between you." He might as well have been talking about South America and Africa rather than two people.

I thought his judgment was a bit abrupt. He had met us only about forty-five minutes earlier. But—unwittingly validating one of the many reasons Tom had for wanting out of our relationship—I didn't say anything at the time. Even at that point I didn't or couldn't say anything.

Tom said, "I understand that it won't happen right away but I hope that eventually we might remain friends." The therapist advised that if we wanted to remain friends, we needed to work at it. "I want you two to try something during the next few weeks. I want you to give each other a long hug of several minutes' duration to let each other know that you don't hate the other person." I thought, *Oh, that's bullshit. Now it's okay to be affectionate with each other after there's no longer any reason to be affectionate.*

I felt that this was an inopportune time to make such a suggestion. I wasn't sure if I could be friends with Tom, and I certainly got along much better with my friends than I did with him right now. The therapist asked me, "Bob, how do you feel about what Tom just said?" I replied tersely, "I don't know if we can be friends." I resented both Tom and the therapist at that moment. They seemed like a pushy waiter and an overbearing host of a restaurant who were rudely trying to rush me from my table when I had just sat down to eat my heart out. They were going to have to wait for me to finish.

On the drive home the first thing I said to Tom was, "I can't believe you couldn't take my hand back there. It really hurt me when the fucking therapist had to insist that you take it. Why would you do that?"

"Bob, I wasn't trying to hurt you. That wasn't why I didn't take your hand. I hesitated because I knew that when I took your hand and said that I wanted to break up with you . . . that it was final. I just froze." I thought that Tom's answer rang true but I wasn't entirely sure. God, even in the presence of a therapist we found a way of miscommunicating.

We started telling our friends that we were going to break up. After our recent dinner together they weren't entirely surprised but everyone was visibly upset by the news. A few weeks later I was having dinner with Glenn and Larry when Glenn admitted, "This is so upsetting that Larry and I needed to talk about it during our therapy."

I was intrigued and asked, "Did your therapist have any ideas that could help?"

Glenn grinned. "No."

"I wish more of my friends talked about me in their therapy because I can use all the help I can get."

Glenn said, "Maybe we should all talk about each other's problems in therapy each week. It would give gossiping a useful purpose."

We had to call to break the news to our oldest friends, Patty and Sharon. Tom called Sharon and later, I called Patty. Patty answered the telephone. In high school Patty had been a six-foot-three-inch girl whose nickname was "Sasquatch," which meant that she was destined to become an aggressively funny comedian.

"Hi, Patty."

"Hi, Bob. Sharon told me. I can't believe you guys are breaking up. What the fuck's wrong with Tom?"

"You know the whole story. We're not having sex and—"

Patty interrupted, "Tell him to get over sex! We almost never have sex. Nobody has sex after a while!"

"Thanks, that's a lot of help. I can't wait to see you and Sharon on the cover of *Time* when they do their story on 'Lesbian Bed Death.' "

"Shut the fuck up. So what else?"

"There's his work problems—"

Patty interrupted once more, "He's not going to find someone else who'll let him take ten years to pick a career. And what are you going to do now? You're going to have a hard time finding someone to put up with you. You know how mental you are."

"Patty! Shut the fuck up. Like you should talk."

"Yeah, but Sharon knows I'm mental and she's just given up trying to change me."

Patty was sympathetic and let me thoroughly blame Tom. But the next day, showing that she wasn't going to play favorites, she called him to get his version of the story and let Tom thoroughly blame me.

"Patty called today," he told me. "You're not going to believe what she said."

"What?"

"She started off with"—Tom began to imitate Patty's

mock-cheerful delivery—" 'Hi Tom, I wanted to let you know that Sharon and I had a long talk about it and we've decided to completely side with Bob and blame you for the breakup. So from now on we're going to have nothing more to do with you. But it's been really nice knowing you, and good luck on the rest of your life!' "

We both laughed at Patty's spiel, and as we shared her joke it only emphasized how much we were going to lose by breaking up.

Shortly after we did our couple counseling, Tom brought up the subject of moving out. After talking it over, we agreed that I would keep our apartment and that he would leave. I wanted to remain in our apartment because I couldn't handle the prospect of moving by myself. When we moved from New York to California, Tom took care of all the packing while I was away performing in Australia. And although I've always acknowledged being selfish, I still couldn't see myself asking Tom, "Hey, while you're moving, would you mind doing me a favor and packing me up too? For old times' sake." I had my pride: it's not good for your self-esteem if you can't cope with being single again without the assistance of the person leaving you.

It appeared to me that Tom wasn't in any hurry to move out. Of course I knew that he was looking for an apartment, but we didn't discuss it. We couldn't discuss it because under these circumstances there was no way to casually debate the pros and cons of various apartments. It was too bad because it was a subject that we would normally enjoy.

Since it was inevitable that we were going to break up I began to want it to happen. I was becoming depressed that we were stuck in a relationship that was over but not concluded.

At the beginning of November I finally said, "Tom, I want you to move out by December first, if you can find a place. If you're going to move out, then let's get it over with. You know I'm not throwing you out but I want to get on with my life."

Tom agreed with me and intensified his search for an apartment. Playing back our messages one day, I heard that his application for an apartment in Studio City had been accepted. We now had to start the dry business of tearing apart our lives, and I was beginning to feel a little vengeful. We agreed that Tom was going to take the sofabed that we had bought together, so, for the next few weeks, I tried to eat every meal while sitting on it. I ate crackers carelessly and sloshed them down with red wine and coffee.

The first time I saw the packed but open boxes sitting near our front door, all of the possessions inside seemed to be a reproach. Sitting on top of a box, I saw a dictionary and thesaurus, which by their departure seemed to be proof that we had nothing more to say to each other. A paperback with the title *Conversational French* caught my eye. French was the language of love. A language that I had obviously never mastered. A box of kitchen supplies was capped by an overturned metal colander. A symbol of a relationship in which the affection had leaked away. There was a cold iron—the warmth having gone from it too. A big jar of glue mocked our loss of attachment to each other while plastic Tupperware containers ridiculed the idea that we could preserve anything. A hot-air popcorn maker was holding its breath to see what would happen next. Tom had split up the spices in the kitchen cabinet and I suspected that he left me with all the bitter herbs. Leaning against the boxes was a large kitschy luminous crucifix from the 1950s that I had never allowed Tom to hang. On the back of the cross were directions that said: *To retain the brilliancy of the corpse expose it to the sun or electric light occasionally*. Jesus stared in mute resignation; forgiveness was leaving with him.

Tom saw me looking at the boxes and said, "I didn't do anything about the photographs. Right now I can't look at them. I definitely want some but I'm going to leave them with you for now and we'll have to talk about them later." How were we going to split up our photographs? Divide them up according to the holidays? "Bob, if you give me the Christmas photos, I'll let you have the Halloween."

"Will you throw in the Thanksgiving?"

"No. That's not fair."

Dividing up our photographs could turn into a nightmare. From now on, I plan on always taking advantage of the photo-processing offer to get an extra set of prints for a few dollars more. It's worth the money to have a backup set of photographs in case of a divorce.

I could understand how hard it was for Tom to look through our photo albums. I still haven't looked through our photographs but many of the images are clear in my mind. Here we are in Provincetown. Proof that at one point in our lives we were able to figure out a way to spend three summers tanned and, for the most part, ecstatically happy. Here we are in San Francisco, where on a day trip to Muir Woods we're standing in front of the first redwood that either of us had ever seen and our smiles suggest that our happiness will outlive the trees. Here we are in Australia, where I'm holding an adorable baby wombat and from the overjoyed expression on my face it appears that I'm the proud father. Oh God, here's a photo of my goatee that lasted for two weeks and here's a photo of Tom's goatee that lasted for two weeks. Here's a photo of Tom having finished the AIDS ride from Boston to New York and from the radiant smile on his face it almost looks as if they found the cure. Here's a photo of us dressed up for our friend Steven's annual Halloween party. It was the year that we wore dresses that we had found at the Salvation Army. We told ourselves that we weren't in drag—we wore no makeup or wigs—we were guys in dresses. My dress was an iridescent rainbow-hued party dress that looked like it was last worn in 1966 by a Vegas singer. As I moved in the light, my dress kept queasily changing colors as if at any moment it was going to be sick. Tom's pink dress was made out of a heavy fuzzy artificial material that looked and felt like fiberglass insulation. It was uncomfortably itchy to wear and to touch, and appeared to be the discarded prototype for a summer party dress designed to allow a woman to go sleeveless in the Arctic and yet still stay warm. In the photo we look happy to have overcome our own sense of propriety for at least one night. Here we are in Washington, D.C., wearing tuxedos when I performed at one of the balls for the first inauguration of President Clinton.

I keep my favorite photograph of us in a pinecone-encrusted frame that our friend Nanette made when she was going through one of her periodic craft phases. We were in Washington, D.C., again for the Gay and Lesbian March in 1993 and we're standing in front of the Capitol building. We have our arms around each other and we both look happy and handsome. The shutter clicked on us at a moment when we were clicking too.

Here are photographs of family and friends, birthdays, dinners, parties, and holidays. Neither of us wanted to look through them as we both realized that we only took photographs during the numerous good times. I wonder why Kodak has never tried to sell more film by encouraging people to take snapshots during the bad times of their lives. "Capture your bleakest moments with our brightest color film!"

One of my keenest-felt disappointments of breaking up with Tom was that I had anticipated spending a really long time together with him. Call me a romantic, but I have always wanted a relationship like my parents had, where things are iffy for forty or fifty years.

Tom moved out the first weekend in December when I was performing in Boston. I was glad not to be there but another part of me, my pal Beelzebub, wanted to be there in order to try to slip the movers a few extra bucks to ensure that they dropped a few boxes and bumped and scratched his furniture. When I returned home, I found our—make that *my* apartment looking like it had been robbed by a very selective criminal who had the exact same taste as Tom. On the dining-room table there was a letter from Tom waiting for me. But I dismissed the feelings expressed in the letter because I was determined to remain angry with him.

Out of habit I kept looking up at the spot on the wall above the sink where the 1950s kitchen clock had hung. Seeing the ghostly outline where the paint had stayed lighter made Tom's absence even more haunting. Larger spooky rectangles of unfaded paint in the living room and hall and bedroom indicated where paintings or photographs had hung.

My first night alone I hadn't planned on doing anything, but as the December sun went down the thought of spending the evening by myself became unappealing. In the afternoon Glenn had called me to ask how I was doing.

"Not too well," I answered honestly. "The apartment feels kind of haunted or something."

"It would bum me out. I would have to be on major drugs."

"I've decided that I'm not going to stay home tonight. I'm going to perform at the Weho Lounge."

"That's good. Where is that again?"

"In West Hollywood, near A Different Light."

"Oh yeah. Is that the place that has the two signs hanging out front that say 'Lunch Specials' and 'Free HIV Testing'?"

"That's it."

Glenn said, "It's like, "Hmm, I'm hungry for a sandwich and while I eat maybe I'll see if I test positive."

"I know. I think it's kind of cruel for a coffee joint to offer free HIV testing and then to be pushing caffeine on people who are already feeling pretty jumpy."

"What time does the show start?"

"Around eight-thirty. But don't come. I'm just trying out new crap and goofing around."

Later on, when I was searching my closet for something to wear for the show, I found that Tom had left me a shirt of his that I was always borrowing. It was printed with a pattern that looked like kitchen wallpaper from a 1950s tract house. It was thoughtful of him to leave it for me, but I registered the fact and then crushed the warm feeling as if it was a smoldering cigarette butt in an ashtray. I was actually looking forward to performing because I often give my best performances when I'm not feeling funny. Anger, disappointment, and depression can sharpen my stand-up almost like a little salt heightens the flavor of candy.

I saw Larry and Glenn walk in the front door as I was pacing in the back of the club wondering whether I could or should try out a joke about the Weho Lounge's dual function of serving lattes and offering HIV testing. I was touched by Glenn and Larry's thoughtfulness, driving in from Studio City on a wet and rainy Wednesday night. I felt that I could almost start crying as they walked over with a you-don't-have-say-anything-we-know smile on their faces. As I thanked them for coming, Glenn dismissed it by saying, "Oh, it's nothing. It just sounded like you needed a bit of support tonight so we thought we'd come down." Looking around the brightly lit room, which was filled with gay men in their early twenties, Larry commented, "This place is nice." Glenn added, "And we are all so old." Later that night, getting into bed by myself, as I heard the patter of the winter rain on the roof and windows I thought, *I wish men were like flannel sheets. On a cold night, flannel sheets have never disappointed me.*

When my mother telephoned the next morning I was screening my calls on the answering machine.

"Hi, Bob. It's Mom. Are you in there? Are you screening?" Becoming impatient, she snarled, "Are you dead or alive?"

"Mom, I'm here."

"I thought you were."

"I'm writing. I'm trying not to answer the phone in the mornings."

"Well, are you okay? Tom moved out over the weekend, right?"

"Yeah, he did. I wasn't here."

"That's a shame. Oh, what are you going to do without your Tom?"

"I don't know, Mom. I don't feel like talking about this right now."

"Listen. You better learn to talk. None of the Smiths talked about their feelings and they all ended up in the bars. Your father, Uncle George, Aunt Lorraine."

"Maybe they talked to the bartenders."

My mother chuckled. "Well, Aunt Lorraine liked to talk. She could talk your ears off, but she had nothing to say that I wanted to hear." She paused, then asked, "Hey, are you eating? Didn't Tom do most of the cooking?"

"Mom, I know how to cook."

"Sure you know how. But you don't like to cook. Take vitamins." If I told my mother a year earlier that Tom and I had stopped having sex, her advice would have been, "Take vitamins." "And watch your cholesterol. You know Toby Garlock, that big criminal lawyer that Dad knew . . ." I had no idea who she was talking about. ". . . Well, he just dropped dead at sixty. Just dropped dead. One minute and then . . ." My mother made a noise that made it sound like a referee had blown a whistle to stop the poor man's heart. "There was a big write-up about him in the paper. Have you been tested for your cholesterol?"

"Yes, Mom. I'm fine."

"Well, you have to watch your heart. The Smiths have bad hearts. Let's hope you get your heart from my side of the family. Nan and Gramp ate cheese, beef, all that shit, all their lives, and it didn't bother them. I just hope you didn't get Nan's mouth. She could be a miserable bitch. And Grampy went blind and he was deaf, so let's hope you don't have his eyes and ears . . ." My mother sounded like a mad scientist who was assembling me from the various defective body parts of members of my family. As she rambled on, I could easily follow her train of thought, and this scared me because it suggested that I had inherited her brain.

* * *

At the supermarket today, while I waited in a slow-moving line, I thought, *What is taking is so long?* In California every fancy supermarket brags about being open twenty-four hours and I've decided that the store's employees believe that this is for their convenience, not the customers'. Since the store never closes they can take a full day to ring up each order. Behind me were two happy men, obviously a couple, pushing their loaded shopping cart with the same glowing look on their faces that another couple might have worn pushing a baby stroller. Of course, no matter how much this couple spends at the supermarket, it won't compare to putting a kid through college. I glanced at my small basket filled with the groceries of an obviously single man or maybe a couple of fashion models who are pigging out for one night.

I dreaded the prospect of being single again. A few years ago I remember seeing a product that was called Soup for One. It was a small can of soup that filled exactly one bowl, letting the single person enjoy the cheering prospect of serving himself as if he was an indigent in his own soup kitchen. Single-serving products assume that the state of singleness is never just a passing phase. It's forever, baby. Why don't they just come out with a line of meals for the solitary? They could be called Hungry for Love®, and their motto "We Put the Wholesome into Lonesome!"™

One of the saddest products ever peddled is called Coffee Singles. It's a package of tea bags filled with coffee that allow the perpetually lonely to brew one cup. I never want to reach the point where I don't feel that I'm worth brewing a pot for myself or that I can't afford to brew a couple of extra cups—I might need that fifty dollars that I extravagantly wasted on coffee for the cans of dog food that I'll be surviving on when I'm old and forlorn. If I woke up each morning to the smell of a Coffee Single, I'd soon be ending each evening with Vodka or Scotch for One.

Being single means a lot of Sex for One too. Masturbation when I was in a couple was an occasional treat, a night out with the boy in myself, but a lifetime of sex for one would be disheartening. A series of one-night stands where you try to avoid thinking, *Oh, it's you again.*

Of course I knew that being single was nothing to be ashamed of. The supposed stigma of the state was all in my mind. I knew a lot of single men and women who were happy, but as Glenn had put it, if you're single past a certain age "you get the weird single thing" and I wasn't sure if being in a relationship for ten years rendered me immune to the weird single thing.

I remember my friend Kevin once telling me, "I'm single by choice." I thought, *Kevin, that's bullshit. If you're single by choice, it's because other people have made the decision for you.*

And I also remember once hearing another single friend affably say, "I leave the television on all the time for the company." The words struck fear into my heart, as I couldn't imagine anything worse than the realization that one was getting a sense of companionship from watching reruns of *Three's Company*. When I heard her say this I thought, *That is something that should never be expressed to another person.* It struck me as being as depressing, sort of like saying, "I started hearing voices for the company."

Of course, people tried to remind me that being single has its advantages. As a joke, I told my mother, "Now that I'm single I can fling my clothes on the floor and put my feet up on the furniture."

She was having none of that. "Bob, you were a slob when you were with Tom. You better not get any sloppier or *nobody* will want you."

After Tom had moved out, my mother starting calling me almost daily to check up on me and see how I was doing. Normally we talked once a week, but now my mother felt that I needed her version of a pep talk more often. I admitted to her that I was feeling depressed. She would say, "Don't feel depressed. He's the one who should feel depressed!" Then she'd soften. "Oh, but we liked Tom and you loved Tom just like I loved Dad." Switching tactics yet again, she belittled my sorrow: "Now you know what I felt when Dad died. And I had my man all my life and you only had yours ten years."

I think the telephone cord must have disturbed the chip on her shoulder—a chip that had broken off from one of the crosses she had to bear. Resenting her diminishment of my relationship, I thought, *If she's going to compare relationships, then let's compare everything.* "Well, Mom," I said unfairly, "at least mine didn't become an alcoholic." I thought she might become angry but she wasn't fazed. "Give him another thirty years!" she hurled back.

I had to laugh at that. Later, when I told my mother that I was considering getting a roommate, she snapped, "Don't get a new boyfriend right away!" She made it sound as if instead of breaking up with a man, a beloved dog of mine had died and I was immediately thinking of trying to replace him with a new puppy. "Just because you're lonely, don't take anybody," she added, as if I was ready to grab the first available man I saw.

I protested, "I'm not getting a new boyfriend." It was a statement that I uttered with bravado, and it betrayed a secret fear.

"Have you spoken to Tom recently?" my mother asked.

I told her no, that when he came by to pick up his mail, I had made it clear that I had nothing more to say to him. I had even told Tom not to call me on my birthday, December 24. He asked, "Why can't I call you and wish you a happy birthday?" I replied, "It would only depress me and I don't need that additional gift."

I was curious about Tom but I never inquired about him when I saw our mutual friends. I didn't want to hear anything because if I was told that he was happy about his new place or already dating, it would only depress me more. I would have liked to hear that he was unhappy and miserable but I didn't want to take the chance that he wasn't. That's the difference between breaking up with someone in your twenties and breaking up with someone in your thirties. In your twenties you insist on knowing what your ex is doing even though the knowledge only makes you miserable. In your thirties you're content to remain ignorant because you know yourself better and possess the strength to protect your own happiness.

In a further attempt to protect my happiness I began to think seriously about moving. I loved our big sunny apartment but it was always going to be *our* apartment and would never be mine alone.

Glenn suggested that instead of moving I consider listing my apartment with a gay and lesbian roommate service called Giovanni's Roommates. I thought it was worth a try and signed up. The day after I listed the apartment I received a telephone call from a potential roomie on my answering machine. She said, "Hello, I'm calling for Bob, this is Amy." She had a breathy, girlish voice that sounded pleasant but there was an odd, tentative, almost pleading sound in her message. "I'm calling about your room for rent that I saw listed at Giovanni's Roommates. You can reach me at . . . or at my work number . . . Once again, I'm very neat and clean and very responsible and respectful and courteous. I'm financially stable. I have a steady income. I have not been late in my rent for over four years. I work in music and entertainment as a publisher, publicist, and manager. I'm drug-free. A nonsmoker. I have excellent references. So if you're interested in showing me the apartment if it's still available, give me a call at your earliest convenience. Thank you and I hope to hear from you soon. Oh, and by the way, I'm a transsexual."

I sympathized with Amy. There had to be no easy way to announce to a stranger, "Hi, I have excellent references as both a man *and* a woman." I was glad to hear that she had a steady income but I found her financial stability almost intimidating. All I wanted was someone who wasn't going to stiff me on the electric bill. I wasn't looking for someone who had never missed a payment on her breasts and vagina. I called Amy to tell her that I had changed my mind and had decided against getting a roommate. Instead I began to look for a new apartment.

"Hi, Bob. It's Mom. Are you there? All right, you must be—"

"I'm here. Sorry, I was screening. I'm trying to finish writing this piece."

I had just seen my mother, and was surprised that

she was calling me so soon. I had flown home to Buffalo to do an AIDS benefit and had stayed two nights. My mother had complained, "You're only here two nights and one of them you're performing. That's not a visit." She was right. It was too brief. In fact when she found out the reason for my visit, she warned, "Whatever you do, don't get AIDS. Don't get that lonely. It's not worth dying."

"Thanks, Mom. Now every time I go on a date I'll always hear your voice saying, 'Whatever you do, don't get AIDS.' That should protect me from all relationships."

At one time her bringing up the subject of AIDS would have made me extremely uncomfortable, but by now it didn't bother me in the least.

"Bob, it's not funny. You have to be careful. You can't trust people. People have a lot of bullshit." My mother then said, "Well, guess what . . . ?"

"What?"

"I found a condom that you left. I saw it lying on the bathroom floor and I didn't have on my glasses, and when I picked it up, I thought, 'What's this?' That was nice for your mother to find." She sounded more amused than upset by the discovery but I was horrified. It must have fallen out of my shaving kit. I had put it in there after Tom had moved out. Just in case. Every gay man thinks that he should always carry a condom. It's the homosexual version of mad money.

"Mom. Do you mind sending it to me by overnight delivery? It's the only condom I have."

"Shut up. I threw it out."

"Well, Mom, you should've been happy when you found it. If I use condoms, I won't get AIDS."

"That's true. But do I have to know about it? We never talked about all of this when I was growing up."

"Well, Mom, when you were growing up, you weren't lucky enough to have AIDS."

"That's enough. You know what I mean. The condoms. Bob, eat a lot of fruits and vegetables. That's healthy."

My friends from all over the country called me regularly to see how I was doing. I was truly pleased by every phone call and the fact that I could say to them, "My life sucks right now."

It was Patty who told me that I had to change the outgoing message on my answering machine. Tom had recorded all of our messages on our answering machine, as he had the deeper and far more mellifluous voice. On the few occasions when I recorded our outgoing message I always sounded as if I was unsure if I was home. Two months had elapsed since Tom had moved out and one day when Patty called, before she even said hello she said, "Okay, you have to have to change the fucking message on your answering machine. Tom is gone and you have to accept it and move on." She continued, "Why don't you keep it till you start dating again; that should really attract guys when they call up and hear your ex-boyfriend tell them that you're not home. Could you be any more of a loser?"

"All right!" I said, perversely enjoying her condemnation. "I'm going to change the message. I'm going to say, "Hi, this is Bob. I'm not home right now and if you're calling for Tom, that *rat bastard's* new number is area code eight-one-eight . . ."

Patty laughed and after we had talked for an hour she ended the conversation by facetiously threatening, "If I call again and get Tom's message I'm never calling again. Call me if you want to talk." As belligerent as Patty could be, she's one of the most thoughtful and generous friends I have. Of course with her level of belligerence she has to be. Patty was serious about letting me know I could call her, but she had to dismiss her good impulse before she hung up. "You better call me, you asshole!"

The next time I had a long conversation with Tom was the result of a strange coincidence. I had moved and I had sent a change-of-address notice for my subscription to *Vanity Fair*. However, a few weeks later I received a postcard that said, *Our records indicate that your subscription was canceled. Please let us know if this is incorrect.* This puzzled me; as I recalled, my subscription ran through July.

The subscription had been an annual Christmas gift from Tom's parents, and while I didn't expect them to keep renewing it in perpetuity, I thought that it would at least run its current course. I called the toll-free number given on the postcard and spoke to a charming woman who sounded like somebody's mother. She checked the records and told me, "Yes, the subscription was canceled on January 22 by the person who ordered it."

As this was the date of Tom's birthday, I immediately thought, *Tom must have told his parents that I didn't give him a birthday gift and his parents became angry and canceled the subscription.* As I was very fond of Tom's parents, this hurt me. I considered goading my mother into calling Tom and demanding the ninety dollars she had given him for quitting smoking. Finally, I decided to call Tom and ask him. To my disappointment he wasn't home and I left a message. That night he called me back, and after I explained what had happened he said, "You know my parents wouldn't do that. They've always liked you. But I'll call them and find out."

As he said this, I knew it was true but so many other things that I felt to be true hadn't been that I distrusted my common sense. It turned out that Tom's mother had written *cancel* on the renewal form when she meant *don't renew* and the company took her at her word and cut me off.

Tom made me smile when he said, "Is this some plot to get back at me through my parents? You know that last night while watching television my mother must have said to my father twenty times during the commercial breaks, 'Oh, I can't get it out of my mind. I feel awful that Bob thought we would cancel his subscription. He must have thought we're terrible.' "

I said, "Maybe she'll renew it now for the rest of my life. Just out of guilt."

"I wouldn't count on it."

It was funny to think about her reaction but it also made me sad. Tom and I were in sync again, even if it was just for a minute.

Months went by and Tom and I stopped talking or seeing each other even occasionally. I started having all sorts of weird, stress-related aches and twitchy pains in my back and neck even though I had been going to the gym four times a week and eating better than I had in years. I felt that I was carrying around this big cargo of hate. I can't imagine how the great haters in history functioned. Walking around with clenched fists all the time gives me carpal tunnel syndrome.

Also, I began to think, *What's the good of hating someone without them knowing it?* Some of the most solitary and antisocial haters, like the Unabomber for instance, tried to keep in touch with their enemies by mail. And I didn't want people to think that I was more fucked up than the Unabomber.

One of the benefits of being in what some people consider an unconventional relationship is that I began to think maybe we could have an unconventional breakup. I wanted to be careful for both of our sakes. I didn't want to fuck up our estrangement in the same way that I felt that I had fucked up our relationship. I didn't feel that I could be friends with Tom yet, but I was beginning to think that maybe he didn't have to be my enemy.

I called Tom and to his surprise I suggested that we might have lunch.

Shortly after talking to Tom I got a telephone call from Glenn and I told him that Tom and I were going to meet. Glenn said, "I think that might be good. It's kind of like Marilyn Monroe and Joe DiMaggio. They couldn't make their marriage work but Joe always sent those flowers to her grave every year." In the three years I had known Glenn this was the closest he had ever come to talking sports. Entering more familiar territory, Glenn continued, "It's kind of like Gwen Verdon and Bob Fosse. They couldn't be lovers but they were able to remain friends and continued to be a part of each other's lives. And look, the musical *Chicago* did come out of it."

I cattily hoped that Glenn was comparing Tom to Gwen Verdon. Glenn is one of those gay men who believes Shakespeare's line about all the world being a stage and all the men and women merely players—only in Glenn's interpretation all the world's a backstage filled with juicy stories, legendary feuds, memorable anecdotes, bits of gossip, and tales of scandal among bickering cast members.

Getting carried away with his theme, Glenn added,

"Sonny and Cher couldn't convince anyone that they were still friends after they were divorced. When they did that second TV series, no one was buying all those supposedly lighthearted jokes about being divorced. Which is the difference between television and theater. Television people can't do what theater people can pull off. And you know I like to think of you and Tom as theater people."

I paused to try to make the connection. "And who knows? Gwen Verdon ended up working with Bob Fosse's other lover Ann Reinking. You know they both worked on *Fosse*. So maybe you'll end up working with . . ."

"I don't think I'm ready to go there," I interjected. "I don't want to have to fight for title credit with Tom's new boyfriend." Glenn thought for a second and said, "No, you're not ready for that."

Glenn turned serious and offered one of the sharp insights that he occasionally stumbled upon after wandering off on a preposterous tangent. "You know, I saw Gwen Verdon and Ann Reinking talking about their collaboration on *Fosse* and I thought, 'These people were in relationships with him and whatever their feelings and differences, they ultimately loved and respected Bob Fosse enough to overcome them.' There has to have been a lot of love to make that possible. I found it very moving. It was kind of sad but it was also sweet and beautiful."

In Glenn's telling, I suddenly found it moving and sad and sweet and beautiful too.

"Mom, you and Dad stayed together a long time. How did you do it?"

"I know, we were together almost fifty years. We met in high school—"

Interrupting, I said, "I know, Mom. You went to Kenmore West. So did I."

"We loved each other. And that doctor in Niagara Falls said that Dad would leave me because I was sick. I was so scared when he said that."

My mother was talking about her nervous breakdown, a subject she rarely mentioned. Her life suddenly became palpably real and was no longer an amusing distraction. "He did? That's a horrible thing to say. I didn't know that. Mom, that doctor was an asshole."

"Oh, Bob. Don't say that!" she said sweetly. "I don't like that word." Then, changing her mind, she said, "You're right, he *was* an asshole! The puke! You can't always listen to doctors. I would've never gotten better if I had listened to him. My other doctor was wonderful.

"It was rough. I couldn't take care of you kids. I couldn't drive. I couldn't take care of myself. I wore that wig because I couldn't take care of myself."

I can remember my mother putting on the frosted brunette wig that was the late 1960s hair-color equivalent to white lipstick and smoked mirrors. At the time I didn't understand that she was wearing the wig because she felt it was the only way she could go out in public. I had thought she was just trying to be groovy.

"But your father came through for me. I never forgot that. He made dinner for you kids. He cleaned the house and did the laundry. We weren't perfect. If you want perfect, stay single! And after I went in the hospital . . . I wanted to get better. Going in that hospital once was enough. I remember going to therapy and people saying, 'I've been in the hospital three time or four times,' and I thought, 'Are you nuts?' " Discovering that she had made a joke, she laughed and said, "Yeah, I guess they were.

"And later on I was there for Dad. People don't know

what I went through. For a while people were bringing him home drunk, right and left, and just leaving him at the back door. It was like they were delivering a package. Then your father fell and broke his nose at the Tiki House because they gave him too much to drink."

"He drank at the Tiki House?"

The Tiki House was a tiny bar in a hutlike structure where I was served my first underage drink. It was a dive where customeers drank to forget their surroundings.

"He fell right in the bar. And they took him to the hospital, dropped him off, and then they called me. I was so mad. They served him the drinks and then just hustled him out of there. So the next day I went up to the Tiki House and caused a scene. I did. And I think they were used to wives coming in because they didn't act that surprised."

I said, "The Tiki House probably has a ladies' night offering half-price drinks to the wives of alcoholics."

My mother didn't react to my little joke. "I screamed at the owner. That wasn't right, but I didn't know what else to do. One woman sitting at the bar shouted, 'We're not all alcoholics in here!'

"And I said, 'Well, you could've fooled me!' "

"Hey, that was a good one, Mom."

"I know. That was pretty good. Wasn't it? I'm funny. I could be a comedian too."

For months after the breakup I had chosen to have no contact with Tom. It now felt strange to be having lunch with him again because I knew everything about his life until a certain point but I didn't know anything about what had happened to him recently. I felt as if I was the subject of an Oliver Sacks medical essay about a man who's lost the ability to retain any short-term memories of his former boyfriend: "The Man Who Tried Not to Think About His Ex."

Tom was more informed about what I had been doing for the past few months because he had finished reading a copy of this chapter. One of the reasons for our meeting for lunch was that I wanted his thoughts on it.

Before I took advantage of his good nature, I asked Tom how he was doing. He answered, "I've been feeling depressed." I responded, "I'm sorry that you've been feeling depressed." Then at the urgent prompting of Beelzebub, I added, "Maybe you should have been on antidepressants last year. We might still be together." Tom flashed a withering, fake smile and replied, "Very funny."

Tom also mentioned that he had bought a new television and a new car. We had shared a 1987 Honda Civic for years and now he had a nicer and newer car than I had. I resented his doing this now. I said to him, "Hey, why didn't you buy all this stuff when we were still together? It might have saved the relationship."

He smirked. "I know. It probably would have."

We were at a chicken restaurant in Studio City and were sitting in a booth that William Shatner had just vacated. Tom had spotted Captain Kirk and pointed him out to me while we were in line.

After we ate, Tom pulled out his copy of the chapter I had sent him and laid it on the table. I noticed that the first page had been marked up in pencil. Tom was understandably reluctant to become involved but I requested that he read this piece because I didn't want him to think I was writing it out of revenge. I assured him that I would change anything that he strongly objected to but I wasn't trying to be scrupulously fair in the story of our breakup because unlike the set of serving spoons, I never offered to give him half the chapter to put forth his point of view.

Ultimately, I knew that only someone who really loved me would consent to read an essay that I wrote about our breakup and then help me improve my composition—often at his expense. During lunch I asked one question that Tom refused to answer. "I knew that our relationship was over when I was in the therapist's office. When did you know that it was over?"

He smiled, "Oh, no. I've helped you more than enough. You figure it out. Or do what you always do when you're not sure or can't remember something. Just make it up."

I followed his advice.

"Mom, I have a date next week."

"You do?" The sound of disbelief in her voice could have undermined the confidence of an entire empire.

"Yes, I do."

"Well, don't just go for anyone."

"Yeah, Mom, that's my usual method of picking up guys. I'm a slut and I go for anyone who will have me."

"Bob, you're not a slut," she reassured me. Then there was a pause. "Are you?"

It was my turn to laugh. "No. I'm not a slut. I'm just easy."

"Where did you two meet?"

I hesitated and thought, *Should I tell her the truth or lie and say that we met at a party?*

I told the truth. "We met at a gay bar."

"Oh, Bob," she said, concerned. "Don't you start hanging out in bars all the time. I don't want you to start drinking too." I forgot that from my mother's perspective the dangerous lure of gay bars would be the alcohol and not the men.

"Mom, I went out to meet men, not to drink. When I go out to meet men I stay sober. Then later, when they break my heart, I go out to drink and drown my sorrows."

It occurred to me that's why many gay clubs have two separate bar areas. One should be designated the pickup bar and the other should be the letdown bar.

"Hmm. I guess that's good, then."

"Yeah, if Dad had gone out to bars to meet women, maybe he wouldn't have drunk so much."

"That's true. Women I could have handled but the drinking will kill you. Women don't kill men." Chuckling, she added, "At least not as quickly." Then she asked, "Bob, is he nice looking?"

"Yeah, he is."

"Well, that's good. Whatever you do, don't go out with someone too short. Tom was tall and you need someone tall." She sounded like I needed help getting boxes down from the top shelf of a closet. "I hate seeing a couple where the man is too tall or even worse the girl towers over the man. That looks terrible."

"Well, Mom, I'm six-two—there's a pretty good chance that I just might be the tall girl in my next relationship."

Unfazed by my sarcasm, she said, "You better not be. I didn't bring you up to talk like that."

"No, you didn't."

"And the next boyfriend you get, don't tell him everything about the family. He doesn't have to know about Dad's drinking and my nervous breakdown."

"Mom, I wrote about it in my last book."

"He doesn't have to know about the book either."

A week later, after I had my date, my mother called and asked me how it had gone.

As I told her, I knew that my worst fantasy had become a reality. It's every sensible gay man's worst nightmare. I had lost my boyfriend and gained a new girlfriend: my mother.

Is He Wearing Hai Karate?

IN THE fourth grade I wrote my first and only fan letter—to Edna St. Vincent Millay's sister. I didn't write to Edna herself because she had died seventeen years earlier and pestering a dead celebrity is rude. Strangely enough, I wasn't a fervent devotee of Edna's poetry. I only wrote the letter because my teacher, Mr. McGaffin, had made the class write to her sister after he had read aloud from *Restless Spirit*, a lengthy biography about Edna's troubled life. I don't believe that children should be shielded from such subjects as melancholy, rejection, or alcoholism, but must we teach those matters in our schools? Isn't it the parents' responsibility to teach them at home? Mr. McGaffin also read aloud numerous selections from Edna's poetry. Reading poetry to children is perilous because a poem can express the ghastly aspects of life with beautiful and appealing imagery. Take, for example, Edna St. Vincent Millay's most-quoted lines:

My candle burns at both ends;
It will not last the night;
But, ah, my foes, and oh, my friends—
It gives a lovely light.

I'm not sure that an ode to squandering your life is an appropriate poem to introduce to nine-year-olds. We could have become precocious wastrels, coloring our crayons at both ends, drawing like there was no Tomorrowland. At the time my favorite poet was Dr. Seuss, but unlike that author of rhymes, Edna often looked upon the sunny side of darkness. I imagine a children's book by "Dr. Millay" would be upsetting:

The Cat in the Hat is old, fat, and gray.
No! No! That poor cat does not want to play.
The Cat in the Hat once meowed to score points.
Now that poor cat just says "Ow!" to sore joints.
The Cat in the Hat gums his jaws when he chews.
I'm sorry to tell you—I have some bad news.
That poor cat can't leap or creep and he hardly
makes a peep.
I'm afraid it's time to put the Cat in the Hat to sleep.

Mr. McGaffin loved poetry and every morning he read aloud a poem by a writer such as Emily Dickinson, Walt Whitman, and Robert Frost. He believed learning about poetry was as necessary as learning the multiplication tables. In fact, whenever he came upon a line that he thought should be singled out, such as Emily Dickinson's description of bees as "buccaneers of buzz," he repeated it several times in the exact same manner that he would repeat "five times six equals thirty." But I gathered that Mr. McGaffin preferred poetry to arithmetic since he never chose to read us a biography of Euclid or Pythagoras.

Mr. McGaffin was what my mother called "the sensitive sort," a term that she spoke in a half whisper, as if sensitivity in a man was a character flaw, like promiscuity or drunkenness. My mother believes that real men should drive their emotions like a Porsche. Our feelings have to go from zero to sixty and sixty to zero at the press of a pedal but we also have to stay firmly in control within one restricted lane of behavior. By my mother's sights, Mr. McGaffin didn't follow the rules of the road.

In *Pilgrim at Tinker's Creek* Annie Dillard wrote a description of aesthetic rapture: "I had been my whole life a bell, and never knew it until at that moment I was lifted and struck." Mr. McGaffin was a bell who was struck by beauty almost hourly. He was constantly clanging as he pealed out the virtues of every subject that he taught. His loudest ringing endorsements were for the five sisters of sensitivity: art, music, poetry, theater, and tidiness. Being a sensitive sort is often associated with being unrealistic but Mr. McGaffin's sensitivity was pragmatic. He never tried to draw the line at his appreciation of beauty because he knew that after drawing such a line, he would have to pause to admire his own draftsmanship.

Out of all the poets he loved, Mr. McGaffin singled out Edna St. Vincent Millay's biography for reading aloud after he met her sister Norma. The encounter changed him from a distant admirer to an admirer who needed a restraining order. Idol Worship and Artistic Appreciation were required subjects in Mr. McGaffin's class but his genius as a teacher lay in his belief that his students would benefit from his own extracurricular devotions. In the fourth grade I was eager to learn about everything because I was still far from jaded. It wasn't until late in the fifth grade that I assumed my world-weary guise whenever the teacher would pick up a globe.

The best teachers, like Mr. McGaffin, make the acquisition of knowledge a revelation. I believed wholeheartedly in Mr. McGaffin because at that age I regarded all of my teachers as gurus; in September of each year, I joined a new cult and I searched my teachers' every word for signs and portents of learning.

I was excited at the end of the third grade when my teacher Miss Hill told me that Mr. McGaffin would be my fourth-grade teacher. I knew Mr. McGaffin by sight—the only male teacher at Thomas Edison Elementary School was conspicuous in the playground huddle of third- and fourth-grade teachers.

Mr. McGaffin was a tall, handsome, dark-haired man in his mid-thirties. He seemed old to me then because I was still inexperienced at aging. When I was nine, Mr. McGaffin seemed elderly because he was four times my age. Whereas now, at age thirty-nine, someone four times my age has become an impossibility. It's obvious now that I had a crush on Mr. McGaffin. Before starting a new lesson, Mr. McGaffin often said to the class, "All right, I want everyone's undivided attention." Usually he didn't have to ask me twice. I realized quickly that one of the benefits of having a male teacher was that I could look at Mr. McGaffin as much as I wanted while he taught. In fact, I was *required* to pay attention to him. I noticed his big hands and how his shirt hugged his chest when he removed his jacket on hot spring days. I studied Mr. McGaffin as if I was going to be tested on the geography of his face.

My grades improved dramatically because while I was studying Mr. McGaffin, I also inadvertently paid attention to every word he said. Looking back on it, if I had had a crush on all of my teachers throughout my schooling, I might have had straight *A*s. Maybe the key to improving children's education isn't smaller class sizes or more computers, it's more attractive teachers.

Mr. McGaffin was an odd mixture of the manly and the fey. His five o'clock shadow could plunge a room into darkness and yet his handwriting was more beautiful than the samples offered in our textbooks. Mr. McGaffin was an orderly man who never misplaced his car keys and had probably never found a forgotten twenty-dollar bill in the pocket of an old jacket. Exceedingly well groomed, he probably wore a part in his pubic hair.

The natty appearance of our classroom was also a source of pride to Mr. McGaffin. It seems he pursued his ambitions in the field of interior design by choosing the unusual path of becoming an elementary-school teacher. On his desk was a small blue pot filled with sharpened number-two pencils. They looked like an arrangement of yellow-barked twigs that Mr. McGaffin admired for their perfectly trimmed stems. He took pride in his immaculate classroom and worked hard to keep it that way. For Mr. McGaffin teaching was a grimy job filled with chalk dust, pencil shavings, and eraser residue, and he had more cleaning supplies in the bottom drawer of his desk than the school janitor had in his storeroom. Mr. McGaffin even had his own feather duster, a shifty cleaning utensil that looked busy but did as little work as possible. On Monday mornings Mr. McGaffin feather-dusted his desk, a task that made him look frivolous and not a little fussy. On Friday afternoons Mr. McGaffin cleaned the blackboards with a wet sponge. Wiping out old ideas like they were superstitions that had to be eradicated, he became the personification of Progress itself.

While taking attendance, Mr. McGaffin always sounded distressed when he discovered that a pupil was absent. I now believe that rather than worrying about the possibility of a serious illness, he was upset because the empty seat spoiled the visual symmetry of the row. In seventeen years of education—elementary school, junior and senior high, college—Mr. McGaffin was the only teacher of mine who ever changed the layout of a classroom in the middle of a school year. One morning we found our desks facing a different blackboard and I was staggered by the discovery. I looked upon the position of my desk as a source of stability, its location in the classroom as fixed and unchanging as Australia's on the map of the world. (Except for the occasional times when the class broke up into small groups. To this day, whenever I look at a map of the Hawaiian Islands, I like to think of them as being in a discussion group.) If Mr. McGaffin could move desks, then what else could he change? Tomorrow, would he ask us to recite the Pledge of Allegiance in rhymed couplets?

Debbie Gruber asked the question that I wanted to ask. "Mr. McGaffin, why did you move our desks?"

Taking her question as an implied criticism, he responded, "Why? Don't you like it?"

Debbie gave a shrug that Mr. McGaffin took for approval. While he never explained why he moved our desks, I like to think that it was my first lesson in the age-old wisdom passed down by generations of fastidious men: maybe you can't change the world but you can always rearrange it.

* * *

Ralph Waldo Emerson wrote, "There is properly no History; only Biography," a sentiment that Mr. McGaffin expanded to include arithmetic, science, reading, and writing. For Mr. McGaffin, every subject was a source of gossip, and for him, history was a long juicy story told over a back fence that stretched from the Great Wall of China to the Mason-Dixon Line.

When we studied the American Revolution, Mr. McGaffin couldn't resist mentioning that George Washington wore false teeth. He even showed us a photograph of these historic and unnatural-looking dentures. I was fascinated and appalled by George's whopping clodchoppers. His dentures were made out of hippopotamus ivory and wood and they looked more like a piece of furniture than teeth. They were a dental masquerade of such obvious falsity that they couldn't have fooled anyone. Seeing Washington's false teeth, I knew why in every one of his portraits he has a tight-lipped expression on his face. When he smiled, it must have been like opening the keyboard of a piano.

I loved history but my favorite subject was science, which Mr. McGaffin made riveting with his flair for digression. His description of the life cycle of the monarch butterfly, for example, was enthralling because in his telling the insects were just big queens. Mr. McGaffin made the process of metamorphosis seem more aesthetic than scientific, almost as if monarch caterpillars were fanatic disciples of the Victorian Arts and Crafts leader William Morris. Morris wrote the maxim that has inspired generations of queens: "Have nothing in your homes that you do not know to be useful, or believe to be beautiful." Only Mr. McGaffin made it seem that monarch caterpillars had taken Morris's ideas one step further. Caterpillars demonstrated that living in a beautiful house could not only change your soul but transform your flesh.

Showing the class a film strip about the monarch butterfly's life cycle, Mr. McGaffin would announce with admiration, "In only a few hours the monarch caterpillar builds a beautiful blue-green chrysalis. Can everyone in the back of the room see how the chrysalis is spotted with gold? The caterpillar spends the winter there, until the spring, when it emerges completely transformed." Mr. McGaffin made the caterpillar's transformation into a butterfly sound miraculous, as if the caterpillar had the luxury of acquiring a beautiful body without the pain of joining a gym or doing any exercise. It's a response to your surroundings that pudgy men with elaborately furnished houses can only dream of.

A trace of spitefulness crept into Mr. McGaffin's lecture when he explained that the caterpillar's diet of acrid milkweed sap made monarch butterflies unpalatable to birds and other predators. He almost crowed, "They're pretty on the outside but bitter on the inside!" His implication being that this was true for all great beauties. He ruefully told the class that "appearances can be deceiving," and for a moment he seemed lost in thought, almost as if he was thinking about a certain someone instead of a butterfly.

I have never met anyone who had a greater love of the holiday season than Mr. McGaffin. Except, for Mr. McGaffin, the holiday season encompassed the entire year. He loved holiday foods, holiday songs, and especially holiday decorations. For his students Mr. McGaffin believed the ability to work a pair of safety scissors and a rubber-tipped bottle of mucilage were essential skills and we were continually enlisted in the class production of holiday decorations.

Under Mr. McGaffin's supervision, the windows of our classroom were trimmed more frequently than Macy's. Since school started after Labor Day, Mr. McGaffin decided not to wait until Columbus Day for an occasion worthy of decorating for and celebrated the first day of autumn as if it was an official holiday, which meant that we had to get to work right away. We made red maple, yellow elm, and orange oak leaves out of construction paper and then affixed them to the windowpanes of our classroom. When the Scotch tape dried out and turned brown in the late September sun and the leaves began to fall, it signaled that now it was time to make Columbus Day decorations. The windows were soon filled with a veritable flotilla of paper cutouts of the *Niña*, *Pinta*, and *Santa María*, names that Mr. McGaffin rattled off like he was introducing the Andrews Sisters—"Maxene, Patty, and Laverne." For Halloween, black paper witches riding on their broomsticks flew in formation across the windows but by the second of November these pagan symbols were eliminated by the God-fearing Pilgrim decorations of Thanksgiving. Mr. McGaffin's favorite decorations, though, were paper chains, which he hung over blackboards and windows, giving Room 319 the air of a Milquetoast dungeon. The gaudy shackles that festooned our class became a symbol of Mr. McGaffin's lack of restraint. And Mr. McGaffin didn't limit himself simply to paper decorations; he also used gourds, pumpkins, Indian corn, pinecones, candy canes, and pussy willows to great effect. His stunning deskscape tableaux were still lifes in name only though, because he was constantly fussing with them.

For Christmas, we made my favorite holiday decoration, paper snowflakes. I was gifted at cutting out paper snowflakes, and if I put my mind to it, I probably could have made them life-size. I felt pretty cocky about my scissoring skills, and in my opinion no two paper snowflakes were alike: they were either good or bad. Some of the kids in my class couldn't cut their way out of a wet paper bag. It irritated me when Mr. McGaffin praised everyone's snowflakes equally, including some that left me cold. But it still mystifies me that my excellent hand-eye coordination when cutting out paper snowflakes never came into play when I needed to catch a ball. I guess in my case the two skills had nothing to do with each other.

It's too bad art class was never as competitive as gym class. Every student should have been forced to draw on the blackboard in front of the entire class and endure public humiliation if his efforts were clumsy or uncoordinated. Having to draw a horse would become as traumatic a memory for some students as trying to play baseball was for others. Mr. McGaffin would say, "Okay, Henshaw, you're up next to draw!"

Rick Henshaw, the best athlete in gym class, would crawl out of his seat and slowly make his way up to the blackboard as the catcalls broke out.

"Oh, no! Henshaw's up! He's gonna choke. He always does. Henshaw can't draw a straight line with a ruler!"

"Henshaw's going to muff it!"

"He's a whiffer! Whiff! Whiff! Whiff!"

Mr. McGaffin would intervene, "All right, you guys. Knock it off! Give him a chance." Henshaw would be moist with flop sweat as he slowly began to draw the wobbly front leg of a horse.

From the back of the class, a smart aleck would heckle, "Is that a rocking horse?"

Mr. McGaffin would start coaching him, "Henshaw, keep your eye on the horse when you draw! Get a better grip on the chalk. No, you have to hold it tight. No! Not like that! You're holding it like it's a powder puff. Get a grip on it!"

Under all the pressure, the piece of chalk would break in Henshaw's hand. That would be it. Instead of allowing Henshaw to continue, Mr. McGaffin would send him back to his seat. "Okay, Henshaw, that's enough for now. That was a good try. Sooner or later, you'll get the hang of it. Let's see if the next artist can do a little better. Smith! It's your turn. Show him how it's done."

At Christmastime, it was customary for the students to bring gifts for the teacher and I gave Mr. McGaffin a box of white handkerchiefs. My mother had chosen them for their virtues of being inexpensive but not cheap, and completely impersonal. Some of Mr. McGaffin's other gifts included almost a dozen neckties, four pairs of socks, three wallets, a fifth of Black Velvet, a lighter that was engraved *Compliments of General Motors*, and several key chains, including one that sported the Playboy Bunny logo.

The gift that made the entire class and a blushing Mr. McGaffin laugh was Carrie Bober's present, a bottle of Hai Karate aftershave. I was impressed by Carrie's gift and thought, *Why didn't I think of that?* without realizing that I would never have suggested such a gift to my mother. My sense of concealment had kicked in early; if I had asked my mother to give Mr. McGaffin a bottle of aftershave, I would have splashed myself with suspicion. Everyone in our class was familiar with Hai Karate because we had all seen the television commercials in which men wearing the aftershave needed to use karate chops and kicks to fight off the crazed amorous women who found them irresistible. When Mr. McGaffin opened his present it's possible that the laughter in the classroom stemmed from everyone suddenly having the same thought: We couldn't picture Mr. McGaffin risking his hands in a karate fight. Valentine's Day was coming up and he had a lot of scissoring to do.

I didn't know then that Mr. McGaffin was gay but I did recognize that he was different. He stood out because he was the only man in Buffalo I knew who read poetry, wasn't fat after the age of thirty, and never talked about sports. It's not that I was unfamiliar with men in Buffalo who possessed at least one of those attributes: my uncle Hal liked limericks; Mr. Alt, the gym teacher, was still in shape well into his fourth decade; and . . . well, no, I didn't know any men who didn't talk about sports. It must have struck me as extraordinary for one man to combine all three of those qualities.

Mr. McGaffin was also different from other men because he was frequently met after school, by his fair-haired "friend" Jeffrey and their German shepherd, Lucy. From my desk by the windows, I often saw Jeffrey standing outside on the sidewalk smoking a cigarette waiting for the last bell to ring. It didn't strike me as strange that Jeffrey met Mr. McGaffin after school because when I wanted to play with Tommy Helmbrecht sometimes I had to wait outside on the sidewalk for him to finish dinner. I was at the blissful age when it was more interesting to me that Mr. McGaffin had a dog than a boyfriend.

But there was something about Mr. McGaffin's relationship with Jeffrey that fascinated me, and the more I saw them together after school, the more curious I became about their lives. I was too shy to broach the subject, but thank goodness Debbie Gruber was a loudmouthed girl and every thought that came into her head fell from her mouth like a letter through a mail slot. One day when we were petting Lucy, she asked, "Mr. McGaffin, do you live with Jeffrey?" Jeffrey and Mr. McGaffin both smiled and then without hesitating, Mr. McGaffin said, "Yes, I do." We were satisfied with his answer, because at our age living with your best friend sounded like a perfectly reasonable thing for an adult to do.

The after-school lives of my teachers fascinated me. Spotting Miss Yakopovich putting groceries in the trunk of her car at Loblaw's Supermarket was exciting—I had never suspected that she liked Frosted Flakes. I was nosy and pieced together biographical information about my teachers from dropped comments about their children or from special occasions such as the time Miss Blodgett showed our class slides from her vacation in Mexico. The stated purpose for the slide show was to give us some information about our neighbor to the south but the only image that I retain is one of Miss Blodgett's traveling companion—Miss Ortolani, the mannish assistant principal who always looked awkward wearing a dress. When she walked it looked like she was trying not to bump into it.

When I learned that Mr. McGaffin, Jeffrey, and Lucy lived nearby on Girard Avenue, I made a point of riding by on my bicycle to see their house. It was the first time I ever sought out a teacher's house and my goal wasn't very well thought out. I knew their street but I didn't know their exact address. I think I assumed their house would stand out from all the others because their windows would be filled with holiday decorations.

Mr. McGaffin was cutting the lawn and saw me first. He immediately stopped pushing the lawn mower and said, "Hi, Robert. How are you? Are you on your way to the park?" Girard Park was one block from his house and I was relieved that he handed me this excuse. I had never expected to run into him and at that moment I would have been incapable of thinking up a lie by myself. Mr. McGaffin was wearing a T-shirt that was soaked with sweat, and as we talked, I tried not to stare at his veiny forearms and the tasseled fringe of dark chest hairs that curled over his shirt collar.

"It's the first really hot day today," commented Mr. McGaffin.

"It *is* hot," I said. We both paused and looked at the lawn. I wasn't aware of it at the time but this was a watershed event in my life. I was having my first awkward conversation with a man that I was interested in. It was to be the first of a long series and it's satisfying to know that since the fourth grade I've been able to clearly see some improvement in my conversational skills.

"Where's Lucy?" I asked.

"She's inside," he replied.

I wanted to know if Jeffrey was inside too, and I regretted that I hadn't asked the inquisitive Debbie Gruber to tag along. She would have demanded, "Can we see the inside of your house?"

"Mr. McGaffin, do you always cut the lawn? Or do you take turns?" I was learning to introduce the subject that I wanted to talk about.

"No. I usually cut the lawn. Jeffrey does it once in a while." He grinned. "Once in a great while."

Mr. McGaffin then said, "I'm going to let Lucy out. I'll just be a minute." He went inside the house and soon returned with Lucy and two ice-cream sandwiches.

"I decided that we needed an ice-cream break. Why don't we sit in the shade?" he suggested. I got off my bicycle and we ate our ice-cream sandwiches on the front steps of his house. The well-behaved Lucy sat near us, hoping to be offered a piece. "It looks like Lucy wants some ice cream too," he said, breaking off a piece of his sandwich and flipping it to Lucy, who snapped it out of the air.

"Can I give her a piece?" I asked.

"Sure. Go ahead."

As I tried to figure out how I was going to break off a piece without squeezing out all the ice cream, Mr. McGaffin said, "Here, you keep yours. I'll let you give her a piece of mine. I don't want all of it." He broke off another piece and handed it to me. As Lucy eagerly came forward, he warned her, "Lucy . . . be good." I tossed it to her and she caught it.

Right about then the front door opened and a sleepy-looking Jeffrey came out and joined us. In his hand was a cup of coffee. "Hi," he said. "Taking a little break from your chores?"

Mr. McGaffin said, "Oh yeah."

"How are you?" Jeffrey said, sitting down in the grass. "You're . . . Robert, right?"

Thrilled that he remembered my name, I murmured, "Yeah. Hi, Jeffrey." He was wearing a pair of gym shorts and was shirtless. He had a hairless, muscular build.

"And what are you guys up to? Robert, I assume you're going to help Jim . . . Mr. McGaffin finish cutting the lawn." They exchanged a look of amusement when Jeffrey referred to Mr. McGaffin as "Jim."

"No, Robert's going to the park. Someone else could help me."

"Maybe, but someone else has to be at work in an hour."

"All right," Mr. McGaffin said.

I was just about finished with my ice-cream sandwich when Mr. McGaffin said, "Robert, I better finish cutting this lawn. It was nice to see you." I understood that it was time for me to go. Acquiring a sense of timing was a skill that would be very useful in my life.

•

"Thanks for the ice cream, Mr. McGaffin."

"You're welcome."

As I was about to leave, Jeffrey called out, "Goodbye, Robert."

"Bye, Jeffrey."

Mr. McGaffin bent down and pulled a dandelion from the lawn. He said with a grin, "The dandelions are coming up everywhere." To my surprise, he sounded unconcerned about this manifestation of chaos in his own front yard and he happily resumed mowing as I rode off.

In 1967, two men in their mid-thirties living together in a house in Kenmore, a suburb of Buffalo, was unusual. There once was a time when the broad standards of pretense made it possible for two women who were obviously devoted to each other to still be called old maids. And there was once a time when two confirmed bachelor roommates in their late thirties weren't suspected of being gay unless they were arrested on a morals charge or talked with their hands. But the Age of Wishful Thinking was finally coming to an end. Mr. McGaffin and Jeffrey were unambiguous—they were a couple.

In the fourth grade, I had never heard of homosexuality and "faggot" wasn't a common word in most children's vocabularies. In elementary school the worst thing I can remember a boy being called was a "big fem." It wasn't until junior high that "fag" replaced "fem" in our lexicon of slurs. It's interesting that the two worst things you could accuse a boy of being were either a homosexual or a woman. No man ever tries to combine the two and accuse another guy of being a lesbian because even the stupidest men sense that accusing another man of being attracted to women is a compliment.

That year I had my first identity tremor—warning me of the Big One that was still to come—when Mr. McGaffin cast me as a leprechaun in a school play. I felt miscast in the role of an Irish fairy, but to my consternation, Mr. McGaffin insisted that I was perfect for the part. For weeks I agonized about playing a leprechaun as if it could ruin my chances of ever playing leading roles of more manly practitioners of magic such as wizards or sorcerers.

Every class at Thomas Edison Elementary was responsible for presenting an assembly, and to celebrate St. Patrick's Day, our class's contribution was an Irish children's play directed by Mr. McGaffin. St. Patrick's Day was clearly his favorite holiday, as he was inordinately proud of his Irish heritage. For several weeks before March 17 we sang such songs as "Danny Boy" and "When Irish Eyes Are Smiling" in a shameless display of Celtic pride.

Being of Irish heritage, I've always thought that St. Patrick's Day was a bogus holiday because I'm aware of how disenchanting Irish pride can be. From observations of my family, I learned that the shamrock is the symbol of Ireland because it's the perfect shape for a drink coaster. A traditional St. Patrick's Day parade is a sordid spectacle where the drunk spectators watch others march while they themselves gradually lose the ability even to stand. Whenever I've seen Irish eyes smiling, it means that someone has offered to buy a round. And I'm convinced that if St. Patrick did drive the snakes out of Ireland, it was probably because he was suffering from the d.t.'s and started having hallucinatory reptilian visions.

I was one of seven leprechauns who were not integral to the play's action. We were shillelagh carriers, small parts that were created to make sure that every student had a moment of stage time. During our first rehearsal Mr. McGaffin informed me and the other six unlucky wee folk, "Boys, for your costumes you'll each need a pair of tights, which are then going to be dyed green by Mrs. McIndoo."

Only girls wear tights.

Doesn't he know that?

To my relief, Rick O'Brien voiced a small protest, "Um . . . Mr. McGaffin . . . do we really have to wear tights?"

Noticing for the first time that the seven of us were not delighted to be appearing as pixies in panty hose, Mr. McGaffin tried to sell us a crock of buried gold: "I know that wearing tights might seem strange at first. But it's important to make our show look as authentic as possible. We want the audience to feel like they're really seeing leprechauns. I know it's a lot to ask but will you boys do this for me?" The luck of the Irish was entirely with Mr. McGaffin. We liked him, and by asking us to wear the tights as a personal favor, he shrewdly managed to gain our reluctant consent.

I dreaded having to ask my mother to buy me the tights. I don't know how I knew that she wouldn't like having to do this, but gay sons are quick studies when it comes to sensing their parents' uncomfortable subjects. I decided to bring up the tights when my mother was in the middle of scrubbing the kitchen floor. My hope was that she would be too busy to follow our conversation closely.

"Mom . . ."

"What, Bob?"

I didn't say anything, having already, at the age of

eight, mastered the deluded masculine belief that if I merely initiated a conversation about a subject I didn't want to talk about, then I had done more than my fair share.

"Bob! What?"

"I need a pair of tights."

"*What* do you need?"

"A pair of tights."

She stopped cleaning and waited—praying, I suppose, that I wasn't about to announce that someday I wanted to become a choreographer.

"It's for the school play."

She still didn't say anything.

"I'm a leprechaun," I confessed shamefully.

"Bob, where am I going to find a pair of tights *for a boy*!"

I shrugged. I didn't know. I stood there waiting for her to say something else. I was unable to suggest, "Why don't you try the Gay Boys' Department of a local clothing store?"

I felt somewhat better about having to wear tights when Mr. McGaffin astutely decided to add two more leprechauns to the cast—Mark Daly, the most popular boy in our class, and Bill Yaskow, the toughest boy in our class. No one would dare tease them about wearing tights and the rest of our blarney of leprechauns could hide under the shade of their popularity.

Rehearsals went very well because Mr. McGaffin was a good director. While he could be demanding and exacting, he also could encourage someone to do better without undermining his confidence. "Debbie, that was great. Your voice carries all the way to the back rows . . ." When Debbie sang, she tried to hit every note as if she was sparring with it. Mr. McGaffin chuckled as he said,

"Debbie, it's wonderful, but this time let's try not to use so much force. You're not yelling for help, you're singing about Ireland."

My leprechaun performance went off without a hitch. I had no lines to remember and nothing to do but enter and walk slowly around the stage with my arms outstretched to give the illusion that I was magical. It also gave my mother a chance to recognize me. Following Mr. McGaffin's directions, I crouched next to a large green cardboard shamrock for the remainder of the play. Feeling conspicuous in my tights, I was almost harder to see than a real leprechaun. After the performance, my mother came backstage. "You were good, Bob," she said. She was congratulatory without giving me too much encouragement. A beaming Mr. McGaffin came over to us. "Mrs. Smith, didn't Robert make a wonderful leprechaun?"

"Yes, he did," she said with a forced smile. My mother helped me remove my costume and after I had taken off the tights she said, "I'll take those home for you, Bob." I never saw the tights again. I have no doubt that on the way home my mother pulled the car over and hurled them in the first Dumpster she saw.

Mr. McGaffin's best quality as a teacher was that he had the ability to laugh when a disaster occurred without making you feel laughed at. Spilled paint, dead goldfish, lost lunches, and split pants; every crisis was handled with a lighthearted but not disrespectful attitude.

I got along well with Mr. McGaffin. My only complaint about him was that he called me Robert. One day, when I flinched involuntarily at "Robert," he finally said, "I'm sorry. Do you prefer Robert or Bob? I prefer Jim to James but the choice is yours."

"Bob," I said. "I like Bob."

I'd revealed my preference because Mr. McGaffin and I were going to be working closely together on a very important bulletin board and there was no need for us to be so formal with each other, although I never did feel comfortable calling him "Jim." Earlier in the day Mr. McGaffin had noticed that I liked to draw. In the fourth grade, I loved making elaborate architectural renderings of floating futuristic cities with colored pencils. My cities were always involved in an intergalactic war or alien invasion because I particularly enjoyed coloring laser-blasted buildings with painstakingly drawn gaping holes out of which little scraggly, twisted girders waved like tentacles.

I can now see that for me, a major part of the appeal of drawing was inventing names for the cities and alien planets, which involved hitting upon the right combination of vowels and rarely used consonants. At the bottom of my drawings would be neatly penciled names of my cities and planets such as Bizxctla, capital of Vzonath III. When creating a name, I was fond of the letter *X* and my spelling rule for made-up alien words was: *I* before *Z* except after *V*. And I might be old-fashioned futurist but I still prefer the more traditional look of Roman numerals to demark my imaginary worlds.

Mr. McGaffin discovered my artistic bent when he walked by my desk and saw me engrossed in drawing yet another doomed civilization. "Robert, what are you working on?"

His question caught me off guard and it took me a moment to rush back from the twenty-fourth century. "I'm just drawing."

I had hoped that was the end of our discussion as I felt that my destroying a planet was a personal matter between me and the four million inhabitants of "Amarkos

V." Mr. McGaffin put his hand on the back of my chair as he leaned in closer to examine my drawings. I could smell his cologne. Was he wearing the Hai Karate? I glanced over at Norma Einhiple seated next to me. She was reading *Little House on the Prairie* and her concentration remained unbroken. He must be wearing something else. "Robert, do you mind if I look at the rest of these?"

"No," I lied.

After examining my drawings, he looked into my eyes and said, "These are wonderful." I was pleased that he liked my drawings but I was also embarrassed by the attention. "I didn't know that you liked to draw. Perhaps you would like to work on our bulletin board next month?"

"Uh, yeah." He was referring to the hallway bulletin board near the top of the stairs. Every two weeks a different classroom was responsible for its decoration. Typically, the bulletin board tried to explain a scientific principle by asking an intriguing question such as "What Is a Rainbow?" or commemorated a moment in history such as "LaSalle Discovers the Mississippi." The less ambitious teachers always went with the safe and predictable "Reading is *Fun*damental!" and lazily posted twelve book reports.

Mr. McGaffin was probably planning something spectacular; maybe an illustrated time line of the life of Edna St. Vincent Millay. *May 21, 1927—Lindbergh lands in Paris after flying across the Atlantic. That same evening Edna tries her first Manhattan followed immediately by her second, third, fourth, and fifth.* As Mr. McGaffin asked me more questions about my drawings, I responded with one-word answers because the rest of the class was following our conversation. As an adult there is still only one superpower I desire: gravity vision, the ability to look at someone and make them drop a subject. From that day on, at Mr. McGaffin's urging, I frequently included illustrations in my schoolwork, everything from a portrait of Harriet Tubman to the Leaning Tower of Pisa. I would have preferred to have shown the tower in ruins after being attacked by spaceships from Disxumalon IX.

There were occasions when Mr. McGaffin pressed his enthusiasms on you like an ungracious hostess offering refreshments; refusal wasn't an option and you could never let on that you didn't care for them. "No, thank you, Mr. McGaffin. I've had enough Edna St. Vincent Millay. If I have any more it will spoil my appetite for all literature." And it happened infrequently, but Mr. McGaffin did sometimes lose his temper. One afternoon I was daydreaming during arithmetic. Throughout my childhood, I believed my head was some sort of musical instrument and I tried to learn to play it by practicing whenever I was bored or restless. I was just running through an arpeggio of squeaking, squishing, and splunching sounds with my cheeks when Mr. McGaffin ceased writing a problem on the board to bark at me: "Bob Smith—are you making those noises? You sound just like a little pig." At least he was finally calling me Bob.

I didn't understand that Mr. McGaffin's overreaction to my playing my own skull as a conch-shell trumpet might have had nothing to do with me. It might have been because of a fight that he had that morning with Jeffrey and he was possibly taking out his frustrations on me.

I wish now that an adult had explained the basic mechanics of emotions to me. As a child, I assumed that all emotions followed a pattern of cause and effect like physical pain. When you burn your finger, your response to the injury is immediate. Whereas I know now that when someone hurts your feelings, sometimes you don't react immediately and it can take you years to feel the pain. Or when your own feelings are hurt, you might try to hurt someone else's. I was terrified by Mr. McGaffin's unexpected outburst and would have appreciated a few dropped hints of approaching fury or preferably even advance notice such as, "Bob, you're really pissing me off."

By the afternoon, Mr. McGaffin tried to make amends by asking me to take a file down to the principal's office. When I returned from the errand, Mr. McGaffin was reading *Restless Spirit* to the class. Mr. McGaffin was quite good at reading stories aloud, as he gave each character a distinctive voice. We were near the end of the book and the melodramatic high point of Mr. McGaffin's reading was Edna's death scene:

> On the night of October 18, 1950, alone as usual, she was reading the proofs of a translation of the *Aeneid* by Rolfe Humphries. She read all night long, until dawn of the nineteenth. Then she poured herself a glass of wine and started upstairs. Halfway up, she must have felt ill or weak. She stopped, sat down, and carefully put the glass of wine down on the step above. That afternoon, John Pinnie came into the house and found her lying there, dead of a heart attack.

I loved the casual insertion of the "alone as usual," making sure that we knew that Edna's last days were sad. After finishing the book, Mr. McGaffin had the entire class write Edna's sister Norma letters on big oversize sheets of pale green wide-lined writing paper. In my letter, I mentioned my favorite anecdote in the book, a story about how one cold winter day the pipes burst, flooding the kitchen. When the water froze, Edna and her two sisters ice-skated around the floor.

Our letters to Norma were never answered. It's understandable; I doubt that I would know how to respond to a large package of childishly scrawled condolence letters:

Dear Norma,

I'm sorry your sister died on the stairs and didn't get to finish her wine.

Your friend,
Debbie Gruber

For a long time after our letters were mailed Mr. McGaffin announced that he expected a reply from Norma any day. Finally there were only a few more weeks left in the school year and he had to admit that our letters were probably never going to be answered. Of course we were disappointed but Edna certainly would have appreciated the irony of children learning about disillusionment from trying to write to her sister.

On the last day of school, in one last burst of holiday spirit, Mr. McGaffin decided to celebrate by having a class award ceremony. He ensured that everybody won a prize by creating categories of accomplishment from the Prix de Pasting to Best Picture. The presentation of the awards was exciting because Mr. McGaffin breathlessly opened each envelope almost as if he himself was curious to learn who had won. After each name was announced, the victor would walk to the front of the class to claim his prize. In addition to the prize, Mr. McGaffin handed each winner his final report card, which had shiny green stars attached to it indicating that the recipient had won an award. Mr. McGaffin then led the class in applauding the winner.

The awards that Mr. McGaffin presented were different types of exotic candies. Most of the prizes were little tins of imported lemon or raspberry drops called "pastilles" or bars of McIntosh English toffee. If I had a choice, I wanted to win the pastilles because I didn't care for toffee. It was one of those vaguely unpleasant candies like black licorice or lavender mints that veered toward the disagreeable.

Soon, almost everyone had received their prizes but I still hadn't received mine. As I sat waiting in sugary anticipation, Mr. McGaffin reached into a shopping bag and pulled out two big bars of chocolate. He said, "The last two awards I'm going to give out are for Scholastic Achievement. I felt the winners deserved something special for all of their hard work." Without opening any envelopes—I felt a teensy bit cheated by that—he announced. "The winners for Scholastic Achievement are Kelly Helmbrecht and Bob Smith."

I walked up to receive my award and my report card. When I returned to my seat I first carefully examined my prize. It wasn't the expected Hershey's or Nestlé's; Mr. McGaffin had bought imported chocolate. The writing on the wrapper was foreign and there was a drawing of an orange. I hoped there wasn't fruit in the chocolate because that would make it almost something good for you. All I could make out was that the chocolate was manufactured in the "Nederland," which sounded like the treacherous dead zone on the outskirts of the Qwetzlian Empire on Disxumalon IX. Then I read what Mr. McGaffin had written on my report card in the space for teacher comments. *A joy to have in class! Dependable. Efficient.* Mr. McGaffin had also faultlessly written in flowing blue script, *Bob was honored for Scholastic Achievement.*

Over the lifetime that passed on my summer vacation between the fourth and the fifth grades, my crush on Mr. McGaffin faded. The belief that absence makes the heart grow fonder can be undermined by the fickle attention span of a nine-year-old. After the fourth grade, Mr. McGaffin and I saw each other in the halls occasionally. We would give each other nods of recognition but it was never the same. He was busy with a new class of fourth graders, and in my heart I knew that I was yesterday's pupil and that he was last year's teacher.

The summer after the fifth grade, on a July night, I saw Mr. McGaffin and Jeffrey once more when I went swimming at Kenmore's public pool in Mang Park. My father had brought my sister and me, since children needed to be accompanied by an adult in order to swim at night. I loved swimming as the sun set and the sky darkened and the submerged lights came on in the pool. It was always a toss-up as to whether my father would swim or not. Sometimes we were able to coax him into entering the water, but he mostly stood by the side of the pool watching us swim and contemplating whether bumming a cigarette from a lifeguard would undermine their code of ethics.

I saw Mr. McGaffin and Jeffrey swimming laps but I didn't approach them. I was still intrigued by Mr. McGaffin and Jeffrey but I felt more embarrassed by the prospect of possibly having to introduce them to my father than I was excited by the prospect of talking to them. I wasn't exactly sure why I felt uncomfortable about my father meeting them. I was reaching the age when any attention drawn to myself made me feel awkward. It also might have had to do with the dawning realization that Mr. McGaffin and Jeffrey were different in a way that was considered disreputable. I had heard some of the boys making fun of Mr. McGaffin for reading poetry to his classes. Trying to fit in, I had professed a hatred for poetry too. Poetry was for sissies and although I didn't live in fear of hearing, "You bard!" I knew that it was a four-letter word.

I stayed at the other end of the pool, repeatedly sliding down the big slide. Near closing time, as I climbed out of the water, my father finally announced, "Bob, it's time to get going." As I stood dripping on the pavement, with my towel wrapped around my shoulders, shivering a little, I noticed for the first time that Mr. McGaffin and Jeffrey had departed. It was then that I felt disappointed that I hadn't said hello to them. But as I stood by the entrance to the pool, a familiar voice said, "Hello, Bob."

"Hi, Mr. McGaffin," I replied. I didn't say hello to Jeffrey. We merely smiled a greeting. Mr. McGaffin introduced himself to my father who was tapping a cigarette out of a pack. My father was perfectly at ease, as the prospect of nicotine was already relieving any tension in him. He stated firmly, "It got a little chilly out there tonight."

"It sure did," Mr. McGaffin replied. My father lit his cigarette and held it aloft as if he was going to ask us to warm ourselves by gathering around the burning tip. Mr. McGaffin and Jeffrey said good night and as we walked to the car, I began to perform a little dance, tipping my head back and forth because I had water in my ears and they were ringing. I was a little disappointed that my ears weren't burning because, even though my crush was over, part of me hoped that Mr. McGaffin and Jeffrey were talking about me as they walked to their car.

Way to Go, Smith!

IN THE fifth grade we needed to move beyond the study of guppies and tadpoles to learn about human biology. We had reached the age when the subject of our bodies could no longer be avoided; this was the year the girls would be given a lecture on becoming young women. I knew that maturing had something to do with Nancy Tirranno developing breasts, but how did this apply to me? I was fairly certain that unless I turned out like Ray Gouchie's father, I wasn't going to be getting a pair.

I knew that for boys, growing up involved the appearance of body hair. From what I had observed, hairiness was to men what stickiness was to boys; some boys were sticky from head to toe while most boys were just sticky in spots. It was clear that all men grew beards. It was like the wallet of physical maturation. Every grown man that I knew had one. You would also grow hair under your arms and around your privates too. They were like your set of house keys and car keys. Every man I knew had both of them too.

But only some men grew hair on their chest, arms and legs, and even sometimes on their shoulders and back. The other types of body hair were like the optional accessories that some men chose to carry, like a pocketknife or a nail clipper or those little rubber change holders. They seemed odd to me because my father didn't have them. But weirdest of all was that your body could get really hairy and your head still could go bald. It was like some man's scalps had got plugged up and hair started leaking out their shoulders.

My body had already started changing. I had lost my baby teeth but they were replaced by new ones. I thought it was cool when a baby tooth became loose and I could rock it back and forth with my tongue. It was a relief that my mother never became angry when I told her that I lost a tooth the way she did when I lost a glove. She definitely would have become furious if every time I lost a tooth she had to go all the way out to the mall to buy a replacement. "Bob, don't tell me you've lost another one. We're spending all your father's hard-earned money on new teeth because you don't know how to take care of them!"

Whenever I saw a man with a bald spot, which often enough was the size of a mitten, it made grown men who had lost their hair seem like boys who were especially careless or played too rough. I could just hear their mothers. "You lost your hair? Well, where did you lose it? You don't know? Well, think! You had to have lost it somewhere. Where do you think you might have lost it?"

I couldn't decide what I thought about pubic hair. Sometimes it looked gross and sometimes it looked kind of cool. I wasn't sure if I was going to like getting it, but I hoped that growing pubic hair was like drinking beer. I had tried a few sips of my father's beer and didn't like it now, but it seemed that eventually all men grew to appreciate it. Maybe it was the same with pubic hair.

The main difference that I noticed about men's bodies compared with boys' bodies was muscles. Having big muscles was neat, but not all men got them. Before the popularization of bodybuilding it seemed that only some men developed muscles while other men either remained boyishly skinny or became fat. I wanted to get some muscles but there was no telling what kind of body or body hair I would have and I wasn't worried or in a hurry to find out. Beyond that, my knowledge of puberty was a complete blank, but I was comfortable in my ignorance and figured that when it was time for me to become an adult, someone would let me know.

I just hoped the news wasn't going to be delivered by Mrs. Geiger, the meanest teacher at Thomas Edison Elementary School. The word on the playground was that Mrs. Geiger wrote on her blackboard with the bones of troublemakers. Barry Folvarcik said, "She once threw an eraser at my brother's head and broke a window!" Mrs. Geiger carried her anger like a purse, always with her, holding all she needed to get through her day. When I became her pupil, she was in her early fifties and even her petrified hairstyle looked afraid of her.

Mrs. Geiger hobbled as she walked because she had had polio as a girl. In the school hallways her footsteps were as distinct as the tread of a monster in a horror movie. She dragged her obstinate right leg and then swung it out and forward almost like she was trying to kick Jonas Salk for dawdling when he should have been working on his vaccine.

Early in the school year Mrs. Geiger and I had the first of many altercations. As my class was lining up to go to lunch, she tried to get the students to settle down by saying, "Boys and girls . . ." After she said this for the third time I impulsively told her, "Cool it, Daddy-o!" Mrs. Geiger's reaction let me know that I had just made a big mistake.

"What did you say?" she asked, livid.

"Nothing."

"Why don't you tell the whole class what you just said?"

I wasn't sure that was a good idea.

"Go on."

I repeated, "Cool it, Daddy-o," but this time I sounded like I was from Squaresville.

"For that you'll be staying after school, mister."

From watching television I had discovered and embraced beatnik slang and now at every opportunity I tried out their already outdated yet still irresistible hipster lingo. (In a few years I would move on to saying "groovy," a word that I still find indispensable.) Before leaving the house, I would say, "Mom, I'm going to Vic Benfanti's. *Can you dig it?*" But she never did dig it, just as Mrs. Geiger didn't dig being called "Daddy-o." In addition to threatening to send me down to the principal's office, Mrs. Geiger wrote a note to my parents that had to be signed by my father. He was not exactly overjoyed to be raising a cool cat and so I thought it prudent to wait awhile before asking him for a set of bongos.

I further established myself as a troublemaker in Mrs. Geiger's eyes the next day, during a free period, when she caught me whispering to Brian Dixon, "Mary Canderby likes you." Mrs. Geiger branded me as a "talker" and she did not tolerate talkers in her class. During her teaching career Mrs. Geiger had ended more conversations than the Angel of Death. In her classroom she wanted quiet. Since the first grade my teachers had acknowledged my chatty nature on my report cards. *He talks constantly* or *Still needs to listen* often appeared as teacher comments. But I wasn't talking too much; it was just that with the constant interruptions it took me until June to finish the conversation that I had started in September.

On the day when the girls were taken to the school auditorium to learn about menstruation, the boys stayed in class and I spent my free time doing an extra-credit project—making an illustrated guide to the nations of Latin America.

I loved getting extra credit. Once I started trying to earn it in school, I wanted to earn extra credit everywhere. I wanted extra credit from God for giving up chocolate for Lent. I wanted extra credit from America for not littering unless my garbage was sticky and I wasn't near a trash can. I wanted extra credit for reluctantly offering a handful of my barbecue potato chips to my brother Greg, who knew I wasn't going to refuse him since he had asked me in front of our father.

But that's not the worst of it. Not only did I want extra credit for doing a good deed but I also wanted extra credit for merely intending to do a good deed. When I was reading a comic book and heard my mother return from grocery shopping, I knew that I should go out and help her carry in the bags. But I would wait a minute to see if one of my brothers was going to lend a hand. When I heard, "Mom, let me do that!" I could return to the exploits of the Legion of Super-Heroes, satisfied that I was willing to help. I wanted extra credit for just considering the possibility of being thoughtful.

When the girls returned to class, knowing a little more about their impending womanhood, I was curious and asked Linda Garrity about the lecture. Linda looked almost as alarmed as she had looked when I forced her to jump off Wayne Newport's garage into a pile of leaves. Only this time I didn't threaten to spit on her. While Linda evaded answering me, an exasperated Mrs. Geiger asked, "Is that Bob Smith I hear talking again?"

I didn't answer her, believing that if I didn't speak now she might think I was incapable of talking before.

"Bob, I asked you a question."

"Yes."

"I hope I don't have to send another letter home with you . . ." When I didn't answer, she asked, "Well, do I?"

I didn't think that her unfinished thought required an answer. For someone who hated talking, she loved to drag out a conversation. I replied with a no.

Mrs. Geiger didn't send a note this time because if she sent one home every time she caught me talking she would have had to hire a secretary to handle the volume of correspondence. With evident relief Linda turned away from me and gave her attention to Mrs. Geiger. I never did ask Linda again about the lecture. I would have to fill in the details two years later in the seventh grade.

Our first lessons about the birds and the bees only covered their digestion. Mrs. Geiger explained the function of the gizzard and the production of honey, which are safe subjects in America, as the stomach is a less controversial organ than the penis or vagina. At a cocktail party anyone can make a comment to a stranger about how their stomach is feeling, while mentioning to a new acquaintance how your genitals feel is still frowned upon—well, in most social situations anyway. By learning about the human digestive, respiratory, and circulatory systems, we were leading up to learning about human reproduction. It was almost as if before we could get to the sex, we needed to understand the physiology of a churning stomach, a pounding heart, and heavy breathing.

I still didn't have a very clear idea of what adulthood would be like even though it seemed that adults had been talking to me about my adulthood since my infancy. My confusion was compounded because the Grown-up Bob was always being represented to me by the same people who told me about Santa Claus and the Tooth Fairy.

When I was very young, I believed in my adult self with all the imaginative force a child can muster. Someday I would drive my train to my job digging up dinosaurs and then at night I would go to the caboose, where my wife and my best friend Tommy Helmbrecht and I would have hamburgers or pizza and then watch television until we decided to go to bed. But by the fifth grade I understood that being an adult would be somewhat different from what I had previously imagined. My idea of adulthood was no longer a fantasy, it was just unrealistic. I no longer expected, at any moment, to discover that I possessed secret superpowers but I still thought that someday I would have a wife and kids.

Throughout my childhood the question I was asked most frequently was, "Bob, what do you want to be when you grow up?" After fainting twice in the fifth grade, my answer should have been, "Conscious." The first time I fainted was when Mrs. Geiger showed our class a grainy black-and-white film made during the 1930s called *Your Digestive System.*

I disliked the film but I couldn't have given a reason why, because when I was a boy I didn't think my response to anything required a rationale. As an adult I'm often envious that children in an audience can express the state of being bored to tears by actually shedding them.

The pace of *Your Digestive System* resembled the speed of the process it described—presented as if we needed several hours to assimilate it. The actors sounded as if they were reading their stilted dialogue while it was still being written and I didn't buy for one minute the performance of the pancreas; it looked like it was faking the production of insulin.

Speaking with a heavy-handed smarminess that would prompt a carnival barker to suggest that maybe he was pushing too hard, the on-screen narrator began the film by asking, "Boys and girls, how would you like to learn about digestion?" Losing his smile when he noticed that the sleeves on the lab coat were too short, he continued. "The first step in the digestive process is the production of saliva by your salivary glands." Suddenly jaunty again—he's made up his mind to ask the script girl for a date—he grinned. "Saliva contains an enzyme, ptyalin, which breaks down starches into sugars that your body uses for energy!"

The film barely kept my attention by showing something disgusting every few minutes. The subject of eating was illustrated by a shot of a typical American family seated around a dinner table, which was then contrasted with a family of Bushmen crouched around a campfire devouring fried bugs. A few minutes after the film had started I began to feel queasy when the subject of carbohydrates was illustrated by a lump of chewed bread being picked apart with a fork. But I didn't make much of the sensation, because for a ten-year-old boy feeling nauseated is often difficult to distinguish from boredom.

The last image I remember before blacking out was an explanation of peristalsis featuring X-ray footage of an esophagus in the act of swallowing. As the bulging lump of food moved down the throat, I suddenly felt dizzy. At first I didn't know what was happening—my head was a birthday cake and someone was blowing out all the candles. Flashbulbs went off as I made a wish but it didn't come true. It was actually happening to me—I was going to pass out.

As a ridicule-inducing activity, my flair for passing out ranked with having a natural talent for ballet—an ability probably best to avoid demonstrating before a large group of ten and eleven-year-old boys. I hit the floor as if I was trying to tackle my own shadow and my smooth move was cheered on by Mark Deffler. "Way to go, Smith!" he called. I didn't acknowledge his sarcastic praise, unsuccessfully trying to pass off my silence as modesty. His words filtering down the long passageways of my ears, I heard Joey Valleria say, "Bob's fainted!" and the heads of twenty-three fifth graders snapped in my direction. I couldn't have drawn more attention if I had hired a publicist.

Mrs. Geiger took control of the situation by turning off the film projector and turning on the classroom lights. She knelt by me and said with surprising concern, "Bob, just keep your head down. Don't get up until you feel completely better." As I sat on the floor with my head tucked between my knees, I don't think she understood that I couldn't follow her advice, since I would have needed to stay in that position for years until I felt *completely* better.

My embarrassment grew as the flow of blood returned to my head—abject humiliation being one of the most efficient means of improving your circulation. Shame is the first adult feeling that children are actively encouraged to participate in once they've mastered the training-wheel emotions of joy and pain. No kindly adult ever warns a child, "Honey, you're too little to be embarrassed. Why don't you wait until you're a little older to feel completely humiliated? There's no rush; believe me, you'll have plenty of other opportunities."

My blackout was as sudden as a break in the film—only Mrs. Geiger couldn't quickly repair my damaged reputation with Scotch tape and my life couldn't resume as if nothing had happened. Unlike a snapped film, I knew that my lapse in continuity wouldn't be completely forgotten by the next day. My gut feeling was that my fainting would be long remembered, as I had completely upstaged the cast of the digestive system.

I was mortified. Even Paul Schneggenburger, who was always called "Spaz," had never fallen down while seated. I had caused more of a commotion than Mark Utley did when he threw up in an aquarium after arithmetic. I wished that I had thrown up instead of fainting. In elementary school there was no long-lasting stigma attached to vomiting because boys have an instinctive appreciation for someone making a huge disgusting mess. In fact, if a boy barfed on a particularly disliked or feared teacher, such as Mrs. Geiger, he could probably have increased his popularity.

Fainting is an entirely different matter. For a man or boy, to faint is to be held to a different standard. While avoiding consciousness is perfectly acceptable for boys and men, losing consciousness is losing control and the unwritten rule is that the only time a man can lose control is when he's either drunk or having an orgasm, and even then, he had better regain control fast.

After ten minutes on the floor spent with my head between my knees, I crawled back into my seat and Linda Garrity handed me my new black "Junior Clark Kent" eyeglasses, which had fallen off. A few weeks earlier Mrs. Geiger had discovered that I couldn't read the word "independence" on the blackboard. At first her questions betrayed a suspicion that my eyes were goofing off. "Can you see this? Try again. *You're sure?* You can't read this? Okay, you need to have your eyes checked." She informed the school nurse, who, after giving me an eye test, called my mother with the news that I might need eyeglasses.

I reacted to the optometrist's announcement that I needed eyeglasses with excitement. I was at the age when I wanted to assert my individuality, and since my major accomplishments at this point were learning to tie my own shoes, make a paper airplane, and ride a bicycle, I was willing to embrace nearsightedness as if it was a talent. Needing eyeglasses made me special. This was the first of many instances of self-deception on my part, moments when I've decided that one of my defects actually conferred a secret advantage. Over the years I would add sloppiness ("you ignore the little things"), stubbornness ("you're not wishy-washy"), and selfishness ("you're staying focused"). When I was fitted for eyeglasses at the optician's, it felt like I was being given a toy that only I would be allowed to play with. In retrospect, *Your Di-*

gestive System was probably the first movie I had ever seen clearly.

By lunchtime, everyone in the fifth grade knew about my fainting, the story spreading quickly, as if *My Weekly Reader* had put out an unprecedented extra edition. Kids who had never spoken to me before were inquiring, with stares of disbelief that varied from the incredulous to the smirking, "Why'd ya faint?"

I wasn't sure what had caused me to faint. By the normal standards of boyhood, I wasn't squeamish. I was used to the sight of blood in movies and television shows, and due to numerous childhood accidents I had seen plenty of my own gushing hemoglobin and had never once swooned. Before the age of ten I was always having accidents and my mother was constantly running me over to Kenmore Mercy Hospital to have my birthday suit mended. Once, while running toward the house, I fell face first through a window, slicing open my nose. Another time I was roughhousing with my mother in the kitchen when I kicked, lost my balance, and split my head open on the footrest of a wooden chair. My bloodiest injury involved tripping over my own feet and putting a T-shaped gash in my forehead that required thirteen stitches. If a surgeon had used all the stitches sewn into my face to make a needlepoint sampler, he could have spelled out the words "Walk much?" in several languages. But none of these experiences caused anything but loud crying at first and curiosity later. When the bandages were changed, I wasn't grossed out, I was impressed at the sight of the stitches in my face. I couldn't believe that they actually used a needle and thread to sew you up.

As a boy, I was thrilled by my own revulsion and

eagerly sought out the gross, the vile, and the disgusting. I liked snakes, horror movies, and amusement parks. The rides at amusement parks are a wonderful preparation for your sex life. You spend more time in excited anticipation of the ride than you do actually experiencing it. You can do the ride by yourself but it's more fun if you do it with someone else. During the ride your head is spinning, but it's over all too soon. And, of course, there are plenty of times when the ride is a big disappointment. And even times when you feel like throwing up afterward.

What made the experience of fainting especially terrifying was the knowledge that we were just beginning to study the human body and that I had years of biology films ahead of me. And while the other students would enjoy these short unannounced breaks, much like fire drills, I was afraid that my passing out was going to be a recurring experience throughout junior and senior high.

The following week we moved on to the circulatory system and Mrs. Geiger showed another film explaining its wonders. Once the film started I tried not to pay attention to it by staring at my desk instead of the screen. My school desk was a vintage model from the 1920s when Thomas Edison Elementary School had been built. The vestigial inkwell in the top right-hand corner was a history lesson in itself. The desk had seen years of hard use and it wouldn't have surprised me to find the date 1772 carved in the surface along with the words "John Hancock Sucks!"

The school was in the process of changing over to new desks, and since the school board didn't have enough money to buy a new one for every student, a few were doled out to each classroom. This gave each student a tantalizing glimpse of the future, with the underlying message that only the lucky few would experience it. The new desks were chairs with an attached laminated wood-grain writing surface. They were a hybrid between a chair and a desk, the centaurs of the furniture world, and as centaurs are too smart to be good farm animals and too human to be good pets, the new chair-desks weren't good at either of their functions. The plastic seats weren't as comfortable as the wooden ones and the smaller writing surface and lack of storage space made them inferior to our old desks. The beginning of the decline in American scholastic standards can be traced back to the moment when boards of education across the country started lowering the requirements for quality school desks.

Deliberately trying not to learn in a classroom was harder than I expected. I could only stare at my desk for so long before I had to look up at the film. As I tried not to listen to the narrator's explanation of the differences between a vein and an artery, I became angry that I had been put in such an embarrassing position. There was no compelling reason that we actually had to see our internal organs in order to learn about them. We had learned about Christopher Columbus's discovery of America without actually witnessing the event. We didn't look at live genitals to learn about the reproductive system. So why couldn't our internal organs also be considered private parts?

In desperation I opened my social-studies book. We were being taught to admire the Iroquois Indians for their agricultural techniques, their bravery, and their democratic values—everything but their actual presence. Mrs.

Geiger had told us that some of the suburbs of Buffalo—Cheektowaga, Lackawanna, and Tonawanda—were Iroquois words and it almost seemed as if after slaughtering the original inhabitants, the pioneers were just too tired or lazy to rename anything.

Periodically I looked up to see what Mrs. Geiger was doing so I wouldn't be caught reading. She was grading some papers. Before I went back to the People of the Longhouse, I inadvertently glanced up at the screen and saw a heart beating in an open chest and I thought, *Well, this doesn't seem too bad.* But then I suddenly felt dizzy, then I felt panicked, and then I felt nothing. This time my fainting happened so quickly that when I woke up on the floor, I felt like the guest of honor at a truly unexpected surprise party, one that I wished had never been thrown.

I had managed not only to faint once while watching a biology film, but twice. I certainly deserved extra credit for that. The first time it happened I felt as if my own body had made a mistake. The second time it happened I felt that my body had betrayed me. Mrs. Geiger sounded a little put upon the second time around. As I regained self-consciousness, I heard her sigh. "It's okay, everyone. Bob has fainted again. It happens when not enough blood flows to the brain." It was my worst nightmare—I was becoming a learning experience. I was afraid that on our next science test, question number eighteen would be, "What causes squeamish people like Bob to faint in class?"

a) Temporary loss of circulation in the head.

b) Bob's fear of looking inside himself.

c) The desire to skip class for forty-three seconds, which Mrs. Geiger is going to insist that he make up later.

d) All of the above.

I never did faint again during a biology film. My powers of nonconcentration steadily improved and soon I was able to tune out not just biology films but entire subjects that didn't appeal to me. When I was a sophomore in high school I had to spend an entire year studying biology. It was rough. I still remember the fall of 1973 and the spring of 1974 in the Chinese fashion—as the Year of the Frog. I was able to get through dissecting my frog by pretending that a beloved pet had died and I needed to conduct his autopsy. In truth I was more like a surgical nurse during the dissection. I handed the scalpel to Diana Bilkey, my assigned partner, having given her the honor of doing the carving. I found that cutting up a real frog didn't repulse me that much, but watching a frog being dissected in a film would probably have caused me to keel over. Maybe I wasn't squeamish; perhaps I was an overly sensitive film critic. I suppose there is something that could have been worse than fainting during biology films. Instead of fainting, I could have been overly sentimental and started blubbering during the slow-motion death scenes in nature films, such as when a lizard shoots out its long tongue to capture an insect.

Learning to occasionally ignore how you feel is an inevitable part of growing up but most of us can't precisely remember when we began to practice that skill. After fainting for the second time, my body was under strict orders to do exactly what I said and I didn't care if

I had to suppress every emotion or thought to achieve that goal. It's a wonder that men ever complain to their doctors about having symptoms of neuropathy at all. Total loss of feeling is something most men spend their entire lives working to achieve.

It took me a long time to understand why the experience of fainting was so humiliating. What I figured out was that fainting violated the strongest taboo of manhood: I let something get to me.

To Grandmother's House We Go

CELEBRITIES ARE familiar strangers. We recognize them but they don't know us, and of course, we don't ever really know them. There are times when I think of everyone in my family as a celebrity: I'm familiar with them but I don't feel that I know them intimately. As I've grown older, I've become more curious about the people in my life but sometimes I feel that I know more about the celebrities in *People* magazine than I do about the members of my family. At what point did I become more knowledgeable about Brad Pitt's favorite pastimes than I am about my own brothers' lives? Certainly my relationship with Brad Pitt is more satisfying than my relationship with my brothers, because when I don't hear from Brad, I never wonder if he's mad at me. I'm not suggesting that everyone should heed my mother's advice on how to better understand your family. When I became an author, she told my sister, "I wish all you kids would write books. Then I'd know what you're thinking."

The first celebrity I ever saw was the singer Perry Como, whom I glimpsed from my hiding place in the backseat of my grandmother's Buick. Waiting for his arrival, my sister and I had polished off half a roll of Butter Rum Life Savers as my grandmother passed the time whittling away at my self-esteem with sharp remarks about my behavior.

"Bob, are you kicking the seat? Sit still. You must have worms with all that squirming."

My sister sat in the front because if she sat in the back my grandmother would exclaim, "I can't see out the rear window because Carol's big for her age." Every time my grandmother said "Carol's big for her age," she sounded like an astonished paleontologist who had discovered a new species of Megatherium from the Paleolithic Era. Neither of us pointed out that I was taller than my sister because contradicting my grandmother was dangerous. We had learned the lesson of Little Red Riding Hood and were always on the lookout for the wolf in our grandmother. As we waited, Carol tried to remain motionless because on the drive to the Niagara Falls Country Club my grandmother had directed her, "Carol, quit fidgeting. It's not ladylike." Obviously femininity and movement were incompatible.

Whenever Carol did something that my grandmother disapproved of ("She plays so rough! We're going to have call her Tiger Lil' "), the source of her aberrant behavior was always revealed in the words "But what do you expect from a girl who has three brothers?" Judging from my grandmother's efforts to instill gentility in my sister through barked orders and ridicule, I assumed she would to try to toughen me up with giggled whispers and dainty hand flutters.

When I refused the last Life Saver and started biting my nails, my grandmother corrected my bad habit with the observation, "Bob, you look retarded sitting there with your fingers in your mouth. Look at me." For my benefit she mimed chomping on her fingers complete with munching sound effects and repeated, "You see how this looks? You look mentally retarded."

Saying the word "retarded" seemed to trigger a sentimental memory for my grandmother. In a complete change of manner she affectionately recalled, "You know, Bob, you didn't start speaking until after you turned two and you didn't start walking until very late. You were a very strange baby. Oh God, I remember you would only walk in your rolling stroller, but if we stood you up, you would stubbornly curl your legs and refuse to put your feet down. You were a little bullhead. We all tried but nobody could make you walk. After a while I thought there had to be something wrong with you, so I told your parents to have you examined. It wasn't normal and I was afraid that you might be retarded."

After sharing her poignant reminiscence, my grandmother paused for a moment and looked at me with dewy eyes. The dew quickly evaporated, though, and a second later she roared with pained exasperation, "Bob, sit up straight! If you don't watch out, you're going to end up hunchbacked and have to work in a carnival." I tried to sit up straight, but it was hard to do that and remain in a position of spineless submission. When my grandmother spotted my grandfather's car, she ordered, "Get down! Here they come." I slumped forward in my seat, knowing from experience that my grandmother believed in the carrot-and-stick approach to raising children—she would hit you with both objects if you didn't do exactly what she said.

As the car carrying Perry Como turned into the country club's entrance, I was tempted to peek out the window but I waited until it drove past and then cautiously raised my head in time to catch a glimpse of a dark green sedan filled with four shadowy passengers. I think the one with silvery hair on the passenger side of the front seat was Perry Como.

Earlier that morning, after breakfast, my grandmother had announced, "Grampy is having lunch with Perry Como today at the country club. So I thought we'd sneak a look at him. How would you like that?" I had no idea who Perry Como was—I was eight years old—but my grandmother's eagerness was enough to kindle my enthusiasm because she was an authority on everything. Once she decided something was the best, her loyalty was unshakable. She would drive thirty miles out of her way to buy Sahlen's hot dogs because "A *Sahlen's* hot dog is the only hot dog I would have in my house," as though the wieners were dinner guests rather than dinner itself. I was intrigued by my grandmother's desire to see Perry Como and assumed that she knew what she was talking about because she made a mean hot dog. Perry Como was my first introduction to the media-age Zen koan: if a celebrity isn't known to you, is he still famous?

I understood that my grandfather was having lunch with Perry Como because of his job. He didn't actually know Mr. Como personally. After his retirement as a vice-president at the M&T Bank, my grandfather worked as a financial adviser for a small Roman Catholic college, Niagara University. Perry Como was having lunch with my grandfather because the university was awarding the silver-haired crooner an honorary degree. I still wonder why the university decided to bestow this mark of respect and esteem upon him.

The year was 1969 but the board of trustees of Niagara University was made up of men who thought of the sixties as an age group and not an era. It was the same year the Beatles released *Abbey Road*, and even to the most conservative college students the songs of Perry Como had to sound as dated as Gregorian chants. I would have loved to overhear the deliberations of the trustees as they came to their decision:

"This year we should give an honorary degree to a singer who will appeal to young people."

"Who are the young people listening to these days?"

"My baby brother loves Perry Como."

"How old's your brother?"

"Fifty-five."

"What about that Singing Nun?"

"No. She makes being Catholic sound enjoyable. It's misleading."

"You know I have to admit that I like Perry Como too."

"It would be good to show our students that you don't need to smoke dope to enjoy music."

"Yeah, whatever happened to enjoying music with plenty of cigarettes and alcohol?"

"Let's go with Perry Como."

"Okay, but are you sure that we don't want to honor the guy who found the cure for polio?"

"Nah."

By 1969 Perry Como was no longer a big star; his radiance having dimmed, he was in the nebula phase of his career—he had been big once but now he was living on past glory. But in my grandmother's universe he was still a star almost as if it had taken light-years for his illustriousness to finally reach Niagara Falls. It was clear to me, though, that Perry Como was still capable of exerting a big star's strong gravitational pull. He drew my grandmother out of the house and normally she couldn't be forced to do anything.

My grandmother was a short stout woman in her mid-sixties who always claimed to be on a diet. She insisted that she never ate, but when she walked in the kitchen, the food in the refrigerator shivered in fear. In appearance my grandmother's style was always correct if not correctional; on a cord around her neck hung a pair of demi-lune bifocals that she used to overlook her own flaws and focus better on everyone else's.

She was always well dressed and wore expensive outfits from "her" clothing store, Berger's. My grandmother would justify her purchases by saying, "You have to pay for quality. It doesn't matter whether you're buying baloney or clothes, when something's cheap it usually means it's not worth the money."

Her polished sheen was almost flashy. From month to month her hair color changed as she flirted with the entire spectrum of blondness without committing the vulgar offense of actually becoming a blonde. Starting with "Coral," a yellowish red, she would eventually dye it every shade of nearly blonde until the color wheel finally reached "Corral," a yellowish brown. She was a prospector who spent her life searching for gold but kept striking every other color.

Her favorite piece of jewelry was a chunky silver charm bracelet that she always wore to make sure that everyone knew all the burdens she carried—a husband, a house, a car, a dog, children, grandchildren, golf, etc. The charms reminded me of the pieces from a Monopoly set, and depending on her mood, I sometimes thought she had either won the game or had become frustrated and quit, picking up all the pieces, deciding that she didn't want anyone else to play.

My grandparents lived in Lewiston, New York, a small town on the lower Niagara River located halfway between the falls and the river's mouth at Lake Ontario. Their house was located in a spectacular setting, perched on the edge of the river's deep gorge. A large porch overlooked the river but the architectural feature of the house that most impressed me was the built-in Harvest Gold refrigerator and freezer that hung over the kitchen counter in the same manner that the house hung over the gorge.

At age eleven I was more impressed by exotic kitchen appliances than I was by unfamiliar celebrities and I drank my grandmother's bitter saccharine-flavored Frescas just to have an opportunity to open the refrigerator. The word "dietetic" was emblazoned on half the food in her kitchen, while all the other foods ridiculed moderation with such aggressiveness that I half expected fights to break out between the hulking one-pound chocolate bar that had somehow found its way into the cupboard and the puny dietetic hard candies. I sometimes think that drinking my grandmother's Frescas and eating her dietetic candies scarred me psychologically; it made adulthood seem like a world where everything sweet would have an unpleasant aftertaste. The artificial grapefruit flavor of Fresca actually reminded me of my grandmother's personality. She also tried to be sweet but there was always a bite to her too.

Before our Perry Como stakeout, we had lunch at

the Whistle Pig, where my grandmother browbeat me into getting a vanilla milkshake because she wanted one herself but was, as usual, watching her weight. Whenever we went to the Whistle Pig, my grandmother would rhapsodize about owning a hot-dog stand. "Look at how busy this place is! Owning a hot-dog stand is like owning a gold mine." Then she would either add, "I wanted to buy McDonald's stock when it first came out but your grandfather talked me out of it. Why the hell did I listen to him?" or she would envision being the owner of her own hot-dog stand. "I'd love to open a hot-dog stand and you know where I would do it? Down in Florida. They don't have any good hot-dog stands down there. With the money we'd make I could put all you kids through college and during the summers you could all work for me." Her grandchildren never encouraged the idea of Charlotte's Hot Dogs because she already bossed us around enough and the thought of being her employee was terrifying. If my grandmother was serious about finding a new occupation at her age, I think she should have considered becoming a diamond cutter—it's one career where looking for imperfections is a full-time job.

Her faultfinding never truly hurt my feelings, though, because even as a boy, I thought she was entertaining. She knew it too and played to her grandchildren as a performer to an audience. My grandmother was extremely generous and loved buying her grandchildren gifts and I could never visit her without coming back with a new pair of pants and a new shirt. When her grandchildren visited she also made a big effort to keep them entertained. During the day we might go to the Niagara Falls Aquarium or shopping at her favorite Kmart. In my mind, both destinations were equally exciting. At night we might have dinner at the Red Coach Inn, a restaurant in Niagara Falls that had a view of the river. Every time we went there, I knew that the price of my dessert parfait was that I would have to listen to my grandmother recall another incident about my being a little slow on the uptake. "Bob, I remember the first time we ever brought you here. You were very little and Dad and Grampy were talking about the rapids in the river and you thought they said 'rabbits' and kept looking at the shore trying to see them hopping. You kept saying to your father, 'I don't see the rabbits.' You know, now that I think of it, you might be hard-of-hearing like Grampy."

My grandmother could be a bully and wielded her merry do-you-mind smile like a sickle to cut down any opposition. She always assumed that everyone liked her—a delusion common to many totalitarian dictators. One day I learned firsthand about her temper when she made me lunch. When my grandmother made sandwiches she always buttered the bread first, which explained why she was always on a diet. Chomping into one of her butter-filled sandwiches was like digging into your own grave. When I asked her whether it was necessary to butter the bread on my peanut-butter-and-jelly sandwich, she took it as a criticism and her attitude hardened faster than my arteries. My question was an affront to her sandwich-making prowess.

She complained bitterly. "I've been making lunches for over fifty years and that's the first time anyone has ever told me that they didn't care for one of my sandwiches."

I tried to backtrack as quickly as possible. "I just wanted to know. It tastes good," I lied. Then I tried to flatter her by saying, "I like the strawberry jelly better than the grape." While the American Indians have always been admired for their tracking abilities, my Celtic heritage should be celebrated for our backtracking skills. Thousands of years of incessant intimidation by Caesars, chieftains, kings, queens, popes, grandmothers, and other authority figures has given my people the extraordinary ability to reverse an opinion without leaving a clue that only moments before a different idea had even passed through our thoughts.

My grandmother's dietary laws were "gentile kosher" and ultimately she was their sole arbiter. For the uninitiated, the laws of gentile kosher are:

a) Certain brand names are holy.

b) It's okay to eat anything from *her* kitchen because it's *always* clean.

c) All food should be unfit to eat in the cardiovascular sense.

Her standards for food weren't simply high, they were inaccessible to reason. Another time her favorite supermarket, Tops, the only supermarket she would set foot in, ran out of her favorite brand of tuna in oil and her only alternative was to buy the same brand of tuna fish in water, which she insisted was inedible. Craving a tuna sandwich and being resourceful, however, she bought a can of the tuna in water and mixed it with corn oil before adding the mayonnaise. Since the bread on her tuna-fish sandwiches was also buttered, this meant that my sandwich contained butter, oil, and mayonnaise. After I finished lunch, the fat soaked through my stomach and left a greasy stain on my shirt.

While making my lunch, my grandmother repeatedly asked my grandfather whether he wanted a sandwich. "Wells, do you want a sandwich or not? Jesus Christ, I wish he would turn on his hearing aid!" Grampy's hearing loss allowed my grandmother to conveniently talk about him behind his back while in his presence. Whenever my grandmother spoke directly to my grandfather, she couldn't resist delivering several supposedly whispered asides about him to anyone else who happened to be in the room. While he watched golf on television, she would say, "I wish he would go play golf instead of sitting around here all day watching it. That man has less to do than my ass." Her derogatory comments about Grampy while he sat two feet away sometimes raised our concern that he might be able to hear her. My grandmother would shoo away our worries. "Oh, he can't hear me, he's not wearing his hearing aid. Wells. *Wells!* You can't hear me, can you?"

"What do want now, Charlotte?"

"Don't talk to me like that! I don't want anything from you. I just wanted to make sure you couldn't hear me." Then, resuming a slightly more sotto voce tone, she'd say, "He's always been a bullhead. There's nothing I hate more than a bullhead."

My grandfather did occasionally reveal that he had heard every word that she had said. He would wait until after she had gone on speaking for some time and then say simply, "Bob, she talks more than the TV." After spending the weekend with them, it was obvious to me that after fifty years of marriage my grandfather wasn't hard-of-hearing but tired-of-listening.

Quarreling with my grandfather never seriously disturbed my grandmother's composure and she seemed to enjoy the event almost as if she was a matador and

Grampy was the bull—or bullhead, as the case may be. With her own family, she was satisfied to anger and tire the bullhead but with bullheads from outside the family she went in for the kill. She had an opportunity to demonstrate her enthusiasm and skill for bullhead baiting when my grandparents' friends the Kramers were almost turned down for membership in the country club.

Alex and Olive Kramer were my grandparents' closest friends and it was natural for my grandfather to propose them for membership. They had been guests of my grandparents many times at the club and Alex was a prominent neurosurgeon and someone my grandfather enjoyed golfing with. My grandmother and Olive were estate-sale junkies and loved trying to get into a house early, before the general public, and then walking out of the place having picked up the best deals on Rosenthal china and cut-glass bowls.

My grandfather submitted the Kramers for membership after being assured that they would be approved. But there was a lengthy delay in the process and finally my grandfather heard that the couple weren't going to be approved for membership because it had been discovered that they were Jewish. When my grandmother heard the news she said, "Oh, that is the stupidest thing I've ever heard. For the love of God, Alex Kramer is a neurosurgeon! He's probably one of the most intelligent men I know. I know he's smarter than most members of the club, because I've had dinner with all of them and I'd prefer to sit at his table any day. Wells, who's the head of the membership committee?"

"Bill Marcott. I think he's the main reason there's a problem."

"Oh, Bill Marcott," she snorted. My grandmother loathed bigots and had on more than one occasion said that people who hated Jews were "stupes" and people who hated black people were "trashy." She believed in defamation only as long as it was restricted to a person's character or personal habits. She sneered, saying, "Bill Marcott has a lot of gall turning anyone down for anything. He's one of the most undistinguished members of the club. One year, at the Christmas party, we sat at his table and he's one of those men who never shuts his mouth all the way. I can't tell you how stupid a grown man looks with his mouth hanging open all the time. I wanted to take a candy cane and pull it shut for him. And his wife's a beaut. She's a lump with no sugar. And I've met the son—Junior's no prize either."

My grandfather was determined. "Well, I'm not going to let one man hold up their membership. I'll go to the full committee if I have to. I spend a lot of money in that dining room every week entertaining clients for the bank. And until their membership goes through I'm not spending another dollar in there."

My grandmother didn't like the idea of a boycott. It was too nonconfrontational for her taste. She was certainly capable of teaching a bigot about intolerance. After giving the matter some thought, she insisted, "Wells, you know what we ought to do? For lunch and dinner we ought to bring every Jewish person we know to the club. Then Bill Marcott will wish he had only two Jews to deal with!"

My grandfather erupted. "Goddammit, Charlotte! Will you let me handle this? Believe me, without you getting involved, the Kramers will become members."

"No, Wells. You're dealing with a bullhead. And the only thing a bullhead understands is someone more bullheaded."

"Listen, Charlotte, don't go doing anything without telling me. You could screw this whole thing up."

"Wells, don't talk to me like I'm a child!"

The next week my grandmother did exactly what she said she was going to do. She didn't bother telling my grandfather about her plan because my grandmother believed that it was unnecessary to ask for a second opinion when she could just tell herself again that she was right.

Grace Silverburg, Marion Rose, and Judith Cohen were invited by my grandmother to have lunch at the country club. Afterward, she was proud to report, "Bill Marcott was having lunch with his buddies. So when he was leaving the dining room I stopped him and said hello and then introduced him to everyone at my table. First and last names. I swear it's the first time I ever saw him shut his mouth all the way."

Ultimately the Kramers did become members of the country club. My grandfather even managed somehow to get their first year of membership declared honorary, and had their dues waived. Later my grandmother confessed to my grandfather what she had done, principally because she knew it made a good story and she wanted to be able to tell it when his hearing aid was turned on. She admitted, though, that she had invited Marion Rose under a misapprehension. "I could have sworn that she was Jewish, but it turns out she's Lutheran." My grandmother beamed as she added, "It doesn't matter. If *I* thought she was Jewish, Bill Marcott probably thought she was Jewish too."

My grandparents' relationship was a mixture of constant sniping and occasional flashes of devotion. When my grandfather began to lose his vision to macular degeneration, my grandmother made sure that every effort was made to help preserve what eyesight he had remaining. By asking every doctor she knew and some she didn't, my grandmother heard about a Dr. Latona in Buffalo who was regarded as the one of the best eye specialists in the country. Being told of his reputation whetted my grandmother's appetite. In her mind Dr. Latona became the premium brand of eye doctor, and since her taste in physicians was similar to her taste in hot dogs or tuna fish, she was willing to pay more and go out of her way to get him. But when she tried to make an appointment, she was told that Dr. Latona wasn't accepting any new patients. Since, according to my grandmother's tuna-fish philosophy, pouring corn oil on a regular eye doctor in order to turn him into a close approximation of Dr. Latona wasn't feasible, she had to figure out another way to get my grandfather an appointment. It was one thing for a store to run out of tuna when she wanted it, but she wasn't about to let the tuna decide if *it* wanted her.

Refusal wasn't a barrier to my grandmother. As soon as she hung up the telephone after speaking to Dr. Latona's receptionist, she was dialing Dr. Kramer at his office to ask him if he could do Wells a favor. Within a week my grandfather had an appointment with Dr. Latona.

Not that my grandmother ever became sentimental about my grandfather's impending blindness. She approached his condition with a commonsense determination to make the best of it. But she was also unable to restrain herself from enjoying a few of its advantages from her point of view. In addition to being able to talk about my grandfather in his presence because he was hard-of-hearing, now when he talked she could roll her eyes and make dismissive faces right in front of him, confident that he was unable to see her. When he first started losing his eyesight my grandfather could still watch television, but in order to see a program, he had to sit one foot away from the set, and since he only retained his peripheral vision he needed to sit with his head turned away from the screen so he could see from the corners of his eyes. My grandmother would see him trying to watch the news and scoff, "Oh, he can't see anything. Why, he could be watching the radio for all he knows."

As his eyesight further deteriorated, my grandmother tried to help my grandfather. Of course, her acts of kindness were problematic, because while she was always willing to lend a hand, her mouth also came along for the ride. After moving to Florida in the early 1970s, my grandparents began to spend their summers with our family. In the mornings my grandmother would try to read my grandfather the newspaper but they would always end up fighting because she was unable to resist editorializing about every story. Often she got no further than reading the headline: " 'A New "Head" of State—President Carter's Brother to Sell Billy Beer.' Isn't that the stupidest thing you've ever heard? That family's not right. The sister's a Holy Roller. The brother's a dopey-looking thing, and if that mother jumped up and said boo she'd scare you."

My grandfather would lose his patience and shout, "Goddammit, Charlotte! Let Bob or Carol read to me. I want to know what's in the paper, I don't want *your* news."

"That's fine with me," she'd retort. "I've got better things to do with my time." She would hand me the newspaper and say in a slightly softer voice, "He's a miserable pup and he gets more and more miserable as he gets older. He's lost his hearing, he's lost his eyesight; once his mind goes—that's it—*he's* going next."

Eventually my grandfather needed help dialing the telephone and doing other minor tasks. He could write checks but he had trouble addressing envelopes and his frequent requests for assistance began to get on my grandmother's nerves. Being a practical woman, my grandmother asked one of her doctor friends to make out a prescription for tranquilizers—for my grandfather. It was typical of her approach to problem solving that she believed that the external source of her nervousness should be on a medication, not she herself. It's contrary to most legal and ethical treatments for achieving mental health but prescribing drugs to the people surrounding the person with emotional problems is tempting to contemplate. Do you feel depressed? Have you ever considered putting your family and friends on antidepressants? Who knows? Maybe they'll begin to be happier and your spirits will improve when they start treating you better.

And indeed, my grandmother's nerves improved rapidly after she started giving my grandfather a Valium every day. My grandfather had no idea that he was taking a tranquilizer because she told him that he was taking what she was inspired to call "vitamins for his eyes." But she didn't foresee that he would actually begin to believe that the so-called vitamins were helping his eyesight. The placebo effect was most likely intensified because for the first time since their wedding day, my grandfather felt tranquil around his wife.

Unfortunately my grandfather began to think that if one "vitamin" was good for his eyesight then maybe two or three would help even more. He began popping a few extra Valiums until one afternoon his brief lie-down on the couch came close to being a dirt nap. My grandfather couldn't be woken up for dinner and had to be rushed to the hospital, where a Valium overdose was diagnosed. When he was released the next day, my grandfather was furious at my grandmother for her deception. "Charlotte, congratulations. I have to say this is the stupidest thing you've ever done." She was quiet for a moment, which made me think that even she knew that she had gone too far. But I should have known better. "Oh, Wells, who the hell in their right mind takes seven vitamins?" she soon announced, unrepentant.

While my grandmother disparaged my grandfather to her family, she also displayed a fierce solicitude about his reputation to everyone else. My grandmother didn't want my grandfather to know that the reason we were stalking Perry Como was because she was afraid that a more overt approach might embarrass him in front of the other university officials. She was still going to do exactly what she wanted but she wanted to do it on the sly. "If we don't tell Grampy what we're doing, then he can't say anything, now, can he?"

Her attempt at subterfuge wasn't very successful. It was impossible for Grampy not to recognize us waiting for Perry Como at the entrance to the Niagara Falls Country Club in my grandmother's distinctive maroon 1964 Buick Riviera with white leather upholstery. Massively bulky yet streamlined, it was a muscle car that was sold as a luxury vehicle. Like a bodybuilder in a tuxedo, the effect was either awkward looking or enticing, depending on your taste. It was an unusual car for a woman in her sixties to drive, but as much as she liked to think of herself as a banker's wife, my grandmother was not the refined country-club type. She had a foul mouth but immediately after swearing would pretend that her tongue was a banana peel and the curse words had just slipped out. After a weekend spent snacking on candy and ice cream with her grandchildren, she would say with a long-suffering sigh, "Jesus Christ, I ate everything but shit with sugar on it."

My grandmother believed in being blunt and she handled life's woes, such as my grandfather's blindness, directly. When they moved to Florida, my sister visited them during one spring break. My father telephoned when my sister and grandfather were out at the pool and asked to speak to Carol. It was an extremely hot day and instead of walking out to the pool my grandmother just came to the edge of the condominium's parking lot and shouted, "Wells! Wells! *Wells!*" The condominium was filled with other retirees and their pallid northern families and someone let my grandfather know that my grandmother was calling him. My grandfather walked to the fence surrounding the pool and stood there as my grandmother, compensating for his being hard-of-hearing, yelled twice, "Wells! Tell Carol her father called and that HER OTHER GRANDMOTHER IS DEAD!"

Fortunately, my sister wasn't devastated by her grandmother's calling her in to announce a funeral in the same manner that other grandmothers might tell you that dinner was ready. It became a joke between my sister and me and for years I would allude to it in the messages I left on her answering machine, "Hi Carol, it's Bob. 'Your other grandmother's dead!' So call me."

Carol and I agreed that the most difficult part of spending time with our grandmother wasn't her tendency to scream obituaries at the top of her lungs, it was enduring her driving. She drove in a stop-and-go motion, gunning the engine and then hitting the brakes, that made her passengers feel as if the car was being rocked instead of driven to its destination. Her driving caused even pedestrians momentary feelings of queasiness. When we made the thirty-mile trip from our house in Kenmore to her house in Lewiston, it took my undivided concentration to suppress the urge to heave. Several times while riding with her I had thrown up, and although I never became carsick with anyone else, she refused to believe that her driving was the cause. My grandmother regarded my carsickness as another bad habit, like my nail biting, that needed to be corrected.

The next time I rode with her she proposed that I sit in the middle between my two brothers. "I think Bob only throws up because he's near a window and he can." She made it sound as if I threw up out of car windows for fun because I wanted to see how far I could project my vomit. A half hour later I refuted her theory by barfing in my brother Greg's lap. After that my grandmother wouldn't even allow me to ride in their electric golf cart at the country club. When we would meet my grandfather after he had played a round, she would announce, "Bob can walk along. He shouldn't ride. We can't risk him throwing up on the greens."

My grandmother couldn't admit that her driving was causing my motion sickness because it would have undermined her favorite moment of personal triumph. Everyone in our family had heard her frequently recounted tale of having once driven Charles Lindbergh during World War II. She repeated this story so often that the listener would begin to believe that her driving was crucial to the Allied victory. She had taken a wartime job as a driver for Bell Aerospace Labs—obviously some Nazi spy was trying to sabotage the war effort in giving her that position—and she was asked to drive Mr. Lindbergh from Buffalo's train station to Bell Aerospace's plant in Niagara Falls.

A fierce blizzard began shortly after they departed, and according to my grandmother, it took two hours of treacherous driving through a whiteout to get Lindbergh safely to his destination. I pitied Mr. Lindbergh. The first nonstop solo flight across the Atlantic was heroic but I'm sure it couldn't compare to the courage required to ride shotgun with my grandmother. From my perspective her driving skills really should have been put to good use after the war ended. I can't think of a more fitting punishment for the Nazi High Command than being driven to and from the Nuremberg Trials every day by my grandmother—her orders being to take the most circuitous route possible.

My grandmother never suffered from motion sickness because she owned what she called a "reducing machine." It was a contraption with a large canvas strap that was attached to an electric motor. The strap was slipped over her butt, the motor turned on, and the vigorous vibrations provided the illusion of exercise without any exertion. It was a bunco "treadmill" that had conned my grandmother into believing that she could lose weight by jogging just her ass while the rest of her body remained stationary.

Every morning my grandmother used her reducing

machine and the sight of her backside jiggling in her brown slip was a good reason to skip that second cinnamon bun. Whenever I visited for the weekend my grandfather would let me try it as a treat. We would take turns vibrating and laughing until my grandmother would finally yell, "Wells, that's not a toy!" I stopped immediately. It was safer to quit playing than take the chance that she would decide to come and join the fun and start turning the switch on and off until I became nauseated.

While I never once heard my grandmother criticize Perry Como or Charles Lindbergh, I'm certain that if they had spent the weekend with her, she would have found something that called for a talking-to.

"Charles, please sit up straight. Don't sit there all droopy. No one likes a hero who slouches."

"Perry, if you're going to sing, sing but don't hum. If you go around humming all the time, people will think you're simple."

My grandmother was the driving force in our family and I now understand that while the driver can talk, she might be too busy to pay close attention to what her passengers are saying or doing. I never asked my restless grandmother why she was such a fan of Perry Como, a singer noted for such a lethargic style that it's surprising that his records even spin. The fact is that my grandparents never even owned a record player, which leads me to believe that my grandmother didn't respond to Perry Como's singing as much as she did to his ability to always sound so relaxed. I like to think that she was a fan because she admired Perry Como's ability to do something well that she couldn't do at all.

Once my grandparents retired to Florida, my grandmother became an inveterate writer of letters to her grandchildren. Her letters perfectly captured her voice, and it was after re-reading her letters to me that I decided to write about her. In one letter she could manage to get in a shot at almost everyone in our family:

Dear Bob,

Just finished my breakfast cereal and I don't need it. I look like Aunt Eppie Hog. I hope Carol is alive, *fat* and well. Tell her I am swimming and look *skinny*. I am down to a size 20 *Petite!* Gramp is good, a little ugly but what else is new? I read my horoscope today and it said a new man is going to come into my life. So I guess that's it for Grampy. The neighbors saw the picture you sent and they all said you were good-looking. I said you resemble *me* but had dark hair like your dad. No sense in mentioning your mother. Did I tell you the last time your mother was here that she wore a two-piece bathing suit? At her age! Please, no one wants to see that after having four children. I said to her, "Who are you trying to impress? The youngest man here is 68."

Remember don't be a sap and work all the time! —Have fun!

Love,
Nan

After my grandmother saw me perform stand-up comedy at a small jazz club in Buffalo, she wrote me her version of a congratulatory letter:

Dear Bob,

You haven't written me like you promised but it's all right because I received a letter from your brother.

Just think, when they read the will, there will be only one name in it: Jim Smith. I thought that would get your attention! It was good to see you perform. I'm proud of you. I still can't believe it. You didn't start talking until you were two! Not one word. And now you're talking in front of strangers! I was worried about you then, but now I think maybe you just knew that no one in your family was interesting. I don't know where you get your sense of humor from. You certainly didn't get it from your mother or your father.

Love,
Nan

P.S. Is there anything else you want before I pass on to a better world!! (Let's hope that it's not too soon.)

My grandmother had recently given me my grandfather's gold pocket watch without telling him. He was still alive and she didn't bother telling him that she was prematurely handing over my inheritance. When I protested, she said brusquely, "Bob, he's blind. He can't use a watch anymore. He's lucky to know what day it is! You haven't asked for one thing from us and if you don't take it now someone else will. Remember if you kids fight over my things when I'm gone—I'll come back and haunt you!"

My grandmother always threatened to come back and haunt us, and I always laughed at her threat until earlier this year. My deadline to finish this book was approaching and I was having trouble with the ending of this chapter. I played around with several ideas but I couldn't find one that struck me as exactly right. They sounded forced and there had already been enough browbeating. Finally, I admitted that I was stumped, and in an attempt to gain some fresh inspiration I called my brother Jim.

When Jim was in the navy, my grandmother had written to him almost every week, and I knew that he had saved more than two hundred letters from her. Jim offered to send me the letters but I told him that there wasn't enough time. Taking a cue from my grandmother, I brazenly asked him to re-read all two hundred letters. ". . . and, Jim, could you do it this weekend? I need it done as soon as possible." His orders were to pick out the letters that were funny or relevant to me. Jim reluctantly agreed to become my amanuensis.

The next day Jim called. It was faster service than even my grandmother could have demanded. He announced, "I found the ending for your chapter. Last night, I was looking through Nan's letters and in the pile I found two unopened letters. I'm not sure how they got in there. Back in college, I must have thrown them in with all her other letters when I moved. In the first letter I opened, I found a check for ten dollars. Right now you know she's probably laughing about that. But wait until you hear the second letter." It was dated September 27, 1980.

Dear Jim,

Thanks for your nice letter! I hope Bob, Carol, and your mother are healthy. I haven't heard from them and we do not get the Buffalo obituaries here in Florida. It's so hot down here. Around the apartment all I'm wearing is my girdle and slip. Your uncle Fred's visiting and he keeps yelling, "Mother, would you put some clothes on! It's indecent." If he can't handle seeing a woman in a slip, maybe that's why he's been married three times! Jo Beth is getting married again! She's a brute for punishment.

I have a good story for you. Your grandfather and I drove Alligator Alley last week to see Fred. Coming back we took a wrong turn. Then we took another one. And another one. Gramp got nervous and started hollering. Gramp doesn't trust my driving, and going out after dark is a thing of the past. I am a prisoner of LOVE! I should have put him in the trunk and dropped the lid. He should be glad he got home alive! Fred called the next day and when I told him that it took us seven and a half hours to drive home—instead of three or four—he was speechless. He said that the next time he'll come and drive us. I said that I would rather take the bus.

This is such a long letter and so I'm not going to redo it to send to Kenmore. I know you're busy, but maybe Bob will want to write it up for his book! So I have enclosed a stamped envelope so you can forward it to him.

Love,
Nan

I had goose bumps when my brother read me the closing to her letter. We were both dumbfounded by her eerie request. In 1980, I certainly wasn't writing a book. I was in college writing a one-act play and occasionally doing stand-up, but I wasn't contemplating becoming an author. My grandmother had to be making a joke in the offhand manner that someone would say, "Someday when you write your book . . ." But then again, she did enclose the stamped envelope.

It is a strange coincidence that this particular letter would be opened nineteen years later, when I was writing a book, and specifically writing about her. I'm not dismissing the idea of supernatural intervention. If anyone could manage to give me the ending to her chapter from beyond the grave, it would be my grandmother, Charlotte Corey. It's an achievement that only a real bullhead could pull off.

My Pen Pal

WHEN SHAKESPEARE wrote about murderers, he produced works of art that expressed a universal point of view. The tragedy of our time is that every participant in a murder feels compelled to express his own point of view. If *Macbeth* was a contemporary true-crime story, no writer would touch it, because even the minor characters would have book deals. Before his death Macbeth would have maintained his innocence in a best-selling memoir; in her as-told-to autobiography Lady Macbeth would claim to be a feminist role model; Banquo's wife would publish a ghostwritten tell-all; and in an attempt to cash in on Macbeth's notoriety the three witches would publish a gossipy cookbook of his purported favorite one-cauldron recipes.

For American writers, knowing a murderer has become as basic a literary credential as having an English degree or a drinking problem. In the 1960s, when Truman Capote wrote *In Cold Blood*, it was still considered unusual to know a murderer; then in the 1970s Norman Mailer wrote about Gary Gilmore in *The Executioner's Song*, both books helping to usher in the Age of Presumed Innocence, in which murderers became tragic heroes. Taking a life and using it for material for a book is an impulse that comes easily to a writer, and while most writers wouldn't exactly kill for a good story, they don't seem to mind taking advantage of those who do. One of the most grisly discoveries of modern life is that as soon as the blows to the victim's head stop, somewhere inspiration is striking a writer.

In my hometown of Kenmore, New York, a suburb of Buffalo, there are two surefire ways of getting your name into the local newspaper—you can either become an obituary yourself or cause someone else to become one. An example of the former was Kevin Lunsford, who had been "the jock" in my high-school graduating class. According to *The Kenmore Record-Advertiser* one day Kevin was tossing a Frisbee to his dog in Mang Park when he was struck by lightning and killed. Ironically, other people who are trying to relax in parks often secretly wish this fate upon annoying Frisbee players. By any standard, tossing a Frisbee and then catching a lightning bolt is an example of a death without dignity; the sudden flash must have been followed by a wisecrack of thunder.

The second person from my graduating class to get

his name in the newspaper was Eddie Gowdy; this occurred when he was arrested for committing a murder in Kenmore.

I first heard about Eddie's arrest when our next-door neighbor Mrs. Brounschidle reported to my mother that the police had taken him into custody. Mrs. Brounschidle was our neighborhood bearer of bad tidings, a task that perhaps explained why this hefty woman always wore a jogging outfit. She was built like a stevedore and regularly delivered loads of hearsay and scandal to my mother. "I always knew that Eddie was trouble," she'd say. "Big trouble." Adopting an effective marketing technique that fast-food restaurants use to push soft drinks, Mrs. Brounschidle offered trouble in only two sizes, Big and Supersize. Unzipping the jacket on her jogging suit since it was a hot day, she started wagging her tongue as if she was fanning herself. "They found the bloody knife and bloody jacket in his bedroom closet. They were neatly wrapped in a plastic bag with a twist tie. I'll never forget the day when he stabbed Bob with a pen on our front porch. And didn't he stab Buddy Letchworth with a pen too?" Mrs. Brounschidle looked in my direction. She didn't need me to confirm what she was saying; it was just that she rarely had the pleasure of hearing any of her stories corroborated and was eager to have the experience.

Picking up on my cue, I said, "Yeah."

Satisfied by my reply, she added, "I always thought Eddie had a screw loose."

Eddie did have a screw loose but everyone had ignored the rattling—they knew that fixing it wasn't a minor repair job. Without even looking under the hood, most people could tell that Eddie needed a major overhaul. Hearing that Eddie had committed a murder wasn't surprising. The news of his arrest was like hearing that a 109-year-old had died in his sleep. Everyone knew that it would happen sooner or later.

My mother declared, "He was an accident waiting to happen." A figure of speech that at least attributed to Eddie the virtue of patience. She added with an air of mystery, "I never liked the way he walks." Since my mother's likes and dislikes are as capricious as the lightning that killed Kevin Lunsford, I didn't question her odd antipathy. Over the years I'd often heard her say, "I don't like the way she talks," or "I don't like the way he acts." Once I had even heard her say, "I don't like the way she sits" about a girl who kept her legs farther apart than my mother considered seemly.

Eddie Gowdy was a creep who only walked upright because of peer pressure. Whether his crawliness was a product of his own volition or some undetermined factor is unknown and begs the question what came first in the life of a loser? Being called "chicken" or having egg on his face?

I met Eddie for the first time on our street corner when we were nine years old. I was initially friendly toward him because he passed my low standards of companionship: he was my age and he had nothing to do that day. Like most boys I was fairly undiscriminating about choosing my friends. I thought I shared a common interest with another boy if we both liked candy.

Many of my early friendships were based more upon proximity than rapport. A nine-year-old boy living five houses away had a better chance of becoming my pal than a nine-year-old who lived three miles away, even if that distant nine-year-old and I did have more in common. Children have to make do with whatever friends are available. Adults on the other hand are leery of becoming friends with their next-door neighbors. We won't settle anymore for playmates who only offer the dubious benefit of convenience.

I didn't care how my friends looked or dressed. Skinny or fat, dirty or clean, buck- or gap-toothed, pigeon-toed or bowlegged, cheap clothes or stylish, they all looked fine to me. During my childhood I never once indulged the spiteful thought *Who is Fat Sam trying to fool with those baggy pants? He needs to go on a diet.*

Also, as a boy I didn't pry into my friends' private lives. I didn't care who or what my friends slept with; stuffed animals or security blankets, it was none of my business. And I didn't care what they did in bed—as long as they didn't wet it when they slept over.

My friendships were easy to maintain as a boy. To earn my trust all you had to do was watch my bicycle while I went into the store to buy a Fudgsicle. To express sympathy and understanding about my problems all you had to do was second my opinion that "Barry Bucholtz is a jerk."

The best thing about childhood friendships is that we never had to make time to see each other. In childhood the hourglass of time is a sandbox and children grab big handfuls and freely toss it without ever worrying that each day there's a little less sand and that someday it will run out.

When I met Eddie he didn't have to earn my friendship, he merely had to accept it. All I knew about him was that his family had moved in a few days before and that he had three brothers. The range of ages of the four Gowdy boys was like a jail term—from ten to twenty—Eddie being the youngest. We walked down to the fire hydrant on the corner where a game of touch football was being organized. Eddie hung back for a minute, letting everyone get a good look at him, until Tommy Helmbrecht spoke to him. "Hey, you just moved in, right? What's your name?"

"Eddie . . . Eddie Gowdy."

Eddie's face was a blank and I didn't know yet that his expression clearly reflected the contents of his mind. His brain was like the bathroom on an airplane. It was very small, and a quick glance always told you whether it was vacant or occupied.

"Where'd you live before?"

"Black Rock."

Black Rock was a grimy section of Buffalo, but since most of our families had also migrated from the city, this wasn't a fact worth commenting upon. Unfortunately Eddie added, "I had a motorized Go Kart but I couldn't bring it with me."

Eddie was telling a lie but children are less cynical than adults about lying. They understand that there are times when it has to be done and approaching a large group of strange boys was a situation where telling a lie was probably unavoidable. Lying isn't offensive to children if the liar is captivating, but Eddie never understood that when telling a lie, the unprovable is better than the improbable and a series of white lies, bereft of all flavor and interest, is less effective than one garish whopper. Claiming that you saw a ghost or that your father was a spy was preferable to claiming to have the fastest bicycle or owning a pony. It's only when a lie is boring or simple to disprove that children turn against the teller, and Eddie had no talent for dishonesty: his falsehoods were as dull as the lies on a tax return.

During our football game, Eddie's social ineptitude became evident when he tried to join in mocking Parry

Middal, whose sister Jennifer, for the third time, had just yelled, "Parry, Mommeeee wants you home *now*!" Everyone had laughed when Tommy Helmbrecht and my brother Greg mimicked Jennifer's wailing but trying to follow their lead Eddie goofed up the word order by saying, "Parry go home to your Mommeeee." As soon as he said it everyone's attention turned toward him. For boys, jumping on an already moving joke requires as much skill as skateboarding; you need a good sense of balance, and if your timing is off, your stumble will earn you ridicule. The joke was on Eddie, as if he had spilled a glass of milk on himself or dropped a pot on his foot.

To successfully mock another boy in a group of boys one must be perceived as either completely intimidating or entirely unthreatening and Eddie was still in the vulnerable position of being the new kid whose neck was on the block. He wasn't anyone's buddy yet and hadn't earned the occasional right to jeer at someone older or bigger than him. Parry Middal sensed this and took advantage of Eddie's blunder by saying, "Eat me, Gowdy. You little ass-wipe." Satisfied that his dignity had been salvaged, Parry headed home.

Eddie's first-day fumble was quickly forgotten, though, and that summer he was included in the large group of boys who played in pickup games of kickball and baseball and he even went along on a few of our neighborhood bicycle trips. We had started exploring beyond our immediate neighborhood, and that year one of our favorite destinations was riding to still relatively rural Grand Island in the Niagara River to go fishing.

The day before a fishing trip we would gather at Russ

Erker's house for the purpose of gathering the earthworms we would use as bait. We always went to Russ's house because he had built a homemade bait-gathering apparatus. The Erkers owned a hardware store, and aided by its inventory of nuts and bolts and tools to tinker with, Russ was developing a neighborhood reputation for his inventiveness.

Inventiveness is a quality that Americans have long prized and we're willing to overlook a few moral niceties in our gee-whiz appreciation of the latest gizmo. We're the country that invented the lightbulb and the electric chair and both inventors probably had proud mothers who bragged about their sons' cleverness. Russ's boyish inventions were closer to the darker can-do spirit creating the A-bomb than to building a Go Kart.

Russ's first invention had been a device he called "The Funnelator." Mrs. Erker was a nurse and Russ had taken some yards of rubber surgical tubing and looped it through a plastic kitchen funnel, which, when held by two boys and pulled back by a third, made a catapult with the power to shoot an egg or a water balloon across a football field. We were curious to see how far we could shoot a rock but after our first test with nonlethal projectiles we realized that shooting rocks with the Funnelator might be ill-advised. My first time behind the funnel, instead of hitting Garner Brounschidle with a water balloon as he rode past on his bicycle, I unintentionally proved to everyone's satisfaction that a small water balloon shot by the Funnelator was capable of shattering a living-room window three houses away.

Russ had responded to the challenge of building a better worm trap by taking an old lamp cord, unpeeling the insulation at one end, and attaching the bare copper wires to the metal shafts of two large wooden-handled screwdrivers. He finished his power tool of death by thickly wrapping the contact points with insulated electrical tape. Before using the worm prod, Russ thoroughly watered his front yard in order to saturate the ground; after that was done, he plugged in the electric cord and carefully held the screwdrivers aloft. Poised over the glistening lawn, Russ stared intently at the ground as if he was looking for a socket. When he shoved the screwdrivers into the lawn, I almost expected the grass to light up an electric green.

As impassive as members of a secret police, we waited patiently for the tortured earth to confess everything. Soon the earthworms staggered out of the ground, live wires fleeing a burning house. It was an impressive sight to a ten-year-old boy. It was as if the earth was an appliance and when we threw the switch the ground starting crawling. As we placed the dazed worms in baby-food jars, they seemed to be more stunned by our brutality than by the voltage.

After a few minutes Eddie asked Russ, "Can I move the screwdrivers?"

"Sure, but be careful."

"I will."

We all took turns rotating the screwdrivers around the wet patch of lawn after we had completely dewormed a section of grass. When the screwdrivers were pulled from the soil you could actually feel the throbbing power of the electric current. Eddie's eyes gleamed as he yanked the screwdrivers from the earth and for a moment he held them comfortably in his hands like an upright knife and fork. Instead of shoving them back into the lawn, though,

Eddie began to calmly electrocute several worms that he had previously placed on the driveway.

Russ said, "Eddie! What are you doing? Don't do that." Russ had a strong sense of responsibility for a boy, and although his inventions encouraged recklessness, he always intervened before someone did anything dangerous.

In a childishly pleading voice Eddie said, "I just want to see what happens."

The sickeningly bittersweet odor of burning worm flesh wafted up as if we were being offered an unwanted free sample of the smell of death.

"Eddie, don't be jerk."

"Oh, that's gross."

Russ became angry. "Stop, it Eddie. What's wrong with you?" He grabbed the screwdrivers. "Give me those. Now get rid of those worms."

Eddie said, "They're only worms." Momentarily shamed by Russ's response, his face changed color as if he had suggested playing an unmanly game of hopscotch to a group of boys. As Eddie attempted to kick the remains of the worms into the bushes, we decided that we had enough bait. In truth, Eddie's unmercifulness had just been premature. We had no compunction about ramming fishing hooks through the worms the next day. Boys think of the food chain of Big Fish eats Little Fish as an aquarium amusement instead of a life-and-death matter. It was okay to disembowl worms for fishing but it was wrong for Eddie to kill worms for fun because that was cruel. The distinction was plain to the rest of us.

We weren't little boys anymore who with a mixture of curiosity, horror, and excitement burned ants with a magnifying glass. We were becoming young men who only inflicted pain and cruelty for a reason—any reason; the justifications can range from "It's over" to "It's war."

The next instance of Eddie's strange behavior might have possibly gone unnoticed if it hadn't been observed by the ever-vigilant Mrs. Brounschidle. During the summer I often sat in the Brounschidles' backyard, where, over a glass of iced tea or lemonade, Mrs. Brounschidle polished her gossip by giving it a first run-through on me. Mrs. Brounschidle thought of me as a good listener, and this was true, because in her presence I rarely had a chance to speak. I was fascinated that Mrs. Brounschilde often warmed up by relaying a tidbit of gossip about her own family before she went on to deep-dish another family.

In passing, Mrs. Brounschidle let out that her son Garner was hyperactive and doped up on Ritalin; that her daughter Gail was caught smoking in the garage and was almost held back one year in school; that her son Graham had been caught making out with his girlfriend in the living room; that Mr. Brounschidle had a spastic colon; and that her own mother had been a secret tippler, which was why she never touched the stuff.

An old-fashioned storyteller, Mrs. Brounschidle began her story with the gossip's once-upon-a-time. "You're not going to believe what I saw [or heard] this morning . . ." As she continued to talk, she passed me a plate of chocolate-covered graham crackers. Mrs. Brounschidle was shrewd; she knew that getting people to chew was the quickest method of limbering up their tongues. After seeing me sitting in their backyard my mother repeatedly warned me, "Don't be telling our business to Mrs. Brounschidle." My mother had nothing to worry about, as I usually ate my cookies without spilling anything except my lemonade.

(Author's Note: I present Mrs. Brounschidle's monologue in full because thirty years later I still find it impossible to interrupt her.)

"...I went up to the attic[1] because I was looking for Fritz's[2] old yearbook," she told me. "I had run into Grace Kotka at the market—she had that terrible divorce—and I said to Fritz that she graduated with us at Lafayette, but Fritz said, 'No, she was a year younger than us.' Anyway, I was looking out the window and I glanced over at the Gowdys' to see if someone had cut the lawn. It beats me that you could buy a house and then treat it worse than a rental. They must have come from the projects.[3] I was hoping that someone had cut the lawn because Fritz said he was going to call the cops if they didn't cut it soon. I said, 'Now, Fritz, don't be doing that. It will only start a

---

[1] Built in the early twenties, the Brounschidles' rambling house had the imposing structure of a Victorian residence but none of the style. It was huge and loomed over the neighborhood but it lacked a turret and had no decorative trim. If Victorian houses are painted ladies showing off their voluptuous figures, then the Brounschidles' house was a large and bulky prison matron in a drab smock.

[2] Fritz was Mrs. Brounschidle's husband who every week unloaded a fresh case of Genessee tallboys from the trunk of his car and whose massive beer gut was a camel's hump that could see him through another Prohibition.

[3] She was referring to the housing projects located near Sheridan Park that were the ultimate in degradation to our middle-class street.

ruckus.'[4] Well, after I got Fritz to promise that he wouldn't call the police about the Gowdys' grass, later on, to my relief, I see Eddie cutting the lawn with a big smile on his face and I thought, 'Well, it's about time.' Oh, and I finally found the yearbook in a box of Christmas decorations—I don't know how it got in there. And I was right; Grace Kotka did graduate with us at Lafayette. Well, when I looked out the window again and I saw that Eddie had cut the words 'F you' in the back lawn, I couldn't believe my eyes. It was out there in the open for everybody to see."

Mrs. Brounschidle wasn't being entirely accurate. Eddie's "fuck you" was out in the open if you were snooping from an attic window but it was still invisible to people from the ground because it was concealed by the surrounding long grass.

Having your lawn say "fuck you" wasn't neighborly. The social convention of the suburbs is to say "fuck you" to the neighbors by letting everyone know that you have more money than they do by purchasing an expensive car

---

[4] Mr. Brounschidle was a cantankerous crank who found the gentle fizz of an open beer irritating and would finish off the bottle quickly just to get it to shut up. Almost every time we played touch football in the street Mr. Brounschidle would call the police to break up the noisy game, but he distinguished himself from the other neighborhood cranks by calling the cops even when his own children were playing. The children of real criminals have more respect for their fathers than Mr. Brounschidle's offspring did for him because the one thing that the children of hoods can rely upon is that their fathers will never rat on them. Whenever you heard the wail of the siren and saw a police car slowly coming down the street, you could see the struggle on his son Garner's face as he tried to fit a grown-up look of embarrassment that was several sizes too big for him into a boy's cramped expression.

or buying a fur coat or putting an aboveground pool in your backyard. These were the accepted forms of fuck-you, but spelling it out with letters instead of dollar signs was considered impolite.

I wanted to see Eddie's grassy expletive for myself. "Is it still there?" I asked.

"Yes, it is," Mrs. Brounschidle said with a feeble attempt at disapproval, undermined by her pride of discovery. "I better not catch any F-yous on my lawn." She said this to herself almost as if her grass was in danger of picking up swearing from the other lawns in the neighborhood. "You and Garner can go up in the attic and have a look for yourselves. I don't want to do it but I think I'm going to have to call Mrs. Gowdy about this."

From the attic window Garner and I could see the astonishing "fuck you" in the Gowdys' backyard. It was as though each blade of grass was giving us the finger. I was always impressed when another boy did something that I would never dare to do or even think of doing. I hated cutting the lawn too, but I never would have expressed my displeasure by using the F-word, and to be honest, I was too lazy to be that rebellious. It probably took more time and effort to cut the words "fuck you" in the grass than it would have taken just to mow the lawn.

Later that day Mrs. Brounschidle called Mrs. Gowdy to report Eddie's landscaped graffiti. Mrs. Gowdy laughed at the news and her response wasn't condemnation but concern for Eddie's well-being. "He had better get rid of it before his father sees it."

Even after Eddie pulled out the lawn mower and began to make his retraction, Mrs. Brounschidle was unsatisfied by the easy removal of the offending message and the lack of any intention on his mother's part to punish Eddie for his behavior. I think she thought Eddie owed her an apology and he should have been made to cut the words "I'm sorry" into the front lawn. It's obvious now that Eddie's fuck-you was a green flag that we were unable to read. He was telling us that his growing anger had a way of cropping up unexpectedly.

For years Eddie's disturbing behavior was excused or explained away because his family was thought to be strange. "As ye sow, so shall ye reap" is an agricultural proverb that applies particularly well to the cultivation of family trees but I find the metaphor of a family tree to be insufficient. (My family tree is a grapevine that has always produced a dependable crop of alcoholics.)

I think a better agricultural metaphor for a family history is the family farm, since in addition to producing fruits and vegetables each family is made up of a varied barnyard of personalities. In most families you'll find big horses, fat cows, stubborn mules, jackasses, dumb sheep, old goats, selfish pigs, sly dogs, scaredy cats, sex kittens, pests, both minor and major, and no family would be complete without its poultry: ugly ducklings, turkeys, chickens, and even a silly goose or two. And it's obvious that every family farm is capable of producing a lot of bullshit.

Eddie was the bad apple in the Gowdy family but do apples spoil because of a malignant double-helixed worm of DNA, or do they spoil because they are neglected or mistreated?

When I started to compare my normal family to other normal families, I began to learn that the normal family is like the average family of two parents with 2.2 children. These families exist in theory but neither of them exists in nature. The problem is that people confuse normal families with ideal families. Ideal families exist only on television and even then I believe that most sitcoms are thirty minutes in length because that's the maximum amount of time most people can enjoy someone else's family—no matter how perfect or funny they are.

I began to see that every family was an alternative lifestyle with its own values and traditions that were alien to my family's. Whether it was their eating foods that my family would never consume—the Giambras, for example, ate octopus—or whether it was their attitude toward sex—Mr. Erker subscribed to *Playboy*, *Penthouse*, and *Oui* magazines and the back issues were kept neatly piled on a table near his easy chair.

After visiting the Erkers' I tried to imagine my mother lining up a stack of *Playboy*s next to our *Reader's Digest*s. Since we kids always looked through his magazines when no one was around, I wondered if Mr. Erker became upset when someone looked at the centerfolds before he did. My father always hated it when we read the newspaper before he did and I could almost picture my dad sitting down in his recliner, picking up his new *Playboy*, opening to the centerfold, and exclaiming, "Goddammit!" and then, using his public-address system of calling his children collectively by shouting in a voice that carried throughout our house, "Listen, if you're going to look at the centerfolds, then fold them back properly!" Later on, when my father wasn't in the living room, my mother would say in a low voice, "Your father doesn't ask for much and you boys know that he hates to come home and find his new *Playboy* all messed up. So either wait until he reads it first or make sure you fold back the centerfolds."

This was purely a fantasy, of course, because I knew that my mother would condemn any family that kept dirty magazines in their house. On more than one occasion my mother judged other families harshly, almost as if a big family-size package of prejudices was a time- and step-saver that allowed her to handle a large load of irrationality while still being able to raise four kids and take care of a house and husband. A short time after the Gowdys had moved in, my mother declared with a grim nod of her head, "They're dirty." At first I couldn't figure out what she was talking about—the Gowdys certainly didn't look any more disheveled or soiled than we did. But I didn't challenge her statement; even as a boy, there were times when I let my mother follow her own path of Christian charity, which for her consisted of loving, or at least delighting in, thy neighbor's shortcomings.

Since most families on our street had either come from or were trying to avoid becoming white trash, everyone was vigilant about catching the slightest whiff of a funky family and became alarmed until the source of the smell could be determined. Kenmore was a mostly blue-collar suburb where infinitesimal social distinctions were maintained with a pride that blue bloods would find snobbish. Most of the men in our neighborhood worked at the nearby Chevy or Du Pont plants or they were cops like my father or firemen like Mr. Nasca across the street or owned a small business like Mr. Gowdy, who was a plumber. By declaring the Gowdys unclean, my mother was drawing attention away from any lingering odors that might be emanating from our own house.

Eventually my mother clarified what she found objectionable about the Gowdys' habits: they lived in a dirty house. This was a term that she used so frequently when I was growing up that I was under the false impression that it was an architectural style. I can still hear my mother's descriptions of a dirty house almost as if she was a realtor trying to sell it by listing its drawbacks:

> Dirty House 4 Sale; Must See 2 Believ!
> 3 dsgracfl BR, lg nglectd Liv Rm,
> 1½ (eat-in?) BA & a pigsty kit.
> U Cdnt Pay Me 2 Liv Thre!

My mother's definition of a house of ill repute was based entirely on the appearance of the structure and not the behaviors that went on inside it. From her point of view a freshly painted whorehouse with a neatly trimmed lawn and beautifully maintained garden would have been more respectable than a rectory with peeling paint and open trash cans in the front yard. I thought the Gowdys' house looked big, tough, and intimidating. The windows glared at you and the soot-covered white shingles made the house look like it was wearing a grimy undershirt. Whenever my mother drove past Gowdys' house she became indignant about their house's appearance almost as if it had bad manners and should have sucked in its sagging front porch in the presence of a lady.

For most of my childhood the first sign of spring was the sound of my mother crying out in early February that the Gowdys still hadn't taken down their Christmas decorations. Their Christmas lights hadn't been lit since early January but until they were taken down in May they burned day and night, at least in my mother's mind. Whenever we drove past the Gowdys' house she would rail, "Four boys and not one of them can take the lights down!"

My mother's drive-by denigrations of the Gowdys

made me wonder what the interior of their house looked like. The first time I got a look inside it we were going to play baseball and Eddie asked Tommy Helmbrecht and me to wait in the living room while he got his glove. It was a sunny day but in that room everything was overcast. Passing through the doorway, I noticed an illuminated floor lamp, but the light didn't so much dispel the darkness as rearrange the shadows. The yellowed wallpaper was covered with a pattern of roses that seemed, to my surprise, to be filling the room with the scent of cigarettes. The house reeked of tobacco smoke and by breathing normally it would have been possible for the Gowdy boys to sneak a cigarette right in front of their parents. I noticed an enormous pile of newspapers stacked in a corner that looked like they'd been saved in the unlikely event that history repeated itself word for word. Half-hidden under the couch was a plate with a partially congealed TV dinner which looked as if someone had stashed it there because his favorite program had ended before he was done eating but he intended to finish it the following week when the next episode aired. The sofa and chairs were so tired and worn-out looking that I wanted to offer *them* a place to sit.

Eddie's mother came down the stairs carrying a basket of dirty laundry and she looked at us as if we had been abandoned on her doorstep. Mrs. Gowdy trudged through the living room without saying hello, and after she almost tripped over their dog she yelled, "Eddie, I told you to put Skipper outside." She was a dour woman who had decided that while she had to raise four sons, that didn't mean she had to raise a smile too. She didn't have a kind word for anyone. On another occasion when I asked Eddie what his father did for a living, before he could answer

Mrs. Gowdy said with unconcealed contempt, "He's a plumber. It's not that hard a job to learn. All you need to know is that shit runs downhill."

As she made her way down to the basement, Mr. Gowdy walked into the room. He always looked groggy, as if he had just woken up or was just about to go to bed. In fact the only way you could distinguish between his two states of grogginess was by first determining his mood. If he was angry he had just woken up, and if he was reasonably content then he was just about to hit the sack. I gathered that he had just woken up because he greeted us with, "Eddie, what the hell did you do with the scissors?"

Eddie was coming down the stairs from his bedroom, shielding himself with his baseball mitt, and he said, "I put the scissors back in the drawer."

"Well, they're not there now. Jesus Christ, you kids never put anything back where it belongs." This accusation was arguable because nothing in the house appeared to have a fixed location.

Eddie said, "I think Danny used them last."

"Do you know that for sure? If you're lying . . ." Mr. Gowdy wasn't making an idle threat. From what I observed he acted as if misbehaving children were like defective televisions. When they acted up, he'd start swearing and then hit them a few times. It was already apparent that the best that Mr. Gowdy could hope for in terms of filial devotion was that someday his sons would start every anecdote about him with the phrase "my old man . . ." When a son describes his father as "my old man" he's trying to pass off his unbearable personality as endearingly gruff because to do so is more socially acceptable than admitting that one's progenitor was a mean son of a bitch.

Mr. Gowdy's anger momentarily faded when he began a long hacking cough that sounded as if he was hoisting a bucket of phlegm from the bottom of his lungs. Taking advantage of his bronchial preoccupation, the three of us sped from the house in one synchronized motion like a flock of sparrows in flight from a falcon. No one said anything as we walked for half a block, not daring to look over our shoulders for fear that Mr. Gowdy, or the mere memory of him, would be trailing us.

We never discussed the behavior of Eddie's mother and father because there was nothing to say. Bad parents were like bad weather; there was nothing a child could do to change the fact. Sadly, Eddie was living in a house haunted by two very scary parents. When Eddie went to bed he probably had nightmares about waking up and having breakfast with his father and mother. And when he woke wake up in the middle of the night, Eddie would no doubt have preferred the monster under his bed to comfort him rather than his parents.

About the same time that I entered the Gowdys' house for the first time my friendships were going through a change and I was making new friends from junior high school and slowly withdrawing from the boys in my neighborhood. Eddie had never developed into a close friend, either of mine or of anyone else on our street. I regarded playing with him the way I regarded eating green beans; I didn't hate them but I never looked forward to seeing them on my plate. Eddie and green beans were both tolerable in small amounts.

As we boys grew older, and hit the twilight of boyhood at age twelve, Eddie's behavior became increasingly unacceptable. One time, to everyone's disgust, he alone laughed when Jimmy Joe Valleria fell off his bicycle and broke his arm. Long past the age when most boys could view teasing the retarded as good-natured fun, Eddie continued to torment mentally retarded Wilbur Whistler by snatching away the sticks and twigs that he used to "smoke."

It takes a while for boys to distinguish between occasional stupidity and consistent meanness but we were connecting the blots on Eddie's reputation and a pattern was emerging: Eddie always did or said the wrong thing. Eventually boys lose patience. Playing with him became like doing homework that wasn't required.

As Mrs. Brounschidle reminded me when I first heard of Eddie's arrest, my tolerance for his company ended the day he stabbed me with a pen. We were sitting on the Brounschidles' front porch playing with Garner's birthday present, which was a Spirograph set. It included a pad of white paper, several interlocking plastic wheels, and pens in blue, black, red, and green inks. The plastic wheels were used as rotating stencils to make patterns composed of elliptical shapes that resemble the symbol of an atom. It had a short-lived burst of popularity but it was soon put aside after we discovered that mechanical drawing became repetitious quickly. Much of the enjoyment of playing with the Spirograph was that while using it there were plenty of opportunities for joking and making stupid remarks, such as when Barry Bucholtz held up his drawing and said, "Look I made a pair of boobs." His blue nuclear breasts with red atomic nipples received our unanimous approval.

A few minutes later Eddie announced, "I'm going to study karate and get my black belt."

To which Garner Brounschidle said, "You are not."

"I am too."

"Hey, Eddie, maybe if you washed more your belt wouldn't be black."

Everyone laughed at my stupid joke and I felt an undeserved sense of accomplishment. Eddie became quiet and then suddenly jabbed me hard in the hand with the black Spirograph pen. I cried out and tears came into my eyes—the pen had pierced my skin. I backed away from Eddie, uncertain whether he was going to proceed to stab me with the red, green, and blue pens as well. Hearing the commotion, Mrs. Brounschidle came out onto the porch, and after being told what had happened, she said to Eddie, "I'm sorry, Eddie, you're going to have to go home if you don't know how to play."

By losing his temper so quickly, Eddie had skipped several steps in the time-honored boyhood path to violence. Fistfights and feuds were usually the result of a longer period of simmering hostility that after a blowup often resulted in making the two combatants friends. Eddie should have waited until I had mocked him a few more times before losing his temper. That wasn't how we played.

Unfortunately, once Eddie became inspired by anger, he began dipping pens into arms as if they were inkwells. A couple of weeks later he poked Buddy Letchworth with a pen in church and then at school he stabbed my brother Greg. When their teacher sent home a note about the incident with my brother, my father didn't at first believe Greg's version of the event—"I wasn't doing anything"—because my father thought that all conflicts could be explained by the truism that "it takes two to tango." But my brother had been telling the truth, because Eddie's ominous response when asked why he had stabbed Greg had been, "I don't know why. I just don't like him."

Eddie might possibly have retained someone's friendship if he had only stabbed one boy with a pen. For a long time a boy can get away with being bad if he varies his badness, but a regular program of bad deeds endows predictability on what should be aberrant behavior. Eddie's serial jabbings left people firmly convinced that there was something wrong with him. In Eddie's overly literal mind there seemed to be some confusion as to the meaning of the saying that the pen is mightier than the sword; it was never meant to be practical advice for the homicidally inclined.

It almost seems like Eddie was taking pokes at people with pens because he was stumped and couldn't figure out how to kill someone more expeditiously. I also remember that after each stabbing Eddie could walk down our street and absolutely no one would say hello to him.

In the movies, the figure of Death is often depicted as either a specter in a cowled robe or a handsome blond leading man, Brad Pitt in a tuxedo. While in real life the figure of Death tends to look more like Eddie Gowdy did as a teenager. Eddie's physical appearance had a lot to do with the poor initial impression he made. His most prominent feature was his dark, mean eyes. When Eddie became angry, they were like two stones packed in snowballs. In high school Eddie grew an unattractive mustache, which seemed to cringe upon his upper lip. His mustache was separated into two halves, sharply divided by the "nose gutter," making it appear that he had won two black ribbons in a hair-growing contest and pinned them to his face. Eddie's thick black wiry hair never achieved a position of repose; inchworming its way across his scalp, the entire corrugated slab of tightly wound hair pushed upward almost as if it was trying to sneak from him.

Eddie's choice of attire did nothing to make up for his physical limitations. Judging from what he wore every day, he attended rock concerts primarily to shop for clothes. Eddie had a large collection of lurid black-and-Day-Glo-colored souvenir T-shirts that promoted heavy-metal bands—Blue Öyster Cult, Jethro Tull. Eddie was trying to look cool but projected the too-eager insecurity of a headbanger—he was perpetually ready to rock if only Mick Jagger or some other dude would ask him.

Given my feelings about him, I saw what Eddie wore every day from a distance. After the stabbing incident I tended to stay at least an arm's length away from him. We never spoke again but in high school I was aware that he had a girlfriend because I often saw the two of them holding hands in the halls.

Haley Gerbec and Eddie Gowdy were brought together by the letter *G*. Seated next to each other for three years in our alphabetically assigned homerooms, Haley and Eddie became a couple and started dating.

In appearance Haley was plainer than water and more nondescript than air. Gazing at her own reflection, she could easily have overlooked herself. To be honest, her best feature was that she was nondescript. Haley was nearsighted—a requirement for dating Eddie—and wore a pair of wire-rimmed granny eyeglasses with octagonal lenses that didn't bestow upon her the sought-for hippie-chick look but instead transformed her into a teenage biddy. Haley's graduation photo in our Bicentennial class of '76 yearbook shows her wearing her lackluster shoulder-length brown tresses parted down the middle in a style that seemed to hang in limp resignation to the prospect of a bad-hair decade.

Yet, despite this, I remembered Haley from my fifth-grade class as a sweet and extremely shy girl who had a warm and merry laugh. It amazed me that she had accepted Eddie for a boyfriend because sleeping with him had to be a yuck-fuck, but maybe for her a dud boyfriend was better than no boyfriend at all.

Unbeknown to Haley, Eddie had gotten another girl pregnant, and out of desperation to conceal the relationship from her, he wanted the girl to have an abortion. Getting the money to pay for it would be a problem, though, since Eddie and the girl were both unemployed and the need for secrecy kept him from asking anyone for help. Clearly, Eddie was not a catch. After high school he was "let go," as his managers worded it, from a series of minimum-wage part-time jobs and he wasn't about to be fired, so to speak, by Haley too. Eddie had to find some way of quickly coming up with the cash, but time was running out: the pregnancy could be concealed for only a few more weeks. It's not surprising that a kid who failed geometry would have trouble dealing with the consequences of a love triangle. You didn't need to know his math teacher to figure this out.

To this day one of the most shocking aspects of Eddie's story is that there were two women who were actually willing to accept his sexual favors. At the time I was hoping my mother wouldn't pick up on Eddie's being something of a chick magnet because for the previous year I had been a fugitive from her scrutiny. I was still living at home and not dating anyone of either gender and my mother was beginning to worry that she was mistaken in assuming that my lack of a girlfriend was due to my being a shrinking violet; she was beginning to suspect the correct botanical identification: a budding pansy. As a response to her suspicions, she began to mention girlfriends like an uneasy preacher who talks too much about salvation; she wanted me to believe in the possibility of heaven while suppressing her own suspicion that I was actually doomed to perdition. I knew that even Eddie's heterosexuality could be held against me by my mother. "If a murderer can get two girlfriends, why can't you get one?"

On Monday, June 3, 1981, Mrs. Pamela Farkas looked out her dining-room window and noticed her next-door neighbor Debra Olwicki lying on the sidewalk in front of her house. She called the police and within a few minutes a patrol car pulled up and the officers found the body of Mrs. Olwicki, who had bled to death from knife wounds to her neck and body. From the evidence—an open window at the back of her house and the nightgown that had been brutally sliced off her—it appeared that Debra, the mother of two young children and the wife of Ted Olwicki, had surprised a burglar, who had then killed her.

It was later revealed that after hearing someone in the house, Debra had dialed 911 and said, "Someone's broken into my house . . . call the police. . . . I'm at 826 Franklin." Before the operator could get more information, Debra had hung up. Her telephone call revealed a flaw in Buffalo's 911 emergency response system. At the time all 911 telephone calls for Erie County went through the city of Buffalo, and since Debra was understandably feeling pressed for time, she forgot to give her complete address and the operator sent police cars to Franklin Place, Franklin Street, and Franklin Avenue in the city of Buffalo. It seems obvious now that a countywide emergency response system for a large city and over thirty towns and villages might need to take into account the odds that more than one street might be named Washington, Lincoln, or even Franklin, but by the time someone figured out this mistake it was too late for Debra.

During his trial it was revealed that every day Eddie had walked by the Olwickis' while on his way to Haley's house. Over time he had struck up an acquaintance with Debra. He had spoken to her about her Siamese cat who prowled around the backyard, and when the cat had a litter of kittens, he had even adopted one. I can imagine the meowing protests of the intuitive mother cat when Eddie took her kitten. She had reason to cry: black cats were superstitious about Eddie crossing *their* path.

While desperately trying to come up with the money for the abortion, it's believed, Eddie learned that Debra and her family were going to be on vacation in Florida and that the house would be empty. A burned-out cartoon lightbulb appeared over Eddie's head as he suddenly had a bad idea: he decided to rob the Olwickis' house. It seems in retrospect sadly predictable that Eddie got the date wrong; the Olwickis were leaving for St. Petersburg the *following* week. Sometimes I think the source of all evil is a lack of imagination, but if Eddie was incapable of seeing that his mustache was a bad idea, then how was he going to see that trying to earn money by robbing a house was a bad idea?

Eddie never considered that most people in Kenmore don't keep large amounts of money sitting in their house when they're home and they certainly don't do so while they're away on vacation. Kenmore's a community where people cash their paychecks and keep just enough spending money to see them through the week stashed in the top drawer of their dining-room buffet. Eddie could have broken into two or three houses in Kenmore and still not cleared enough to pay for an office visit to a gynecologist, let alone pay for an abortion.

For the next two weeks the unsolved murder became *the* topic of conversation in Kenmore. Mrs. Brounschidle found the murder an inexhaustible source of idle speculation, idle sympathy, or thoughts of idle vengeance, depending on her mood.

"I'll bet the killer was on dope."

"Those poor children . . . she was only thirty-two."

"Whoever did it should get the chair."

A believer in old-fashioned hospitality, Mrs. Brounschidle insisted on murderers getting the electric chair almost as if good manners demanded it. A few days after Eddie was arrested Mrs. Brounschidle revealed her biggest scoop to my mother. It was revealed in confidence, because her husband Fritz had asked her not to tell people that it was Mr. Brounschidle himself who had called the Kenmore police to report that Eddie was acting more suspicious than usual.

What Mr. Brounschidle had noticed was that immediately after the murder, Eddie had cut his hair short, shaved off his mustache, and no longer wore the shabby green jacket that he had worn every day for the past three years. Eddie had made the most common mistake a creep could make in trying to avoid suspicion. If he had continued his normal manner of behaving strangely, it's possible that he might never have been caught. It was when he tried to act innocent that people began to suspect that he was guilty.

Mr. Brounschidle's report alone wasn't enough to cause a warrant to be issued for Eddie's arrest; there were no doubt a few officers who recognized Mr. Brounschidle's name and looked upon his tip as another crank call. The clincher was when Eddie's girlfriend Haley reported to her father, a lieutenant with the Kenmore police, that Eddie was acting strange. Haley's report carried some weight with her father; he had always thought Eddie was weird, but now if even Haley was beginning to be spooked by his behavior, something must be up. A warrant was issued to search the Gowdys' house.

According to Mrs. Brounschidle, "When the police entered the Gowdy house the first thing Eddie's father said was, 'I *thought* he did it.' " Mrs. Brounschidle paused to let this sink in. "That tells you everything you need to know about the Gowdys, doesn't it? Well, when Mr. Gowdy said that, Eddie's mother started crying. The whole thing is a shame." She went on to say that Eddie, who had been trying to act innocent for over a week, quickly shed that ridiculous pretense and resumed his natural guilty manner. He kept saying over and over, "We were friends." He even said it after the police found the plastic bag with his bloody jacket and the knife. For two weeks Eddie had played hide-and-seek but in the end he was caught by the police. As I recall he was never good at hide-and-seek.

We all know that we're going to die someday but only murderers have the unforgivable insolence to mark the date on someone else's calendar. Stories of murders and murderers remind us that life and death seem to be decided by the toss of a coin, and that's an idea that many writers find irresistible. In fact I'd like to propose to the United States Mint a change in the design of our coinage. As a helpful if chilling daily reminder, a memento mori, a black Post-it note, of the swiftness with which our luck can change, I suggest that on the obverse of the Lincoln penny and the Kennedy half-dollar, instead of having images of the Lincoln Memorial and the bald eagle, why not have portraits of John Wilkes Booth and Lee Harvey Oswald? It would be a more striking image if every time we flipped a coin and called out heads or tails, we were unable to forget that misfortune can turn up at any time.

When I think about Eddie Gowdy I find myself, to my own surprise and against my better judgment as the son of a policeman, feeling sympathetic. Part of me thinks that Eddie's life took a wrong turn when he left his mother's womb and I also feel that love must be extremely scarce in your life if you're willing to kill someone to keep it. I don't think that I can be accused of unwarranted softness. My feeling for this one devil is a cold pity, it doesn't make me feel better about myself. To me Eddie is a chilling reminder of the fact that the most easily concealed weapon is a human heart.

Now I'm another writer who has written about a murder; I too have guilty ink on my hands. Am I exploiting a tragedy? Yes, and how do I justify this? I don't, but unlike all the other writers who have exploited our fascination with murder, I can make one claim: Eddie picked up a pen before I did.

Our Fathers

EVERY DAY I sat with my father in his hospital room from ten in the morning until about two o'clock in the afternoon. We were all taking turns watching him. After he had broken the restraints on his hospital bed twice, his doctor insisted that someone from the family had to stay with him at all times. I had flown home three days before, after my brother had called with the news that Dad was near death from his drinking. However, this afternoon he was showing signs of renewed vigor and had suggested several times, "Bob, there's forty dollars in my wallet. Why don't you go down to the Liquor Locker and get me a bottle of vodka. No, maybe scotch. No. You know what would be good? Some beer. Why don't you get me a six-pack of beer, and while you're at the store get something for yourself."

I explained, "Dad, I can't get you a beer. They don't allow drinking in the hospital." To my relief he seemed satisfied with my answer and didn't try to argue. He mumbled, "Okay," and then promptly fell asleep. After being admitted, my father became so noisy and disruptive—the initial symptoms of alcohol withdrawal—that the other patient in his room, Mr. Friddle, left his hospital bed and slept on the couch in the waiting room. Mr. Friddle was recovering from open-heart surgery but wasn't even angry that he was paying for half a room that he couldn't use. He was too concerned about passing a stress test that he had to take later that week. Mr. Friddle said, "I'll tell you, your father's a talker . . ." He made it sound like my dad had been bending his ear reminiscing about the good old days instead of cursing at the orderlies as he went through delirium tremens. Mr. Friddle smiled and shook his head ruefully, and then, almost as if he wanted to apologize for being difficult, he continued, "But I can't sleep with him talking like that, and if I don't get some rest, I'll never get out of here." The panic in his voice slipped out almost involuntarily. I thought, *No wonder the poor guy has heart problems; if he can't express his anger in this situation then he must hold in everything.*

Mr. Friddle was about the same age as my father, mid-sixties, and I found myself thinking how vulnerable men are. Men are like quarts of milk; once they hit their expiration date, they can go bad overnight. After his retirement from the state police, my father changed rapidly. Seeing my dad become an alcoholic was like watching a strong solid snowman melt into a puddle of vodka simply because winter had ended. At some point as an adult I began to feel that I knew and understood my parents. Not that they didn't surprise me now and then, but after my parents reached their sixties I assumed their surprises were going to be pleasant or innocuous ones. I would have been happy if my father had impulsively started to paint watercolors or revealed that he had once wanted to become a baseball player. I never expected the devastating bombshell that after his retirement my father's dreams of "hitting a double" would become a life of "make that a double." I shouldn't have been surprised that my father was a different man than I thought because I've too often learned that I'm a different man than I thought. One of the most troubling consequences of my father's alcoholism was my realization that I didn't know him and that, in the end, he might be unknowable.

My father's condition had vastly improved since his admission to the hospital. The first time I sat with him, he was hallucinating. He repeatedly asked me, "Bob, do you have any quarters? I want to buy a lottery ticket." He wanted the quarters because he thought the volumetric pump by the side of his bed was a machine that sold lottery tickets. I had to admire the resiliency of my father's spirit. It was remarkable that a man who had almost drunk himself to death could still believe that he was lucky.

Today I was feeling fortunate myself. During my shift my father had mostly slept and didn't try to leave the hospital as he had done the the previous night when my sister was taking her turn at his bedside. "Carol, why don't we go out for a drink?" As he dozed, I left the television tuned to a football game that he had wanted to watch. I didn't follow the game but during the commercial breaks I looked up from my book because the principal sponsor was a beer company. The commercials were clever and entertaining and I almost felt like a spoil-sport for not becoming an alcoholic myself after watching them.

I couldn't decide whether the frequent commercials urging us to pop open a cold one were a taunting form of torture to my father—contemptuous jeers that turned the ordinary act of watching television into a form of harassment—or whether in a strange way, they were a source of comfort to him. Perhaps he was able to watch beer commercials like an injured athlete might still enjoy following football after he can no longer play the game.

I had made sure that I had brought a book to read. As a boy, I discovered that books can make an excellent doorstop to prevent anything from entering your mind. When I was growing up my mother used to say with amused tolerance, "When Bob's reading I have to tell him that dinner's ready three times before he even looks up."

Today, when my father saw me open my book, he asked, "Bob, what are you reading?" I was mildly surprised because my father hadn't asked me that question in years. When he asked me that innocent question when I was in high school and college, I would become flustered and evasive. He never asked me that question when I read Mark Twain or Hemingway but always unerringly chose to ask me when I was engrossed in a gay writer such as E. M. Forster. It's possible that my all-consuming interest in the book was what had triggered my father's curiosity. My face would flush as I looked up from the book and responded, "*Howards End.*" In answer to his follow-up question, "What's it about?" I always felt that I was lying when I replied, "An English family"—even though I was unquestionably telling the truth. Meanwhile, in my mind what the book was really all about was, "An English family as seen by *a big homo*!"

Today I told my father, "It's a book by Edward Abbey. *Down the River.* He's an environmentalist who writes about the west." I was willing to talk about this book because Edward Abbey was an author whose unquestioned heterosexuality was as integral to his literary persona as being gay was to Christopher Isherwood's. Satisfied with my answer, he asked, "Bob, how's Tom?" Tom hadn't come with me on this trip, as he would have had to quit his job to do so. And frankly, I didn't want him to come for my own selfish reasons. I knew that talking to Tom each night would be more comforting. Were he here, he'd probably make me feel guilty that I had brought him. Then I'd need to comfort *him* because he would have to endure it too. And at this particular juncture of our relationship, I didn't want him to come.

My father laughed. "Your mother was all worked up the first time you brought him home. When you got there you must not have brought a book because you read everything in the house just to keep your head in a book and not have to listen to your mother. And I mean everything. Do you remember? You read my state trooper magazines that I just glance at, all the *Reader's Digest*s, the Sears catalog—you even read the Burpee seed catalog and there's nothing in it to read except descriptions of plants. Maybe you were thinking of becoming a farmer. Remember the time you tried growing potatoes?"

I had never thought that my father noticed me reading the Burpee seed catalog but I knew from other comments over the years that he was extremely observant of his children's behavior.

In his hospital room my father appreciated my preference for tuning out by reading instead of watching television. The previous day as my sister Carol finished her shift she told my father, "I don't know who's coming next. It's either Bob or Greg." My father replied, "Send Bob. Greg keeps flipping the channels with the remote every second and it drives me nuts. Bob just sits there and reads."

My brother Greg's impatience as he watched television was a reflection of his impatience with my father's drinking problem. As a successful corporate executive, Greg was used to having problems fixed by having the person responsible for the problem fired. Unfortunately our father was a longtime "family employee" whom we couldn't let go and Greg was having a hard time accepting this. Greg suggested having an intervention for my father but my sister made a good point. "Who would we get to intervene? Dad drinks with everyone in town." During Greg's shift, when my father suggested to him that he run out and pick up a bottle of scotch, Greg decided to apply what the twelve-step people call "tough love." From what I observed Greg's tough love is traditional masculine cruelty in sensitive self-help clothing. Greg repeatedly told him, "Dad, you're an alcoholic. You can never drink again. If you drink anymore you're going to die."

Of course I didn't try to dissuade my brother from telling our father that he was an alcoholic because as a fellow man I too sort of believed that tough love might be the right thing to do. For men, being tough is an unquestioned virtue. But it does seem strange that a lifetime of self-willed toughness tends to make men's hearts weak and subject to all sorts of cardiac damage.

I never pointed out to my brother that maybe being tough with someone who needed help getting up to go to the bathroom was unfair. I couldn't really be honest with my brother because we had made a deal after we became adults: I won't tell you what I think of you if you don't tell me what you think of me. It was a nonverbal agreement not to communicate and therefore a binding contract.

Shortly after I arrived for my shift my father decided that he wanted to get up to go to the bathroom. His doctor said that he could stand although he was unsteady and attached to an IV bag. I tried to help, and Dad took my arm until we reached the bathroom door, where he insisted, "Bob, I'm all right. I can do this by myself." Feeling relieved, I left him there hoping not to hear him fall after he shut the door. When he safely returned to his bed, his hospital gown became tangled in the sheets, and as I went to untangle him, I received an unwanted look at the loins from which I sprang.

After making him comfortable and myself uneasy, I was ready to get out of there. I was thrilled when at two o'clock my mother and my sister, Carol, arrived to relieve me. While we sat talking quietly there was a knock at the open door. A nun stepped into the room and announced, "Excuse me, if anyone would like to partake of Holy Communion we'll be offering it downstairs in half an hour." With snarling disbelief my mother growled, "Are you kidding? I'm the only one here who goes to church." My mother gave the nun a look of contempt as if a sinful soul was a family trait that should have been obvious to the most casual observer. Startled by the bitter tone of her response I exclaimed, "Mom!" Carol piped in, "Oh, that's great, Mom." Then my sister and I laughed out loud.

The nun's expression changed from benign goodwill to a sickly smile that implied that she would pray for us. She departed hurriedly with a stoically murmured "God bless you" that she uttered like she was administering last rites to our hopeless family. My mother had been through a lot in the past few years. In addition to losing her ability to mollycoddle nuns and her children, she took out her frustrations with my father in unpredictable spasms of suddenly withdrawn affection. It was as if she had recklessly spent her love for years, and having finally reached her spending limit, she suddenly balked at forking over another penny's worth of affection.

We had witnessed another instance of my mother's newfound emotional thrift a few days before. My father had asked her to bring him a pair of slippers because his feet were cold. The next time my mother came to the hospital the first thing my father asked was, "Did you bring me the slippers?" She responded, "No, I didn't have time to go to the store." "Mom, they sell the kind of slippers he wants down in the gift shop," my sister suggested. "I saw them," my mother snapped. "I'm not paying eight dollars for a pair of slippers. He might not even make it. They have the same slippers out at the mall for two-ninety-nine." Contrary to conventional wisdom, my mother could put a price on love. After forty years of marriage and ten years of drinking, it's worth five bucks.

I couldn't stop thinking about the nun. "Mom, was that necessary?" I asked.

She wasn't contrite in the least. "Well, it's true, isn't it?" she insisted. "None of you do go to church?"

We didn't bother answering her question because she knew that we didn't go to church. "Mom, don't act like you're so holy," Carol said. "You only go to church on Easter and Christmas." Bridling at Carol's insinuation that her relationship with Jesus was more social obligation than metaphysical, she shouted, "So what? At least I feel bad about missing church!"

It was true that I hadn't been to church in years. When I was a boy I went to church every Sunday and soon decided that going to St. Paul's Roman Catholic Church with my father was a better deal than going to church with my mother. My parents rarely went to church together because my father preferred early mass while my mother always went to the noon service. I preferred attending church with my father because he skipped most of the sermon by arriving late and passed on Holy Communion by leaving early. My mother, on the other hand, would arrive early and stay to the closing hymn. I suspected that she felt it was her duty to stay and participate in Holy Communion each week because the priests had gone to such trouble to fix her something to eat and it would have been impolite not to sample it. Or perhaps she was merely trying to get her full money's worth. Each week she put our family's one-dollar contribution in a green collection envelope, and since she had paid for her share of the lamb of God she didn't want to see it go to waste. Whereas my father always hurried away before Communion as if the priest had offered to buy him a meal and he didn't want to feel obligated to stay and eat with someone he barely knew.

At heart I think my father was an easygoing Protestant by nature who revealed his religious leanings by the time-honored American tradition of reluctant participation. Before walking in the door of the church, my father always took one last long puff on his cigarette and then flicked the butt away in one smooth motion. It was a skill that impressed me because it was done casually but the butt shot to the ground as if he was trying to bean an ant. Once inside the church, we each dipped a hand in a stoup of holy water located near the entrance and crossed ourselves. I felt grown up doing this but holy water was always slightly disappointing—I wanted it to tingle or maybe fizz with blessedness. After dunking my fingers, I took my time and carefully made the sign of the cross as if I had hit a home run and needed to touch all the bases. My mother always dabbed the holy water on herself elegantly as if she was applying scent, while my father made the sign of the cross by patting himself quickly as if he was wiping away beads of sweat. I never felt any spiritual buzz from the holy water but my father couldn't smoke in church and it's possible the H_2 God helped prevent his fingers from itching for a cigarette during mass.

My father's brief visit to church each week made it seem like Jesus was a patient in a hospital who was slowly recovering from his injuries. My father made it clear that we were just stopping by to pay our respects but unfortunately we couldn't stay long. We never sat down in the church even if seats in the pews were available. Instead we would stand in the back of the vestibule since my father's idea of "communion" was to remain aloof from our fellow Christians. He believed that it was possible in a manly fashion to fulfill the commandment to love thy neighbor by remaining undemonstrative and minding your own business. The vestibule was filled with other members of our faith who, like my father, believed in attendance but held back from full participation, which, fittingly for Christians, is how God behaves toward man.

When I first started going to church with my father the mass was still said in Latin, which only emphasized how out of touch God was with our lives. I couldn't understand what the priest was saying and his speaking a dead language made it seem like we were all children and the priest and God were talking about an adult matter that they didn't want us to understand. It didn't make sense to me but I was relieved that the priest didn't protract the mass by spelling out the word "sin" and every other "bad" word.

I excused myself from the Latin lesson. The sound of the Mass had become a background noise, *humina-humina-humina.* It sounded like the priest had been transformed into Ralph Kramden stupefied by the idea of speaking directly to God. I tried to follow my father's example of patiently waiting but I found standing for over a half hour to be dull and tiring. Since the church offered no toys or games to play with I had to figure out different ways to keep myself entertained.

I'm not sure when I decided to bring my hamster, Doris, to church with me each week. I first started bringing her on the occasional times when I went to church with my mother and my sister. I should have known better than to bring Doris to church, as hamsters are native to Iran and so she probably wasn't even a Roman Catholic. Before leaving the house I would slip her and a handful of sunflower seeds into the inside pocket of my blue sport coat and her constant wiggling made it feel like my heart had jumped out of my chest and was trying to tickle me. In the church I couldn't play with Doris, but occasionally I would open my sport coat to flash her to my sister. Carol's look of disbelief as she saw Doris's sunflower-filled cheeks peer from my pocket was satisfying enough to keep me entertained. I was able to flash Doris for at least half the mass until my mother shushed Carol and me. It was just as well, because whether it was from eating all the sunflower seeds or from listening to the sermon, Doris always fell asleep.

Doris's churchgoing ended the first time I brought her to mass with my father. She had been so well behaved that I was confident that she wouldn't embarrass me. I didn't know that for weeks Doris had been chewing a hole in the pocket of my sport coat and that she was ready to make her prison break. We were standing in the back of the church when I realized that she was clambering up my shirt. I began to panic when she made a detour, traveling down my coat sleeve. As I started twisting myself inside out in order to get the hamster to reverse course, my father bent over me and whispered, "Bob, are you okay?" Before I could reply Doris came crawling out of the sleeve into my hand.

I expected my dad to become angry but he looked astonished and, with a tightly held smile on his face, slowly shook his head back and forth. Then he led me to the door as I gripped Doris tightly in my hands. A few people saw what had happened and they seemed to enjoy the sudden appearance of a hamster in our church almost as much as they'd enjoy a visitation by Our Lady. Outside on the front steps, as my father calmly lit a cigarette, he asked out of curiosity, "Bob, why the hell did you bring your hamster to church?"

I knew that if my father didn't become angry immediately, he wasn't going to become angry at all. "I don't know," I replied. "I thought it would be fun."

Inhaling deeply on his cigarette, he said dryly, "Well, I'm glad you don't have that garter snake anymore."

We decided to put the hamster in the other pocket inside my coat and that day we set a new record for the brevity of our church attendance. My father decided that Doris had picked a reasonable time to leave even though we had been there such a short time that the spots of holy water on my shirt were still damp. From then on, before leaving for church my father always asked, "Bob, are you all ready to go? And is Doris coming with us or is she sleeping in today?"

At first I just smiled and rolled my eyes in reply, but

soon I began coming up with a different response each time because I liked to make him laugh. I'd say, "No, she's going with Mom later." I got my biggest laugh from him when I said, "No, she's tired. She was on her wheel all last night."

Leaving Doris in her cage meant that I had to find other ways of entertaining myself at church. To help pass the time I started reading every word in the church bulletin, pondering cryptic announcements such as *A special thanks to all who helped make our Chinese Auction so successful, especially Eileen Capucci.* It sounded almost like the women's sodality had sponsored a night of slave trading. But then, I'd wonder, what the heck is a sodality?

Usually, when I finished reading the bulletin, my body would start to wobble and I would start shifting from one foot to the other. My father would place his hands on my shoulders, reassuring me that we were in this thing together.

When overcome by boredom, I could always stare at the other people in church. What was that old man's tattoo? Hey! That guy wore sneakers to church. Ewww, did Mr. Lathrop step in dog do? That bald man has a big dent in his head. That woman's yellow shoes match her purse and her hair. That skinny guy is carrying the church bulletin with his fake arm. Did he pick it up first with his real hand and stick it in the pinchers or pick it up with the pinchers? That man with big arms is handsome.

Shortly after I had exhausted all diversions, it was usually time for the collection. My father never put any money in the basket but he always gave me a dime to put in myself. Clutching my coin, I would watch the communion basket being passed slowly from hand to hand waiting for it to finally reach us. My father would grab it and hold it near me, but before I tossed my dime in the basket I would stare intently at the salad of dollars and collection envelopes garnished with shining coins. Suddenly I wanted to keep my dime and even help myself to some of the money. I was being led each week into temptation but I resisted, less out of fear of my Heavenly Father above than fear of the earthly dad over my shoulder.

After I had thrown in my begrudged offering, the communion procession began. This is when my father would tap me on the shoulder and indicate with a nod that it was time for us to go. As soon as we walked out of the church my father would start bantering with me. He would light up a cigarette and say, "Brrr, it's cold out. Bob, bundle up or your nose will freeze off." Then he would feign grabbing my nose and show me his captured thumb poking out from between his fingers. "You hungry?" he'd ask. "Yeah." I was always hungry during church. There were times during the mass when I was tempted to nibble on Doris's sunflower seeds.

"How does going to Your Host sound?"

"That sounds good."

"Then let's go."

Before and after church my father and I would talk in short bursts punctuated by periods of quiet of equal or longer duration. I don't think my father, like many men, ever looked upon conversation as an art. He regarded it as a sport. The action is punctuated by frequent lulls while the players wait for the pitch. It was perfectly acceptable to take your time making contact with the ball. Since my father seemed to calmly accept frequent time-outs and breathers as part of the game, I never felt uncomfortable when there was silence between us.

After church we always went to a nearby Your Host

restaurant, one of a popular chain in Buffalo. While driving to the restaurant we would pass the Amigone Funeral Home. Part of our weekly routine was that my father would always grin and crack the same joke. "Am-I-Gone? I'd say you were." It never occurred to me until recently how appropriate the name Your Host was for people who were dining after attending mass. Going to Your Host was also a weekly ritual that had an unvarying sequence of actions that required you to listen and respond before you were fed.

We might have stayed for the end of the mass if the priest had offered the kind of welcome we received from Katie, our favorite waitress at Your Host. If Katie had been our priest, as soon as we walked up to the altar, she would say, "Hi, Matt. Body of Christ?" because she knew his usual order, and then my father would say with a mischievous smile, "How do you know that, Katie? I might be in the mood for something different today. I hear that Buddhism is awfully good . . ." And her sarcastic response would be, "Yeah, and I might marry a Rockefeller tomorrow" just before she placed the Host on his tongue and repeated "Body of Christ" and my father responded with an "amen" and a wink.

Now that I think of it, perhaps churches could stand to be a little more like coffee shops. It would make church more inviting if everyone sat on stools at a counter instead of sitting in pews and the priest offered free refills and Communion at any time. And it's not demeaning to suggest that a good priest should try to be more like a good waiter. A good priest might try to handle each parishioner like they were his regulars. He would know who's in a hurry, who wants it to go, who likes to linger, and who just needs somebody to talk to—and at the end of mass, instead of taking up a collection, everyone would be encouraged to tip heavily.

Later in life it's true that my father might have preferred that churches should be run like neighborhood saloons, with the wine served on tap and bowls of heavily salted communion wafers left sitting out on the bar. But I've always felt that the dreariest coffee shop is more cheerful than most bars and more restorative than most churches. When you stop in a coffee shop, often after spending the night in a bar, it's a blinking neon sign of hope; you're not going there to withdraw from the world, you go to a coffee shop to fortify yourself to reenter it. I know there have been mornings and nights when I myself have found a friendly waitress or waiter offering a bottomless cup of coffee to be the perfect symbol of a love that is miraculous, abundant, and unconditional.

At Your Host, we always sat at the counter, where my father would have coffee and smoke Pall Malls. I had the cheeseburger deluxe and a chocolate milkshake. The "100% All-Beef Cheeseburger Deluxe" came with crinkle-cut french fries and a tiny paper cup of coleslaw that kept its distance at the edge of the plate. Coleslaw's the wishy-washy side dish that doesn't know whether it's a vegetable or a salad and no matter how much unhealthy mayonnaise-based dressing it wears, it's still a Goody Two-Shoes trying to tag along with the cool greaser crowd. When it came time to order my cheeseburger from Katie, I always emphasized, "And no onions, please."

"No onions, Bobby. You got it."

Katie was an excellant waitress and every week my cheeseburger arrived as ordered. But the first time we went to Your Host, I forgot to mention the dreaded onions because I had assumed that no one would deliberately put onions on or in any food. Still innocent of culinary double-dealing, I was unsuspecting when Katie placed the large white oval platter in front of me with a hurried, "Enjoy." I immediately took a big mouthful of cheeseburger, which I quickly spit out as if the cheeseburger had bit me back.

"Bob, what's wrong?" my father asked.

"There's onions. I hate onions!"

Onions! Onions were an abomination unto my mouth. I had read the menu and there was no mention of onions anywhere in the description of the cheeseburger deluxe. I wanted no onions, onions being a word that in my mind should be spelled ØniØns. Removing the top of the bun, I gingerly lifted the cheeseburger patty, turning it over like a rock and finding, with a shudder of disgust, that little slimy pieces of onion were secreted there. It was at that moment that onions became a bogey-food for me, a horror that I was afraid was hiding in every sandwich or lurking in every sauce.

I told my father, "I hate onions."

He smiled and said, "I know." My opinion of onions was as well known in my family as Senator McCarthy's opinion of communists.

"It's all right, Bob. We'll just scrape them off. Here, let me do it."

My father took a knife and removed the onions and most of the cheese, and then after I double-checked for any stowaways, I smothered the burger with ketchup in an attempt to blot out their memory. But it was too late. After that one booby-trapped cheeseburger, I started inspecting all my food with a hardened cynicism that belied my age.

As a boy I was a picky eater; I was fussy; I was hard to please; but those are mild terms that hold out the possibility that I could be reasonable or open to compromise. It wasn't just onions that I hated. I was on a hunger strike against anything healthy—vegetables, fresh fruit, anything. If Adam in Eden had possessed my finickiness he would never have been tempted.

To my mother's consternation I started each day not breaking my fast but resuming it. My mother tried to force me to eat breakfast but at eight in the morning, she couldn't win. After getting four children ready for school, she had no appetite for fighting and she certainly couldn't threaten me with, "If you don't eat something you're not going to school."

Switching tactics, my mother decided that you can catch more flies with honey than with vinegar. So she began trying to entice me by offering with a series of different breakfasts. One morning she would fix bacon and eggs, then the next day she would prepare pancakes or French toast or waffles or oatmeal or even Pop-Tarts, but nothing satisfied me. She was like a zookeeper trying to get an orphaned baby animal to eat, though the scientific literature offered no hint of what it subsisted upon in its natural habitat. Finally, after months of trial, I agreed to drink a glass of Carnation Instant Breakfast every morning before going to school. Instant Breakfast became a form of nutritional hocus-pocus—we were being sold a snake-oil mixture of chocolate powder with an abracadabra of vitamins which was added to eight ounces of milk. But my mother didn't regard Instant Breakfast as a magic formula. It was more of a breakfast superstition with her. She needed to believe in it because she had tried everything else.

For lunch I was more adventurous and would eat one of four sandwiches: peanut butter and jelly, grilled cheese, tuna fish, or boloney with ketchup. For dinner, I ate meat and potatoes with my two approved vegetables: corn or string beans. But even my eating of corn was qualified. I wouldn't eat the corn *on the cob;* it had to be sliced off the cob. I can't even remember why I hated eating corn on the cob. I was lazy, but I never asked for my Popsicles or lollipops to be taken off the stick. More mystified than angry, my mother would slice off the kernels while informing me, "Bob, it's the same corn off the cob as it is on the cob." Irrational dislikes are to children what irrational loves are to adults. They can't be explained, they can only be allowed to fade.

Getting me to eat corn off the cob had to feel like a victory to my mother since I hated liver and lamb and corned beef, I didn't like the skin on chicken (I didn't like chicken on the bone either), and I wasn't crazy about pork chops. (The pork-chop bone didn't bother me but I would only eat pork chops if *all* the fat was cut off.) I hated fat more than the editors of *Vogue*. At dinner I hacked away at my pieces of steak or roast beef, cutting off every bit of fat until the rejected trimmings crowded out the remaining meat. I would push the glistening slugs of fat to the edge of my plate but I couldn't allow them to stay there. My plate was surrounded by enemy foods and I couldn't afford to let down my guard. Sure I had won this battle but the war was never ending.

When I ate out with my father, he let me eat whatever I wanted and never insisted that I eat the coleslaw that came with cheeseburger and french fries. I think my father felt that he was doing his paternal duty to see that I was eating well by allowing me to have a real chocolate milkshake with my cheeseburger. It looked more substantial than a glass of Instant Breakfast.

It was time to leave Your Host when I made a second slurping sound with my milkshake straw and my father gave me a look that squelched the desire to make a third. "Well, Bob, should we get going?" I would mull over his question for a moment, as if our staying or going was really my decision, before decisively replying, "Yeah, let's go."

"Well, I'm ready if you are." While my father paid the bill I would ask him about one of his friends who had stopped by the counter to say hello. "Dad, why does Mr. Van Alstine wear sandals in the winter?" Stubbing out his cigarette, letting the smoke fall from his nose and mouth as if he was tired of carrying it, my father would reply with a slight shake of his head, "He thinks we're living in Florida."

I could handle the prospect of being bored at church but it was harder to accept the feelings of desolation that descended upon me as we drove home. The rest of Sunday loomed before me like purgatory. As preparation for my first Communion, I had attended religious instruction classes at St. Paul's on Tuesdays; there, Sister Annette had explained purgatory as a place where people who weren't bad enough to go to hell but still hadn't made the first cut to get into heaven were punished by being made to wait before they could try again. Purgatory was a remedial heaven or a special hell, where you had to work on improving your goodness before you could join the rest of the class.

Sister Annette made becoming an angel sound like trying out for football or becoming a cheerleader. To get out of purgatory required teamwork and to make God's starting lineup you had to be helped by our prayers or improve your score by atonement—an act of contrition that she made sound like being forced to stay after school and having to chant one hundred thousand times "I will not sin anymore" as punishment for misconduct. A stay in purgatory must put a big dent in your heavenly social status, which will matter because heaven is snobby. It's based upon the most discriminating form of exclusivity: you've got to be good enough to get in. Once the ex-purgs make it to heaven they must feel like ex-cons. Even though they're officially forgiven and have paid for their crimes, they're always going to have a record.

"You know Bob, don't you? He's new. He didn't get in right away. Bob spent some time in purgatory . . ."

"Oh, I see."

In addition to purgatory, Sister Annette also explained that there was a place called limbo, another of heaven's waiting rooms for people who through no fault of their own were out of the salvation loop. This included anyone born prior to Jesus's birth, any current heathens, and all unbaptized babies. (It must irk God when impish smart-asses call limbo "Baby Hell.") The thought has occurred to me that to make limbo or purgatory more punishing while you're stuck there, I'll bet that the only reading material is the Bible. The one good book that no one ever reads for pleasure.

The concept of limbo troubled me even as a boy. Not letting unbaptized babies into heaven made God sound unbelievably petty. I still find it hard to believe in a God who is meaner than me. I can be really nasty and spiteful at times but even I would relent and let unbaptized babies into heaven. I've always felt that God must understand the concept of extenuating circumstances because He is, by definition, exceptional.

The problem with organized religions is that they try to bring comfort to the living by explaining what happens to us after we die and I've never liked any of the descriptions of heaven that I've heard. Uncertainty makes life interesting and if our afterlives are predictable, then it's quite possible that they'll be dull. I understand that organized religions need to be careful about how they present the afterlife. They have to make their heaven sound appealing by presenting it as an attractive fringe benefit to members in good standing of the faith but they can't make it sound too appealing or people whose lives aren't going well might try to head on over early. It's almost as if religions invented the almost universal prohibition against suicide to serve as a police line to keep the crowds from rushing the gates. Religions also need to keep descriptions of heaven cloudy because if the portrayal is too specific, they might lose more members than they attract. A heaven where everyone has a pair of wings isn't that appealing to people who are allergic to feathers.

It's sad when people spend their whole lives working to earn a place in heaven, almost like being alive is a job that they hate but they're really looking forward to enjoying their retirement. The afterlifestyle of a religion is such a big selling point in winning converts and keeping the faithful happy that I think you could start an extremely popular religion in America if you professed a belief in a Permanent Vacation All-You-Can-Eat Heaven with heated swimming pools, unlimited tennis and golf, and rooms with free cable TV. Basically I'm content to believe that something will happen to us after we die but I don't need to know exactly what. I think it would be better if all religions regarded death as if it was a trip to the bathroom. Once you pass through that door we don't need to know what happens there. We can assume that death will be pretty self-explanatory.

The most ridiculous version of heaven is the fool's paradise of fundamentalist Christianity. Some fundamentalist Christian preachers have claimed that there won't be any homosexuals or Jews in heaven, which means that everyone stuck in their heaven will have to go to hell to see a good play or movie. What really seems to tick off fundamentalist Christians is that gay people and Jews don't seem to care that we might not get into their heaven. As I get older I realize that having a halo isn't all it's cracked up to be. Direct overhead lighting is always unflattering and it would only accentuate the dark circles under my eyes.

It's sad when the narrow-minded try to guess the presumed community standards of heaven by excluding entire groups of people; as far as I'm concerned a so-called heaven without Jews or homosexuals is my definition of hell. In my heaven I would even want bigoted fundamentalist Christians because in my selfish vision of paradise there should still be people that me and my friends can make fun of.

As a boy, I saw the difference between heaven and hell as simply as the difference between a Sunday morning and a Sunday afternoon. After a morning at church and Your Host with my father, Sunday became a day where my mood always changed from blissful to forlorn. The remainder of Sunday was a day off that invariably felt like an off day. Sundays always felt like the afterlife of the week and during the long eternity of Sunday afternoons I felt that I was stuck in limbo. I wasn't being punished but I wasn't having any fun either. For a boy hell could just be a heaven where there was nothing to do. Sunday was a day of restlessness that I spent awaiting the new dispensation of Monday.

On the drive home I seemed to slip away from my father's attention. On Sundays my father, being a state trooper, often had to work, and if he had to go in to work at three o'clock, I could tell because after we left the restaurant he would become quietly lost in thought and almost never made a joke as we drove home. He would turn on the car radio and by the time we arrived I understood that he had already wordlessly said good-bye. I was beginning to see that when adults went to work they started early just by thinking about it. Still, I didn't resent my father's silence and it didn't diminish the time we had together. It appeared to me that my father dreaded Sunday afternoons just like I did.

The few hours I spent each week with my father mirrored the few hours I spent each week with God. Going to church on Sundays was our time together but during the rest of the week my father and God had other responsibilities and I understood that they might be busy or tired or in a bad mood and it was better not to bother them.

I tried to get through Sundays by killing time. As a boy I killed time in the same manner that I killed my pet turtles; each minute died of neglect because I didn't know how to properly care for it. For a while I would hang out in the living room reading the newspaper. In the afternoon I poked around the basement and before dinner I would lie on my bed reading comic books. I kept moving around the house, hoping to run into someone more interesting than my family.

Outside of going to church, my family wore its Catholicism lightly. A few dried palm fronds hung over the living-room mirror all year as remembrances of Palm Sunday, but they were less a mark of our faith than a symbol during the long Buffalo winters of our longing for the return of warm weather. We clearly weren't heavy-duty Catholics like the Petulas, the elderly Polish couple next door. They had framed pictures of Jesus,

Mary, and Joseph hanging in their kitchen, making their house look like a restaurant where the celebrated Holy Family had once enjoyed a meal.

On Fridays my mother's perfunctory attitude about our faith became plain. Catholics were supposed to avoid meat on Fridays, but if my mother ran out of tuna or peanut butter, she had no qualms about making us baloney sandwiches. I would argue with her. "Mom, if we eat meat, it's a sin."

Exasperated by my recourse to a religious belief to restrict my diet even further, she would blurt out, "Oh, just eat it. It's a sin to waste good food too." She had had her fill of fussy eaters, and God and I were just being too picky. But not wanting to completely undermine my faith, she held out the possibility of redemption. "If you're really worried about it just go to confession tomorrow." She recommended taking confession as if it was an antacid that would relieve the stomach upset of a sinful meal.

My parents went through the motions of being good Catholics, but after having four children in five years, on Sunday mornings they were tired, all they wanted was a little peace and quiet, and the baby Jesus was just another kid demanding attention.

Do I think God is a mother or father? I don't know. A great case can be made for the belief that God is a mother. The idea of a female God is appealing, as life is filled with maternal images of birth and growth and nurturing. But if I had to choose a sex for God, the notion of God the father works for me better than that of God the mother. It's purely personal. I think that I have some understanding of my mother but I don't think that I'll ever understand my father and it's that mystery that I respond to.

God's the strong silent type. We've been told that He loves us but He remains physically undemonstrative and emotionally unavailable. He's impossible to read, keeps His own counsel, and while He'll listen to you He never talks about Himself. God watches over us but He's not really too involved in our day-to-day lives. Is it neglect or is God just busy?

It seems to me that one of the things that the Judeo-Christian tradition avoids questioning is that if God is our father, then there has to be a better way of teaching children lessons than by His overreliance on corporal punishment. I avoided some childhood traumas because my father had a sense of humor and handled my mistakes lightheartedly. For example, one time when I was three or four our family went to the drive-in to see a movie. When I had to go take a tinkle my father took me to the men's room, where I used a urinal for the first time. I understood what I had to do and I confidently walked up to a urinal, pushed my underwear down to my ankles, and then let my shorts drop to the floor. As I started peeing, I had a vague feeling that people behind me were laughing as they walked past but I couldn't imagine why.

My father was using the next urinal over and glanced down at me to see how I was doing. Noticing my bare-assed condition he started to softly chuckle and said, "Hey, Bob, you feeling a little draft over there?" I smiled at hearing my name and my father's amused tone of voice without exactly understanding what he was saying. But I didn't reply because I was concentrating on targeting the soap in the bottom of the urinal. When I finished my father gently explained that it wasn't necessary to drop my pants to use a urinal. This was a valuable lesson for a boy to learn and advice that I follow to this day.

After I made my confirmation I stopped going to church, as did my brothers and my sister after their own confirmations. My mother continued to attend church but gradually even she stopped going. I assume she realized that she would be all alone in heaven while the rest of her family roasted in hell and she decided to go for the devil she knew rather than the God she didn't.

My father stopped going to church around the same time that he quit smoking. He had two heart attacks when he was in his early forties and his doctor told him that his smoking had contributed to them. Each cigarette put to his lips had been a Judas kiss and this betrayal by an old friend seemed to make him question all his beliefs. My father had been able to accept the changes in the mass that included the adoption of English instead of Latin, but not being able to light up a cigarette before and after church was a change in ritual that he found intolerable.

When I became older I started to feel that Christianity was just a story that refused to die. I've always had a problem with the central tenet of the faith—letting His son get nailed to a cross because God wanted to make a point—that's not my idea of healthy parenting. It's been said that God sacrificed His only son to show His love for us. Maybe it's just me but couldn't God have shown His love for us by letting His son suffer psychologically instead of physically? God could have let Jesus spend a long miserable life in a lousy marriage, working a crappy job, and dealing with His screwed-up kids. It's conceivable that fifty years of that misery could have been an equally powerful symbol of inconceivable pain and sacrifice. I think Christianity would been a better religion if God had sacrificed His need to control and be judgmental instead of sacrificing His son; founding a religion with bloodshed, even a religion of love and forgiveness, is a bad idea.

When I moved to New York I became a Buddhist for six months, but eventually decided that Eastern religions are no prize either. Reincarnation is a lousy deal as far as I'm concerned. Out of the billions of people who are born there seem to be only a handful who have reached nirvana through repeated incarnations. For most people every incarnation is a sucker bet that this time they're going to be a winner. From what I understand karma is a form of spiritual credit and the system of reincarnation makes God into an all-seeing collection agency hounding people to pay off their debts, and unlike MasterCard the finance charges don't end with your death. The debt is carried over to your next life, where you have to pay for things that you don't even remember buying. And if you have any questions about the bill, good luck, there's no way to dispute a charge. When it's your word against the word of God, you don't stand a chance. I don't want a God who makes us pay for everything; how about a free sample of forgiveness?

On the other hand, the most attractive aspect of Christianity is that the entire faith is built on a bizarre father-and-son relationship. The most moving words in the New Testament are said by Jesus when He is dangling like a trophy and asks God, "My God, why have you forsaken me?" The pain of that father-and-son relationship is still capable of stinging across two millenniums. I would say that the ultimate example of tough love is God letting His only son die for our sins. A God that twisted is actually almost comforting, because inexplicable and unforgivable behavior that will have to be forgiven is inevitable in all relationships with our parents.

I've never believed in simple faith. Faith should be complex and open to doubts, irony, inconsistencies, alternate meanings, and confusion. On that basis alone God does a great job. Christianity is a religion in which God is constantly asking us to prove that we love Him and of course we constantly want Him to prove that He loves us, and therefore the relationship is always going to be unsatisfying.

I had to learn to love my father for who he was, the loving father and the stumbling alcoholic, and it seems to me that that kind of love is the basis for some sort of faith.

On my last day with my father in his hospital room I sat quietly reading. His condition had improved and one of the first signs of his recovery was that he had resumed wielding the remote control for the TV. He would flip through the channels, stop for a moment, sample the program, become bored, and then change the channel. After a while he would either leave the television on CNN or shut it off and take a nap.

My father had stopped suggesting that I run out and pick him up some scotch and since he couldn't drink he began to eat again. He was still on his IV—the hospital version of Carnation Instant Breakfast—but he was also eating solid food. His lunch was always brought in by a dour nurse, and after she departed, my father would say, "She has the personality of a hubcap." He offered to order me a meal and he gave the food his endorsement. "Bob, it's not bad. I've had worse." He added, "Since your mother doesn't cook anymore, this is the closest to a home-cooked meal I've had in years. She probably wishes I'd stay in the hospital all the time." After lunch my father asked, "So, Bob, you're leaving tomorrow?"

"Yeah."

"It was smart of you to figure out how to work your summers on the Cape."

I was working in Provincetown but my parents almost never said the name of the place on the Cape where I was performing. I like to think that this allowed them to maintain the illusion that I was spending the summer at the Kennedy compound in Hyannisport instead of in a town where you were not likely to rub shoulders with Jackie Onassis but it wouldn't be out of the ordinary to bump into a man dressed as her.

All morning while I sat in his room the thought ran through my mind that I might not see my father again. His doctor had said that his heart was permanently damaged from his drinking and that even if he quit now he would still have health problems. I wanted to tell him that I loved him but I felt completely self-conscious about saying it. I had seen enough television melodramas to know that I should do it and that if I didn't say it, then according to the rules of melodrama, I'd regret it for the rest of my life and possibly even end up an alcoholic myself.

"Hey, Dad, you know . . . um . . . I love you."

"I know, Bob." He took an audible breath and said, "I love you too, Bob."

"Um, Dad, I don't want you to die, so can you try not to drink?"

"All right." He didn't promise me that he wouldn't

drink and we both were aware of that. I decided to ask him a question.

"Dad, why do you drink?"

"I don't drink that much."

"Dad. You're in the hospital because you almost died from drinking."

"Boy, I knew I was in trouble when you all showed up here. You never all visit us at once. I thought, 'It must be worse than I thought if they're all here.' I'm dying, aren't I?"

Stunned by his question, I answered truthfully, "I don't know, Dad. You're still alive, but your doctor said that you're going to die if you start drinking again."

"He keeps asking me for a state trooper's hat. I'm not giving him a hat. *Anyone* can be a doctor. There's a height requirement to get into the state police."

It looked like he wasn't going to answer my question and I decided not to pursue it. But my father wasn't finished. "Bob, everyone in Buffalo drinks. In case you forgot, in Buffalo there isn't that much to do."

I laughed at his joke although I didn't think the chamber of commerce would use "Everyone in Buffalo drinks" in an ad campaign to raise the city's profile.

"And I love sports. And we lost three Super Bowls. Jesus, if you really want to see people drink, go to any sports bar in this city."

"Come on, Dad."

"Hey, and you try living with your mother. She can drive you nuts."

I have to admit that idea had crossed my mind.

"Well, Dad. If she's driving you nuts then maybe you two should split up."

"No, I'm going to stick with her." He added with a

grin, "Anyway, you need two people to operate the boat. I can't get it out of the dock by myself."

After talking to my father, it wouldn't surprise me to learn that God's a wise guy too. You can ask all the questions you want, you just might never get a straight answer.

I've stopped trying to figure out God's reasons or purpose for me and everyone else in the universe. There are times when I can't figure out my own behavior or my parents', let alone God's. Can anyone explain to me why my mother writes the alphabet over and over, *A B C D E . . .* and then writes down disturbing reminders to herself such as *You're not a bitch. You're a good mother*?

What's missing from Christianity is any acknowledgment that Jesus had to forgive His father's behavior or His mother's if that be the case. And of course, it would be nice if God acknowledged that sometimes He probably hasn't seemed like such a good father and that while He may disagree with our interpretation of the relationship we can certainly discuss it.

In fact my relationship with my parents leads me to the only reason that I can think of to ever assume that God is either a mother or father. My spiritual beliefs can be boiled down to this: God's irrational, irritating, and often a huge embarrassment, but what are you going to do? God's family.

I'm Just a Love Machine

TURNING THE pages of my three *Kenitorial* high-school yearbooks recently, I was surprised to see how much could be learned about who I was as a teenager from reading the inscriptions that my friends and classmates wrote at the end of each year.

"Maybe in another 200 years, Brian won't be a total zero" tells you that I graduated from Kenmore West Senior High School in the bicentennial year of 1976, an anniversary that reminded all Americans of their deep-seated love of that most democratic of ideas: universal apathy. My hometown, Kenmore, commemorated the two-hundredth anniversary of the American Revolution by painting all the fire hydrants in the village red, white,

and blue. It was not the most stirring of patriotic tributes but it was fiscally responsible, as the village department of public works only had to spring for blue and white paint since the hydrants were already red. Nineteen seventy-six was a historic year for my friends and me, and we celebrated our declaration of independence, at least from high school, by hitting a dozen graduation parties at which the parents reluctantly agreed to serve beer because we were adults now. As teenage boys, we prided ourselves on knowing how to party and we could tell that our country's birthday blast was going to suck. Our idea of a great bicentennial celebration would have been the president's inviting us to party at the White House. The Who's national anthem for the teenage wasteland, "Baba O'Reilly," would be cranking from the Oval Office as Betty Ford encouraged everyone to chug beers and do shots of amaretto while a totally spent Gerry passed around a bong stamped with the presidential seal. As my friend Vic Lugchenko put it, "Fuck that shit. I'm having my own fucking bicentennial celebration every day. I have blue balls and my dick's red and white."

"I have a little of the stuff in my locker" tells you that my friends and I enjoyed getting stoned. There was never any hesitation on my part about smoking pot because as a teenage boy I was already under the influence of a mind-altering substance and I knew that marijuana was never going to fry my brain as badly as testosterone did. In the social hierarchy of our school my friends and I were never considered "heads" because, while we smoked pot on the weekends, we never smoked on a school night. We sang along with Kiss, "I want to rock and roll all night and party every day!" but in practice we upheld

suburban values and confined our partying to Fridays and Saturdays.

I believe the number of your closest friends in high school is limited by the number of guys who can comfortably fit into one car. There were eight guys I hung out with in high school, but my closest friends were John Sorrell, Vic Lugchenko, and Pete "the Turk" Petrocelli. On Saturday nights we would drive around in Vic's car smoking a nickel bag and then, after we were high, we would listen at full volume to an eight-track tape of Pink Floyd's *Dark Side of the Moon.* We would be mesmerized by the growing sound of a heartbeat turning into the ticking of a clock and then space out on the hypnotic pulsating sounds of a Moog synthesizer. We waited in anticipation for the moment when the synthesizer faded and the listener was misled into thinking that the music had stopped. Suddenly the music started up again with the loud chiming and ringing of dozens of clocks, which would cause us to scream and yell because "it was such a rush." The chimes also functioned as a dinner gong of sorts, announcing the onset of the munchies, which would be assuaged by hitting a nearby convenience store. Oreos were the ultimate munchies, and it was an indication of our still being boys that we rewarded ourselves for being bad by giving ourselves cookies.

"Soul-man," "To a Main Man," "A bad dude like you" tells you that in addition to rock music, my friends and I loved funk. We were white boys playing the funky music of the O'Jays, Earth, Wind and Fire, the Ohio Players, Parliament, the Isley Brothers, Kool and the Gang, the Miracles, LaBelle, B.T. Express, and we even liked the music of the two bands of white guys who played funk,

Wild Cherry and the Average White Band. We were absolutely committed to getting dowwwwwwn but our true level of getting the funk was revealed when we also embraced the bubble-gum "funk" of K.C. and the Sunshine Band's song "Get Down Tonight." I can't help but think that our commitment to funk might have been more authentic if any of us had actually known black people. But in Kenmore our opportunities for interracial bonding over the merits of James Brown were few. Our graduating class of over seven hundred students listed only three African-American girls, and it was clear from their sweaters that they were more into preppy than funky.

"Everything seemed to center around the Turk, I wonder why?" Pete "the Turk" Petrocelli was the most funkadelic main man at Kenmore West, which was a considerable accomplishment considering that he was a plump redheaded teenager whose nickname in the tenth grade was the less than cool "Turkey." But then, in an almost miraculous transformation, by the twelfth grade "Turkey" became "the Turk" and he was Dy-No-Mite because he owned every funk album, knew the words to all the songs, and in the eleventh grade even began to dress like a badass pimp who had just stepped from a blaxploitation movie. Dressing like a pimp was wishful thinking on the part of the Turk because while we had reached the age and height requirement to take a spin on the Ohio Players' Rollercoaster of Love, in reality, we were still adolescent boys riding solo.

The centerpiece of the Turk's pimp outfit was a long tangerine-colored leather trench coat that he had purchased with money earned at his after-school job pimping Cookie Puss ice cream cakes and Flying Saucers at Carvel's. The coat was bought on sale and its vastly reduced price was a clear indication that it was rightly considered unsellable. From its pebbled surface and citrusy color most shoppers assumed that the hideous coat had been pieced together from orange rinds instead of cowhides. Spotting a once-in-a-lifetime opportunity to unload merchandise that was proving harder to move than a glacier, the salesperson convinced the Turk to try on the coat along with an oversize wide-brimmed white pimp's hat and a white silk scarf. Standing in front of a three-way mirror, the Turk tried to catch one of the mirrors lying about how cool he looked, but each reflection backed up the other two as if they were in cahoots. Underneath his coat the Turk wore, as we all did, wide—extremely wide—flared pants. If he placed his foot on a manhole cover, the manhole cover would be obliterated by his pants leg. In our eleventh-grade yearbook the Turk and I are both seen wearing plaid flared pants with white belts, and even in black-and-white photographs the fabrics manage to look garish. Complementing the Turk's pants—like a sycophant—was one of the many glossy Qiana "silk" shirts he owned. Qiana shirts were always printed with airbrushed portraits of macaws flying through snowy pine trees or polar bears loping through cactuses or some other ecologically improbable landscape. I treasured my Qiana shirts and appreciated the fact that the imagery had been cleverly designed to look as good painted on the side of a van as it did on a shirt. An artificial fabric, Qiana had a greasy sheen that revealed that it was made from petroleum, and conspiracy theorists have speculated that the fuel shortage and the soaring price of oil in the 1970s was a prescient and praiseworthy attempt by the Arabs to crush this fashion in its infancy. As it turned out, though, Qiana's demise as a textile was decreed by our own government, when it was discovered that under the right conditions the Ohio Players song "Fire" could cause shirts made of the fabric to burst spontaneously into flames.

The finishing touches to the Turk's pimp look, and this really indicated that we were funk-free, was a puka-shell necklace and a pair of blue suede wooden clogs. I'm not sure why clogs for boys—and not just for the faggy boys; the jocks wore them too—became popular for a few years in western New York. Certainly the Buffalo area doesn't have a sizable Dutch community. All I know is that for a brief period of time I wore a pair of blue suede clogs and a puka-shell necklace, and so did almost every other boy in our high school.

We thought the Turk's orange trench coat, wide-brimmed white hat, blue suede clogs, and puka-shell necklace made him into one super-funky dude, although his stature was diminished slightly whenever he had to remove his hat just to get into his "pimpmobile," a used 1969 Chevy Nova.

"And you can't forget Myron's. I like to see you drool" tells you that in high school I went with my friends to a bar that featured topless dancers, and it also reveals that at least one of my friends assumed that I was straight. We were underage when we started going to bars named the Tiki House, the Golden Pheasant, and Myron's. They were neighborhood joints that were rapidly turning into local dives and the only proof underage drinkers needed to be served was having the money to pay for a pitcher of beer. It was as if the bartender regarded George Washington and Abraham Lincoln's pictures on the one- and five-dollar bills as our references. If those two guys

didn't make a face when we ordered, then we must be old enough to drink because everyone knew that Washington never told a lie and neither would Honest Abe.

Located on the west side of Buffalo, near the factories on the Niagara River, Myron's had a long narrow bar with a tiny stage upon which four women would take turns dancing topless for twenty minutes at a time. When they weren't on stage, the dancers worked as waitresses hustling drinks. The topless dancers at Myron's worked as hard as the autoworker-patrons who ogled them, but instead of assembling parts for Ford or Chevy the strippers worked the night shift showing off how their own parts were assembled. Since a playbill to the show was never handed out, much less printed, in my mind the four women were named by the distinguishing quality of their breasts—"Big Tits," "Small Tits," "Uneven Tits," and "Strange Tits." Having no erotic interest in the dancers' performances, I was nonetheless fascinated by Myron's and enjoyed the thrill of doing something that was "adult" in the dirty and grown-up senses of the word. One stripper—I think it was Big Tits—always played the same song during her set. The song had the refrain "How long has this been going on?" and to me it seemed like a commentary on the existence of heterosexuality itself.

"May you always have a J. R. R. book to read!" tells you that in the tenth grade I became obsessed with J. R. R. Tolkien's *The Hobbit* and *The Lord of the Rings.* Clearly, other members of the class of '76 were also reading Tolkien, as quotations from his books were used as epigraphs on the frontispieces in two of our yearbooks. His novels enraptured me, as no books ever had before, and for a week I ignored my schoolwork as the geography of Mid-

dle Earth became my best subject. My teachers were tolerant as I journeyed with Bilbo and Frodo, and they never became angry when they repeatedly caught me reading during class. Mrs. Fishlock would interrupt her lesson on *The Merchant of Venice*, sigh patiently, and then say, "Excuse me, Bob." A moment later she repeated herself: "Excuse me, Bob." Recognition dawning on me, I would look up from the book in my lap, groggy, as if I had woken up from a dream. She would then say kindly, "I know that an English teacher should encourage reading . . . but, Bob, would you please put your book away?"

"What a year in that strange Russian class" tells you that Vic Lugchenko convinced me to study Russian with him during our junior year. I had been taking French since the seventh grade but was willing to drop it because, after four years of study, the one phrase I could use conversationally was *Voulez-vous coucher avec moi, ce soir?* It's a useful phrase to know and the first time I visited Paris I tried it out in a few gay bars in the Marais, but credit for my fluency in propositioning belongs more to Patti LaBelle for "Lady Marmadade" than to my French teacher, Mrs. Monga.

Vic wanted to study Russian because his father was a Ukrainian immigrant who wanted his son to know how to read Cyrillic. And I wanted to study Russian because Vic suggested it. In the tenth grade my friends could talk me into trying almost anything but heterosexuality.

Our teacher Mrs. Dyrek was a plump matronly-looking woman who taught psychology and social studies as well as Russian. She was fluent in three languages, and after taking her classes in Russian and psychology I suspected that this was because she liked the sound of her own voice so much she decided to triple her opportunities to hear it. Mrs. Dyrek believed in ESP ("I'm sometimes psychic," she told her students), slept for only four hours a night ("That's how I get so much done"), and bragged that unlike most people, she was able to put her brain into an alpha state at will. She explained that our brains generate alpha, beta, and delta waves and that the alpha state was the primo brain wave. Standing in front of her blackboard, she'd claim, "I'm in the alpha state, right now." This declaration made her sound like a character in a science-fiction movie who was about to evolve into a higher life-form before the viewer's very eyes.

One afternoon, after considerable pleading, she agreed to try to put our entire Beginning Russian class into the alpha state. I followed Mrs. Dyrek's instructions faithfully, and although I never achieved the exalted alpha state, I did become sleepy, a mental condition that I had always been able to easily achieve simply by attempting to pay attention in geometry class. I was disappointed that my brain was stuck playing one beta tune over and over, and after class I asked Vic if he had been able to achieve the alpha state. He replied, "No. My brain didn't go into the alpha state but I think my nuts did. They began to tingle when I started meditating on Connie Giordano's tits." I never mastered Russian but hanging out with Vic improved my swearing, and as an adult I've found knowing how to speak foul language to be more useful than either French or Russian.

"Bob, you're a fantastic humorist. I hope you become a commedian" [sic] tells you that in the eleventh grade I realized that I wanted to be a comedian, and it also tells you that Donna Pobywaylo never won a spelling bee. I

wasn't a fantastic humorist by any stretch of the imagination and my style of humor at the time is revealed by Tim Ellison's inscription in my yearbook: "*To a great kid who is and always will be a class clown.*" Tim's wish that I always remain a class clown was meant kindly but to an adult it sounds almost like a curse, because there's nothing more pathetic than spending an evening with an erstwhile class clown who doesn't realize that he graduated from high school twenty years earlier.

In the eleventh grade I discovered that I was funny. After presenting in English class a piece I had written about the sordid real life of Santa Claus, my teacher Mrs. Prince changed my life when she commented, "Bob, you're very funny. Have you ever considered writing some sketches for the junior-class show?" Her question struck me with the force of a revelation. I was funny but no adult had ever pointed it out to me.

So I started to study comedy, trying to learn more about being funny by reading, listening, and watching every example of the genre that I could. I studied S. J. Perelman's essays, George Carlin's stand-up comedy albums, and Woody Allen's movies more than I read my textbooks. And while the Turk was able to sing the lyrics to every funk song, I expressed my sense of funk by repeating the catchphrase of the Aunt Esther character on *Sanford and Son.* She was played by the comedienne LaWanda Page, the dowager empress of snap queens, and in every episode of the show she always warned Fred Sanford, in her signature line, "Watch it, sucka!"

My appreciation of LaWanda Page should have been a dead giveaway of my sexual orientation but I can understand that it was difficult for my friends and family to figure out that I was gay because I was too reticent to publicly impersonate Lily Tomlin's Ernestine character. In the decade before Stonewall, the most common way for a man to declare his homosexuality was to follow the lead of Montgomery Clift, Rock Hudson, and Roddy McDowall and publicly announce that he was a close personal friend of Elizabeth Taylor, but in the decade after Stonewall, being able to do a good Ernestine was always the clearest indication that a boy was gay. For many parents in the 1970s the wake-up call to their son's queerness occurred when they overheard him, alone in his bedroom, intoning, "One ringy dingy. Two ringy dingy . . ."

"It was a great if not fantastic year. From Petrocelli's campaign to the littluns to Radicalism to the KLA . . ." tells you several things. "Petrocelli's campaign" refers to my running the Turk's bid to become student-council president. My contribution as the political mastermind behind the campaign was to make signs and hang them over the school's drinking fountains. I was also responsible for the Turk's one campaign "commercial." The day before the election every candidate was allowed to deliver a short plug during the morning announcements over the school's public-address system. The Turk asked me to do his commercial, as he was already a little nervous because he was going to have to deliver a campaign speech in front of the entire junior class. He was confident that he was a bad dude in front of seven of his friends, but asking seven hundred people to make you the Main Man of the student council was a little daunting.

I went to the office of Mr. Becker, the principal, to read the Turk's commercial. First, the principal read the day's announcements. Mr. Becker was directing the school custodians to cut down the bushes and hedges along Delaware

Road because "students have been using them as a cover to smoke cigarettes and marijuana." I wanted to report to Mr. Becker that he should lay off the students and start worrying about drug use by some of the younger members of the school's faculty. My sister's friend Joe had been making anthropomorphic pot pipes out of clay in his art class (the bowl of my pipe was the open mouth of ex-President Nixon) and he was baking a batch in the school's kiln when one of the pipes was stolen. Joe was certain that his art teacher had swiped it because he had extravagantly complimented Joe on the craftsmanship of his pipes and he was the only other person who had access to the kiln that particular day. Understandably Joe couldn't report the theft because he assumed that Mr. Becker would be less than sympathetic given the purpose of the object that was stolen, but I felt strongly that the teachers should set an example and buy their head gear from the students instead of stealing it from them.

After Mr. Becker ended his antidrug tirade, each of the four candidates or their representatives made their announcements. I listened as the other three hopefuls made boring campaign promises and pledges to improve school life. "If elected, I promise to work diligently with the school cafeteria to change the current system and make sure that the gravy is served hot and the Jell-O cold instead of the other way around." Finally, Mr. Becker indicated that it was my turn and I leaned into the large old-fashioned radio-style microphone. "Vote for . . ." I was nervous and started again. "Vote for Pete 'the Turk' Petrocelli for student council president," I announced. "The Turk needs all the support he can get. Especially around the hips!" No promises, no pledges. Pleased with myself as I finished my announcement, I could see from Mr. Becker's face that he was not equally so. Perhaps I should have used one of my other slogans, such as "Don't be a yellow-belly; vote for Pete Petrocelli!"

Frankly I didn't understand why Mr. Becker had a problem with my campaign slogan. In homeroom, when I had told my friend John what I was going to say, he thought it was funny. After signing off, the principal turned to me and said, "I don't know what you think you're doing but this campaign isn't a joke. I'm really disappointed that you took this opportunity to make a mockery of our election." I didn't say anything to defend myself but the truth was that I *was* taking the campaign seriously. I've always taken my jokes seriously. In hindsight what was sophomoric about the whole episode wasn't just my asinine campaign slogans, it was my firm belief that *with* my slogans the Turk could win the election.

"Littluns" was a term taken from William Golding's novel *Lord of the Flies.* In the eleventh grade we read the book in Honors English but I didn't care for it because it was so obviously trying to deliver a heavy-handed message about the nature of Evil. *Lord of the Flies* concerns a group of boys who become killers when they're stranded on a deserted island, but my friends and I had spent a week camping in Allegheny State Park and I thought it was just as possible that the boys would have had fun until they were rescued. The one detail in the book that I did enjoy was that the older boys called all of the younger boys the littluns. In English class my friend Mark and I adopted littlun as a derogatory name to describe anyone who was overly studious and conservative.

* * *

"Radicalism and the KLA" refers to my self-proclaimed status as a "radical" and "cofounder" of the KLA, the Kenmore Liberation Army. Founding the KLA was our homage to Patty Hearst's kidnapping by the Symbionese Liberation Army. The KLA was a goof, and our radicalism was limited to talking about being radical. I primarily responded to Patty Hearst's story because the situation was farcical. "After being kidnapped by revolutionaries, a madcap heiress becomes a radical terrorist" is the plot of a screwball comedy starring Irene Dunne or Katharine Hepburn. But I could also identify with Patty's situation. When you're young, uncertain, and a little bored with your life, you're grateful when people show an interest in you. I could see that it would be easy for a person to confuse her kidnappers with her rescuers because we all want to feel valued . . . and being held for a ransom certainly shows you that you are worth something.

"Don't forget who's the coolest. MY MOTHER!!" tells you that in high school I was a Mama's boy but it was my friend Vic's mother that I adored. At age thirty-six, Mrs. Lugchenko was the youngest of all of our mothers and the Lugchenko's house became our hang-out. John and I started going there to watch television with Mrs. Lugchenko even on the nights when Vic was working his part-time job at a fried chicken restaurant. Ostensibly, we were waiting for him to get off work, but talking to Mrs. Lugchenko was almost as much fun as talking with Vic.

While we waited for Vic, Mrs. Lugchenko usually sat curled up on the couch reading a novel while we sprawled on the orange and brown shag carpeting watching television. One of the many shows that we watched was *Happy Days.* Mrs. Lugchenko was as nice as the 1950s mom portrayed on the show, but she had more of an edge than Mrs. Cunningham. Mrs. Lugchenko smoked, drank an occasional glass of chablis, and worked as an office manager for a trucking company. During the commercial breaks, she would look up from her book and offer an astringent observation while lighting another cigarette. "Please, I lived through the fifties and I can tell you, it wasn't fun. I knew guys like Fonzie in high school and they usually had to drop out because they knocked up a girl and then they had to sell their motorcycle when they needed the money for diapers."

The reason I would walk five blocks to watch television programs at the Lugchenkos' wasn't that I wanted to see the programs; I liked to crack jokes and talk during the commercial breaks, and Mrs. Lugchenko was an appreciative audience. The shows were easy targets because most of them were awful. I watched TV shows at the Lugchenkos' that I would never have sat through at my own house. I endured tedious police dramas like *Adam-12* and *Hawaii Five-O* or soporific medical dramas like *Medical Center* and *Marcus Welby, M.D.* I guess after watching television with my family for sixteen years, I was restless and ready to change families for a while and see if they enjoyed my humor more. As a teenager, I definitely felt the reception was better at the Lugchenkos'.

In high school, I never dreamed that my life as a gay man would ever be represented on television. It would have made the TV programs we watched at the Lugchenkos' much more compelling if I had known the sexual bios of the stars. I was unaware that in 1974 I could have watched gay people on television almost every night of the week. Rock Hudson starred in *McMillan and Wife*, Robert Reed was on *The Brady Bunch*, Paul Lynde was on *The Hollywood Squares*, Will Geer and Ellen Corby were on *The Waltons* (Yes, Grandpa *and* Grandma Walton were gay). Raymond Burr played a wheelchair-bound police office on *Ironside*, and baby Chastity Bono was making guest appearances on *The Sonny and Cher Comedy Hour*. And I can't really complain that none of them publicly acknowledged being gay, because at the time neither did I.

Oh, and just in case you were wondering, the subject of homosexuality was alluded to, not once, but twice in my yearbooks. All of my closest friends were straight but they handled my being gay better than I did because in high school I was afraid to talk about homosexuality even when Vic Lugchenko asked me directly in his inscription:

> *What are you a homosexual? No girls signing your yearbook. Oh, but then you have Turkey to make up for it! Even though you've been a bore, a littlun, and "gay guy" it's digible knowing you. But remember don't call me, I'll call you!*
> *Alias Fatman, Soul-man, Metro-cal, and really,*
> *Vic Lugchenko*

I was extremely angry when I first read Vic's inscription, and I wanted to forcefully deny his accusation. Plenty of girls had signed my yearbook. I was just glad that Barb Gunther, my date for the prom, didn't express her curiosity with an inscription, "*Bob, how come you never tried to get to second base with me? Are you gay?*"

I wasn't happy that Vic had made my sexual orientation the theme of my junior-class yearbook. Although part of me was relieved that he used the words *homosexual* and *gay* instead of *fag*, as it seemed to indicate a certain respect. I understood that Vic was my friend and he wasn't trying to hurt my feelings. It wasn't until years later that I gave Vic the answer to his question even though he seemed to be informing me that knowing a "gay guy" was "digible." I never considered that Vic might have been trying to tell me something; he could handle my answer to that question.

John Sorell wrote in my junior-class yearbook:

Bob,

To a main man who helped us dominate the Junior Show. Your man from Myron's.

John Sorell

P.S. Dennis Drapo is Gay!

When I first read John's postscript I assumed that he was trying to insult Dennis and never considered that he could have been kindly trying to fix me up with him. In high school I knew that I was gay but one of my reasons for not telling anyone was Dennis Drapo. Dennis had been graded by every boy in our high school and he had received the failing mark of an F for fag. As far as I know Dennis never declared his homosexuality but he was the only boy studying cosmetology in the vocational program. It was universally known that when a boy was eager to get his hands on a woman's hair, he was never going to get them in any woman's pants. And if there was any doubt about Dennis's sexual orientation, he wore a "girl's" bracelet on his left wrist; worn on a boy, it was the same as wearing an ID bracelet that was engraved "homo." Dennis was so well known in our school for being a fag that boys who probably had never even spoken to him commonly used his name as a slur. I can recall hearing one of my friends saying to me, "Hey, 'Dennis Drapo,' are you coming with us or not?"

I did *not* identify myself with Dennis Drapo. I was gay but he was a *big* fag. (I didn't understand until much later that there is no such thing as a big fag. Homosexuality is one size fits all.) And I had no sympathy for Dennis's choice of vocation. If he really had to be a hairdresser, couldn't he have fudged the issue and studied to become a barber? In high school, I couldn't always afford to take a stand when I heard someone, or even myself, being called a fag. If I had chosen not to associate with anyone who used the word *fag*, my circle of friends would have been limited to newly arrived foreign exchange students. Very newly arrived. I would have had to meet Jorge at the airport when he arrived from Argentina because, by the end of his first day of classes, he would have been shouting, "Bob—amigo—last one out the door is a big fag!"

In high school I accepted the fact that homophobia and heterosexuality were stupid required subjects, like gym class, which I was obliged to take for three years, and I vowed that after graduation I would never listen to another fag joke, pretend to be attracted to women, or play baseball again. I was trying to put off my homosexuality until college unless one of my fantasies came true and Scott Rundell, our track-and-field team's champion shotputter, insisted on making me his boyfriend. In my fantasies it was okay to be openly gay if you did it with a really popular guy, but being gay by yourself was something that you only did at home. If you're a straight boy you're confident that your boner points at chicks, but if you're gay you know that your boner points directly at yourself.

* * *

"Hey, Bob, did you 'forget' your gym clothes?" tells you that in high school—for the first time in my life—gym class became almost tolerable. I never learned to enjoy or look forward to gym class, but I was able to lose my fear of it. This was because my friends helped me get through it. Most of them played junior-varsity football or other sports, and when it came time to choose sides, while I was never picked first, they made sure I was never allowed to be picked last. John, Vic, Bruce, the Turk, or Matt would usually either be the captain or else tell the captain, "Pick Smith!" And once I was on my friends' team it didn't matter if I made a bad move or clumsily dropped the ball, because I could rebound quickly with a joke.

In order to survive three years of compulsory heterosexuality, I adopted the same strategy that I used to get through three years of gym class: I participated as little as possible by inventing excuses. It was never necessary, but if I had needed to forge a note from my mother excusing me from participation in dating, I was willing to do it. I found, though, that heterosexuality was, in the end, easier to get through than gym class because being straight was mostly all talk and no action but in gym class you had no choice but to get physical.

My problems in gym class virtually disappeared when I discovered that you could be excused from participation if you told Mr. Wildhack the gym teacher that you forgot to bring your gym clothes. Once I discovered that alibi I began to suffer from chronic athletic-apparel amnesia. At the start of gym class I would apologetically announce, "Um, Mr. Wildhack, I forgot my gym clothes."

My weekly lie was transparent to Mr. Wildhack but he didn't seem to care. He merely became sarcastic about my forgetfulness. "Smith, you forgot your gym clothes again? Maybe I should send you down to the school nurse to be checked. You must have suffered a concussion the last time you actually did take gym class. Are you sure you didn't get popped in the head by a fly ball? Why am I asking you? You probably wouldn't remember." Pointing to the bleachers, he would smile and say, "Okay, Smith. Have a seat."

One time he even mocked, "Okay, you're telling me that you don't have your gym clothes even though you're wearing a brand-new pair of Pumas." I had forgotten that I was wearing my new black suede Pumas. Mr. Wildhack smiled. "Well, I don't suppose that you can play in them," he said. "You wouldn't want to scuff 'em up." Dropping any pretense that he wanted me to take gym, he examined my sneakers more closely and said, "Those look pretty sharp. How much did you pay for those?"

I never played sports in high school but I must have attended every sporting event that my friends participated in. (As a boy I had played football, but after puberty I shunned contact sports, fearing that once I made contact I probably couldn't have handled the pain of separation.) I went to swim meets, basketball games, baseball games, football games, and then there were *Monday Night Football* games with the Buffalo Bills, Sabres games, and Braves games. (I was disappointed that my friends' interest in spectator sports didn't extend to bodybuilding contests.) To my surprise I actually learned to enjoy attending sporting events although I never became a sports fan. If a friend of mine was playing football, the game held my interest in exactly the same way that seeing a friend perform in a dull play could still hold my interest. I felt very comfortable sitting in the stands watching everyone else play sports. It was like being in gym class, except I didn't have to make up excuses for why I didn't participate. Being rail thin and uncoordinated were valid and perfectly acceptible reasons.

On Fridays at Kenmore-West, the day before the football game, it was traditional for the members of the team to wear their jerseys to school. It favorably singled out the jocks from the rest of the student body. I never felt envious that this one extracurricular activity was being lauded over all other extracurricular activities in school. I was smart and creative, but it's an irrefutable fact that for most people, myself included, being a jock is sexier and cooler than being a brain or an artist. If the school cast of *The Sound of Music,* wore their dirndls and lederhosen to class the day before opening night, or the brains wore their lab coats and safety goggles to school the day before the Science Fair, it wouldn't have improved their social status. Everyone would still have thought they were geeks.

"It has not been dull with you humiliating David and the Turk"; "You're really a good person when you're not cutting me down or the Turk"; "I don't think anyone takes your wisecracks personally, but they've been really funny" tells you that I was known among my friends for my mock-outs. Appropriately enough, it was at one of my friends' hockey games that I first became aware that I was able to handle myself when someone tried to slam me. The game was over and afterward in the changing room, I was volubly cracking jokes when suddenly Phil Harlach, a portly, moon-faced jock, said in a loud and contemptuous voice, "God, Smith! You are such a fag!"

A total hush fell over the changing room as everyone turned and looked toward me and Phil Harlach. I was horribly embarrassed but I was also indignantly angry.

There was no reason for Phil's unprovoked attack, since I barely knew him. But the unexpectedness of the remark helped me. I might have been intimidated if I had known beforehand that Phil didn't like me but the suddenness of his attack made me feel cold and hard inside even as my face flushed. On every level I knew there was no reason to be intimidated by Phil Harlach. Although he was a member of the football team, he had the soft porky physique of someone who played the game primarily because it gave him an opportunity to guzzle free Gatorade. I had no respect for jocks who looked out of shape years before they retired from their sport. What was the point of being a jock if you didn't at least *look* athletic? One of the most important turning points in every gay man's life is the discovery that being called a fag isn't the worst thing that can happen to you. Phil Harlach made me understand that a word has no power when you have absolutely no respect for the oaf who is saying it. At that moment I didn't care what Phil Harlach thought of me, but I did care about what my friends thought of me.

Instead of backing down, I thought for a second and then replied with a sneer, "Oh yeah, Harlach. Well, there's a three-letter word that starts with an *F* that describes you too!" I considered puffing out my cheeks to lend a visual emphasis to my retort but it was unnecessary. To my immense satisfaction and relief, an explosion of derisive laughter erupted at Phil's expense. My friends began to congratulate me and Vic even attempted to high-five me—an attempt that I clumsily flubbed, as my palm didn't connect evenly with his. But my high-two-out-of-five didn't matter because Vic had shouted, "Nice one! When he said you were a fag, I could see the little wheels spinning in your mind and I knew you'd nail him."

The tension in the room evaporated as everyone went

back to changing but I was stunned that I had pulled it off. I'm not claiming my comeback was of Oscar Wilde's caliber—and a fat joke is certainly as mean as a fag joke—but for me it was a clear break with my past. For the first time I understood that my friends were rooting for me to win, and that being quick and funny was a skill that even jocks respected. I had found my sport.

"Bob Picasso?? Yes, I still have your drawings. Someday you'll become a famous artist..." tells you that in the tenth grade I fancied myself a painter and had jokingly told Maureen Dimmick to save my work because someday it would be worth a fortune. But it doesn't tell you that I talked the hunkiest boy in the tenth grade into becoming my model.

If suppressing my desires had been a form of "progressive resistance" exercise, by the end of high school I would have had a body like the guys I fantasized about. There were moments when resisting the impulse to touch another boy was the hardest physical challenge I had to face in high school. This didn't happen on a daily basis but there were times when the strain of my crushes became almost unbearable and other times when the weight of a crush made me shiver with ecstasy. Thankfully, I wasn't physically attracted to my friends in high school; I don't think I could have survived the frustration if I was. I was attracted to guys I didn't know or guys I barely knew, although I always somehow managed to learn the names of all my crushes.

Walking to Mr. Stewart's European Cultures class from Mr. Ross's geometry class, I would look forward to seeing Anthony Sansone, a senior and star wrestler, getting his books from his locker. I didn't know Anthony, but seeing him in the hall was the highlight of my day when I was in tenth grade. On the few days when he missed school, I almost wanted him to bring me a note from home explaining his absence.

Having a crush on someone I barely knew was more conducive to my fantasy life than a crush on a friend because if I didn't know much about the guy, I could at least hope that maybe he too was gay. If I had employed the same level of diligence in my academic work that I employed in my sexual fantasies I would have been my class valedictorian. I don't want to overstate my lasciviousness in high school. I did not walk the halls in a state of continual tumescence. My moments of feral lust always pounced on me unexpectedly. But when they did, as, say, on an occasion when I found myself in close proximity to a dreamy boy in the flesh, that's when I understood that the penis not only has a mind of its own, but that its mind is positively Machiavellian.

I first realized what a little perv I was in my art class in the tenth grade. (Pervs, unlike fags, come in big and little sizes.) Mr. Finley, our teacher, had asked a few students to model so the class could draw their likenesses with charcoal pencils. Sketching the fully clothed Beth Rubenstein sitting in a chair was interesting but I wanted to stretch my artistic abilities. There were no Greek-god-like bodies in our class to inspire a budding Michelangelo like myself, because once art was no longer a required subject, the students who chose to study drawing and painting consisted almost entirely of plump brainy girls and skinny brainy boys.

But artistic inspiration struck me during study hall, where I sat in the back of class, next to Kirk Bradley. Kirk was a dreamboat and I wanted to use him as a bath toy: I had a crush on him that caused my heart to squeak like a rubber duck. In fact, I think the continual squeaking prompted by a multitude of boy crushes over the next three years did eventually drive me crazy.

Kirk was a handsome dark-haired gymnast and had a thickly muscled physique that he put on display as soon as the weather turned warm enough to wear tank tops to school. He had a body that just wouldn't quit bothering me. One afternoon I idly thought, *I'd like to draw Kirk.* It was a passing fancy that my brain quickly dropped, but as the idea fell it somehow managed to hit my penis, and a startled penis always asks, *What was that?!* The biggest drawback to having two heads on one body is that each is always within hearing range of the other. And it might sound cynical to say, but one of the first things a boy learns as he becomes a man is that when a penis blushes it never does so out of innocence. The brain and the penis are the Leopold and Loeb of body parts; separately they don't cause much trouble, but when they team up, it can be murder.

I asked, "Hey, Kirk, are you doing anything?"

I could see that he wasn't doing anything. He was scribbling his name on the cover of his notebook but I was following the first rule of trial lawyers and perverts. Never ask a question that you don't already know the answer to.

"No, I'm just doodling."

I boldly asked, "Kirk, would you mind me practicing my drawing by using you as a model?" The oldest trick in the dirty old man's book is to ask a beautiful man or woman to model for him, but the fact that we were both in the tenth grade lent the ruse some novelty.

My question didn't faze Kirk and he put down his pen and said, "No, sure."

"Hey, I've got an idea," I added as if the thought had just occurred to me. "Why don't you make a muscle? You've got really great arms."

He grinned. "Yeah, I know."

Kirk's ability to accept a compliment effortlessly made him even more desirable. There are times when a penis is a cold-blooded animal. I felt as deceitful as a spider who was trying to lure a butterfly to its web by offering to knit it a sweater.

Kirk put his arm on the edge of his desk and then flexed his right biceps. Seized by something like inspiration, I started my pencil drawing. As the work progressed, it began to look like I was answering an ad on a matchbook cover: *If you can draw this muscular arm, you too can become a homosexual artist! Many of the most famous painters in history were gay—da Vinci, Michelangelo, Caravaggio—and there's room to add your name to the list! Send in your drawing now and we'll send you your information on how to study with the Famous Gay Artists School!*"

I tentatively gave Kirk a few compliments as the drawing began to take shape and then I blurted out, "Can I feel your arm?"

Kirk said, "Sure. Go ahead."

I put my hand on his arm, gave it a squeeze, and then stored the memory away to scrutinize later in the privacy of my own bedroom. The agony of my adolescent sexual frustration wasn't simply that I wasn't able to have sex with boys that I was attracted to: I knew that straight boys were also frustrated. But my straight friends were able to achieve some release by talking and joking about their hopeless crushes and unrealizable desires. Joking about sex at least lets straight boys gain some relief. Not being able to joke about my desires was probably the hardest part of being in the closet. There was nobody I could brag to about the success of my scheme to cop a feel of Kirk's arm.

Unfortunately, I didn't know how to deal with my predicament because Homosexuality 101 was never offered as an elective subject. One of my favorite funk songs is the Miracles' "Love Machine Part 1," which has the lyric, "I'm just a love machine and I won't work for nobody but you." I identified with the song because while I too was a love machine, I seemed to be missing any accompanying operating instructions.

"Summerfest was good last year (the Stones)" tells you that I went to see the Rolling Stones in concert. The recording industry still tries to deny it, but listening to rock music, I believe, does lead to drug use; at least, good rock music should. During the 1970s my friends and I never thought of getting high while grooving to the sounds of Neil Sedaka or the Captain and Tennille—that would have been a really bad trip—but head-spinning songs such as "Space Oddity" by David Bowie or "Bohemian Rhapsody" by Queen were an inducement to catch a buzz.

In the summer of 1975, funk temporarily receded in the Turk's musical affections when he announced that "we have to get tickets to the Stones!" I love how the Rolling Stones are always referred to as "The Stones" as if the band's full and proper name is only used by their parents and librarians. The Stones were going to be giving a concert at Rich Stadium in suburban Orchard Park and Summerfest that year was going to be our very own Woodstock. A commuter Woodstock, where we would drive out for the day, rock on, and return home that night to sleep in our own beds.

At the time I wasn't a big fan of the Stones but I agreed to go because all of my friends were going, and if I didn't accompany them, I knew that would be the night that Mick Jagger would ask the Turk to come up on stage and I would kick myself for missing it. I've learned from experience not to always condemn peer pressure, because it's often been a force for good in my life. Going along with the herd might not be original but it does get you moving. I have a tendency to procrastinate and I might have missed out on much of my life if I hadn't blindly imitated what my friends were doing. Over the years peer pressure has served as a goad to get me to go to the gym, to work on my comedy act, to read more, to dress better, to clean my apartment, to try boogie boarding, and most important, to overcome my shyness. Admittedly, peer pressure also encouraged me to do some really stupid things, such as sniffing amyl nitrate once in a disco and buying tickets to see Peter Frampton and ZZ Top in concert. But I don't feel it's stupid to give in to peer pressure and do a particular thing once. Stupidity is giving in to peer pressure a second time to do something that you already know that you hate.

All of my friends were going to the Stones concert: Vic, John, the Turk, David, Bruce, Matt, and Bill. We made our plans for Summerfest sitting in the Tomasellis' "patio," a tent with mesh sides that the Turk's father erected in the backyard in June and then proceeded to furnish with all the comforts of a living room. It was decided that Vic would buy the tickets for the concert after he collected the money from everybody. After that was settled, John announced, "We have to get some pot." Vic quickly seconded the idea, "Fuck-yes, we need pot." (In the language of teenage boys, "fuck-yes" always endorses a proposition of indisputable veracity while the "fuck" in "fuck-no" lifts mere refusal to the height of human impossibility.) The Turk agreed that yes we had to get some pot but he also asked that we watch our language because his mother had just let out the Petrocellis' dog, Mitzi.

It was decided that the Turk would buy the pot and it was suggested that I go along with him to "make sure he doesn't get ripped off by buying oregano!" Buying bad pot—"oregano"—was a crime for which the victim was always blamed and which you could never live down. I don't know why I was entrusted with safeguarding the potency of our pot. After all, the Turk was Italian and knew more about oregano than I did.

Our high-school pot dealer was Jerry Brunsing and appropriately enough he was as skinny, white, and tightly wound as a well-made joint. Jerry was always irritated or pissed off and I took satisfaction in his seeming to hate his after-school job selling pot more than I hated my after-school job selling hot dogs and ice-cream cones. In some ways, Jerry was a model student. He worked hard, kept his word, and was responsible for a great deal of money. The principal could well have held him up as an example to the PTA had it not been for the fact that Jerry had developed such sterling qualities from years of dealing pot.

The Turk and I knew that you had to "be cool" around Jerry. Jerry never sold pot at school. That wasn't cool. If you wanted to buy pot, you talked to him at his locker in the morning. But a stranger couldn't just approach him; you had to be referred to him by one of his regular customers. And when you talked to Jerry at his locker, you could never say the word "pot" aloud or the deal was off. You had to discreetly ask, "Jerry, can you get me some stuff for the weekend?" If Jerry thought you were cool, he answered, "Sure," and then he arranged for a time to meet him. The Turk and I knew all this and arranged to meet him at four o'clock at his house.

Jerry, his mom, and his sister lived in a tiny ranch house. At four o'clock sharp the Turk rang the doorbell. Jerry's mother answered the door, and from the smirk on her face, we suspected that she knew what we were there for. Jerry's mother was in her mid-thirties but she looked much younger. She had long inky-black hair parted down the middle and on her eyelids she wore the faintest amount of dark blue eye shadow, making it appear that she wasn't wearing makeup but that her eyelids suffered from poor circulation. She was wearing a pair of worn blue jeans and a tight pink sweater that had an embroidered rose over her left breast.

The Turk asked, "Is Jerry home?"

"Yeah. Come on in," she said, waving us inside. As we passed through the door, Jerry's mother screamed, "Jerry!"

We heard a muffled "What?" in response.

"Someone's here for you!"

"Mom, who the fuck is it?"

I had never said the word "fuck" in front of my mother.

"It's some friends of yours."

"Okay! I'll be right down."

"Have a seat, guys. Do you want something to drink? A beer? Or maybe something to eat?"

"No thanks," answered the Turk.

"No," I seconded.

We had made no motion to sit down and Jerry's mother ordered, "Guys, sit down. I know you're here to buy some pot. You can relax." We had interrupted her in the middle of making a meat loaf and she resumed mixing the meat and the bread crumbs as she mentioned, "You guys must be going to the Stones concert."

I spoke up. "How'd you know?"

"Because Jerry's been so busy this week. That doorbell hasn't stopped ringing. I feel like having the damn thing disconnected. But then again, let's face it. The money's nice." Again, she screamed, "Jerry!" Then she smiled at me as if his name was a secret that only she and I shared. I liked Jerry's mother. She was even cooler than Mrs. Lugchenko. How cool was it that your mom helped you sell pot? I wondered if the Brunsings had dealt drugs for generations. I imagined Jerry's great-great-grandmother dealing vials of laudanum to nineteenth-century teenagers who were going to hear Jenny Lind sing at the local lyceum.

We were sitting at the white Colonial-style kitchen table in white Windsor-style chairs with avocado vinyl-covered cushions. The kitchen table had yellow daisies painted on the surface and the walls were covered with a white wallpaper that also featured a pattern of yellow daisies. There was even a yellow-daisy-shaped lazy Susan sitting in the center of the table. The impossibly high standards for cheerfulness set by the kitchen decor seemed to explain why Jerry was always in such a bad mood. When he finally dragged himself into the kitchen, he got right down to business. "How much do you guys want to buy?"

"We want to buy two dime bags," replied the Turk.

"All right. That will be forty dollars." A dime bag cost twenty dollars and a nickel bag cost ten dollars. The Turk got the money out from his wallet and handed it to Jerry. His mom then went to the clown cookie jar on the counter, lifted the lid, and took out two rolled Baggies filled with pot. As she handed them to Jerry, she said to us, "This is really good shit you're getting. It has a lot of buds and I didn't break them up when I rolled the Baggies." I was impressed by her thoughtfulness and I wondered if she packed a joint in Jerry's lunch box when she sent him off to school each day. With a characteristically sullen expression on his face Jerry asked, "Do you guys want to check out the pot?"

The Turk and I glanced at each other and I shook my head no. The Turk answered, "No, man. It's cool."

For the first time, Jerry smiled. "That's great. I'm glad you guys don't want to sample the pot. I hate that shit. Fucking Danny Buffomante wanted to smoke an entire joint of his fucking pot before he paid me. I told him, 'All right. I'll let you try your pot if the next time I order a pizza from your dad's pizzeria, I get to eat a slice first to see if your fucking stuff's any good.' " We laughed at this comeback while Jerry added, "What a fucking asshole!" The Turk and I commiserated with him about the insensitivity of his customers. We basked in Jerry's approval of our business manner, and instead of feeling like wimps who were too nervous to ask for a sample, we thought of ourselves as guys who really knew how to be cool.

I shattered our newfound camaraderie, though, when I noticed a Spanish textbook sitting on the kitchen counter and, suddenly curious, asked, "Jerry, do you take Spanish?"

"Yeah."

"Oh, that's great," I joked. "Someday you'll be able to negotiate directly with your Colombian connections."

Jerry frowned and I realized immediately that what I said wasn't cool. Jerry's mother suppressed a smile, though, and turned away to wash her hands. Interestingly enough, though they're on opposite sides of the law, drug dealers and the police share one trait in common: they take their jobs very seriously, and when working, they don't appreciate smart-asses. Drying her hands, Jerry's mother asked, "Before you go, do you boys need some rolling papers or a pipe? Because I could sell you some beautiful teak pipes if you need one. The teak burns really clean. I also have some great roach clips." It turned out that Jerry's mother had a profitable sideline dealing head gear. I almost expected her to open the refrigerator and show us Tupperware containers that we could use as stash boxes.

"No, thanks, Mrs. Brunsing," I said. "We don't need anything." Before we left the Turk asked, "Jerry, are you going to the Stones concert?" Losing any hint of pleasantness he might have shown, Jerry snarled, "Are you fucking kidding? No. I hate rock concerts. There's way too many fucked-up people."

"Yeah, you're right," I answered, thinking that the Turk and I were going to be among the fucked up.

As soon as we were away from their house, I asked the Turk, "Can you imagine your mother helping you to deal pot?"

"No, I can't."

"I'm sure my mother would love it." I mimicked her saying, "I like dealing pot. You get to meet so many people." Having been a housewife her entire adult life, my mother believes that any job that allows you to meet people is good. What she would have found criminal about the Brunsings' business was that it was house-based. "What's the fun of that? If I was dealing I would want to get out to the school playgrounds and get some fresh air."

"Remember being stoned at the Stones?" tells you that after buying the pot and getting the tickets we were ready to party. Eight of us drove to the concert in two cars. We took Vic's dad's Ford and Bruce's parents' station wagon and planned on arriving at around ten o'clock in the morning in order to get good seats. To pass the time while we waited for the doors of the stadium to open, we planned to have a tailgate party. Tailgate parties are picnics in which the beverages are more important than the food, and in a sign of rebellion against our provincial background we no longer drank Genessee Beer but only Molson's, which had the cachet of being imported.

It had traveled all the way from Canada, a distant five miles, but all the same, in Buffalo, every cool dude knows that Canadian beer rules.

As soon as we arrived at the stadium, the Turk suggested, "Why don't we fire up a joint?" Everyone agreed that it was a good idea to get high now because in only eight more hours the Stones were going to be on stage. After his first hit off a joint, the Turk could always be depended upon to declare, "Man, this is really good shit." Then, after his second hit, he would contend, "I think this shit might be laced with hash." The Turk had a sensitive pot palate and I suddenly pictured him wearing a smoking jacket and holding a bong as if it were a brandy snifter, in order to better appreciate the bouquet of a rare and costly sinsemilla. Every time we bought pot, one of my friends voiced the belief that it was laced with hash, as if the drug dealers in Buffalo commonly threw some hash into their weed in the same manner that an auto dealer might throw in a free stereo system when you bought a brand-new Pinto. The Turk acted the part of the marijuana connoisseur with such authority that I believed that if he was blindfolded, he could swallow an aspirin and say, "Hey, is this *Bayer*? I thought it was. This is good shit. It must be extra-strength. Fuck! This shit must be laced with Bufferin. Oh yeah, this is going down nice. It's really smooth and gentle on my stomach."

"Jesus, Bob! What are you, blowing that joint? Quit sucking it off. Now it's all wet."

"Fuck you. You asshole." I coughed then inhaled deeply again and then began a fit of uncontrollable coughing. I actually think that for the first few years that I smoked pot, I got more of a buzz from hyperventilation than I did from the THC. After smoking an entire joint and hacking and coughing continuously for fifteen minutes, I was usually as out of it as a patient with advanced tuberculosis.

After we finished our first joint, the Turk decided to roll some more before we got too fucked up to do so. It was a prudent measure, because even when we weren't stoned our doobie craftsmanship was laughable and our fragile joints had to be smoked quickly before the saliva that held them together dried and they crumbled and fell apart. It wasn't until college that any of us became skilled at rolling a proper joint. In high school our joints reminded me of the projects that we had made in junior high in wood or metal shop. (My mother hung the uneven cutting board I made in wood shop above our dishwasher because using it to slice a tomato put you in serious danger of self-mutilation.)

As the Turk rolled the joints and we watched him intently, a little of the pot spilled and we yelled in unison, "Watch out! You're spilling it."

"Fuck you all," the Turk said with regal hauteur. "Let me finish without your petty interruptions." We usually smoked pot in Vic's car because it was the most beat-up of any of our cars. The speedometer, mileage gauge, radio, and heater didn't work. The only instrument on the dashboard that did work was the cigarette lighter. And it worked too well. It could have lit a cigarette underwater. It generated a heat so intense that glassblowing was a viable option if the windshield ever cracked. Every time we lit a joint with Vic's car lighter it was an exercise in fire hazards and their prevention. You couldn't hold the joint too closely to the lighter or most of the joint would burn before anyone got a hit. Rather, you had to carefully "broil" the joint until it ignited.

We kept smoking joints until someone finally announced, "I've had enough." Then one other person would say, "I've had enough too." At this time the joint was usually burned down to a small roach and the last person holding it would say, "I'm going to finish this off," and then proceed to burn his fingers or lips trying to inhale on a tiny glowing ember that was about as easy to smoke as a spark.

The doors to the stadium opened exactly at one o'clock. There was a mad rush to get seats in front of the stage on the floor of the stadium, but we made no effort to do this. We might have been high but no amount of drugs could make us reject the comfort of having real seats in favor of sitting on the ground or even standing for hours. We grabbed two rows of seats in the stands that gave us a good view of the stage and then we began to drink some more. Every rock concert that I've ever attended had one requirement: someone had to throw up during the show. It was usually one of my friends but theoretically it could have been one of the performers as well. Throwing up was an expected part of the offstage show's special effects. A showier and messier version of the audience salute of holding up a lit match.

During the afternoon, while we waited in the sun for the concert to start, the Turk went down to the floor of the stadium and bought four hits of speed. I had never done speed, but when the Turk offered me a hit, I decided to try it. It turned out to be the slowest speed you could buy. My hit had the get-up-and-go of about two cups of weak coffee, but since none of us drank coffee at the time, I thought I was flying! Hopped up on my Dexie, I decided to walk around the stadium by myself because I wanted to stare at all the shirtless guys. Since most people at the concert were getting high, my being glassy-eyed and staring wasn't considered rude or provocative and I was able to look to my heart's content, but by the time I finished my loop around the floor of the stadium my libido was speeding faster than my brain.

I don't remember much of the concert itself. Does anyone ever remember much of an outdoor rock concert? There were a few opening bands but I don't recall their names. Taking a cue from the Beatles, the name for all opening rock bands should be "The Decibells," because the main requirement for an opening act at a rock concert seems to be to test the limits of the sound system instead of playing music that anyone recognizes or enjoys. Saying that an act "opened for the Stones in Buffalo" denotes an undeniable achievement but it also damns the group's ear-shattering music with faint praise.

What I clearly remember about the concert is sitting right in front of the Turk, who at one point during the Stones' "Jumpin' Jack Flash" started playing air guitar and doing Chuck Berry moves, first straightening out his right leg and then going into a half crouch and hopping along the row of seats. We all laughed hysterically at his performance, not in spite of but because the Turk was never really able to pull off that he was rocking. He always looked like he was playing acoustic air guitar. But on that day he made acoustic air guitar look cool and by the end of the concert we were calling him "Mick."

We actually did get some good looks at Mick Jagger himself because I had brought along a pair of binoculars. These also gave us close-up views of the ravaged trick-or-treat face of guitarist Keith Richards. I've never understood why an antidrug campaign hasn't been built around his ghoulish complexion. I didn't really care about my brain when I was a teenager but I was, and still am, susceptible to being worried about my appearance.

When I had to use my fake ID to get into better bars than Myron's, I always hoped that the muscular bouncer checking my proof at the door would think, *He looks really good for his age. He's eighteen but you'd swear that he's not a day over sixteen.* Antidrug, cigarette, and alcohol campaigns should appeal to our vanity. A head shot of Keith Richards paired with the slogan *Just Say No to Ugly* would make me have second thoughts about snorting coke or shooting up heroin.

The other song that I clearly remember hearing was "Satisfaction." When the Stones started playing it everyone in the stadium jumped to their feet and cheered. They were playing *my* song. "I can't get no . . . satisfaction" was a lyric that spoke to me and about fifty thousand other teenagers that night.

"I have one suggestion—get more perverted!" tells you that my classmates were urging me to be myself. But I see now that kinky behavior should never be done on the spur of the moment. I should have pondered the idea before I impulsively decided to get more perverted at Mickey Rats Beach Club, Buffalo's leading beach bar. We decided to stop off there on the way home from the concert. We smoked several joints on the way there, and as we drove—with all the windows rolled down because Vic's father was going to use the car the next day and Vic decided now that he didn't want the interior to reek of pot—we were followed by a flicked comet's trail of burning ashes. Mickey Rats Beach Club was located on the shore of Lake Erie in Hamburg on a beach that faced in the direction of California, which, I assume, was the inspiration for the club's surfing theme. Opening a beach club with a surfing theme on the shores of Lake Erie is about as sensible as opening a ski lodge in Malibu, but whenever we drove out to Mickey Rats, we ignored the

huge steel mill and grain elevators that we passed on the waterfront and pretended that we were cruising along the Pacific Coast Highway. Mickey Rats was a magnet to teenagers who wanted to believe for a few hours that the cool breeze coming off the water was salty instead of sooty and that the tang in the air wasn't from harmful levels of ozone and sulfur dioxide.

I loved Mickey Rats because to me it seemed as if I was at Muscle Beach. It was filled with tanned teenage boys who all seemed to work out and who were dressed in tank tops, shorts, and sandals. But this was the first time I had ever arrived at Mickey Rats in a less than sober condition. I wasn't completely fucked up but I was woozy and a little fried from all the sun, the pot, and the beers. Almost as soon as we entered the club I became separated from my friends when I went to the bathroom. But I knew I would find them again and actually enjoyed being by myself as I walked around sipping from a plastic cup of soda. I didn't want another beer by this time. Every man in the bar looked beautiful until I spotted the most beautiful man that I'd ever seen on the shores of Lake Erie and experienced one of those moments when my lust turned feral and pounced.

He was radiantly sexy and handsome. He had light brown hair, a deep tan, and was wearing a tank top that showed his huge shoulders, big arms, and powerful chest. We were perfect for each other. We were the same height and I was willing to overlook that he he outweighed me by about seventy pounds of muscle. I started following him around for ten minutes because he also seemed to be by himself and I wanted him.

My only explanation for what happened next is that maybe the pot we smoked really *was* laced with hash. (All right, I don't believe it either but I thought I'd try.)

I wanted to touch this guy so badly that I didn't consider that his response might be to make bodily contact with his fists. I went up to him and said, "Hi. You have really great arms." And then I reached out and touched his arm.

When I look back on it I'm still surprised that he didn't punch me in the face. Instead he rolled his eyes and shook his head as if stoned gay teenagers were always trying to grope him in public, and he said, "Hey, you can't do that here." He sounded as if he was correcting a misbehaving child. "This isn't the right place. You're going to get beat up."

Right at that moment John and Vic showed up. Sizing up the situation, they saw that I looked terror-stricken but they assumed I was afraid because of something the guy had said to me and not because of something that I had said to him. He had to have started it because they knew that I would never try to take on *that* guy. Vic and John didn't know that I can be quite a bully when I choose a boyfriend and often pick on someone twice my size. Vic asked, "Bob, is there some sort of problem?" Nobody said a thing as they waited for me to answer. I was too stunned to think clearly then, but on the ride home, as I sobered up, I thought, *Yeah, there's a big problem. I'm gay and I just flipped out because I can't take pretending to be straight anymore.* Since I didn't want to tell the truth I lied and said, "No." The nameless god whose arm I had groped didn't correct me but he told John and Vic, "Is this your friend? He's drunk and he's going to get in trouble. You guys better watch him." When he departed Vic asked, "Bob, what the fuck was that all about? I wasn't sure if that guy was going to beat you up or ask you to dance. What were you doing? Making a pass at him?"

I didn't answer because I couldn't believe that my

friend had nailed it right on the head. I was still reviewing what had happened in my mind and I was almost in a state of shocked disbelief but I managed to say, "It was nothing . . ." as the Turk, Bruce, and Matt joined us.

The Turk asked, "What happened to you guys?"

John said, "Oh, we had to rescue Bob. He was having a fight with his boyfriend." Everybody laughed at the absurdity of that.

Years later, after I came out to my friends and they all reacted with a big so-what, I asked John if they ever thought that I was gay. He admitted, "We had many long conversations about it but none of us thought you were gay." He added, "Bob, we thought you were funny haha, not funny la-di-da!"

"Thanks, John," I said sarcastically. "I'm going to write that down."

I found it hard to believe that my friends in high school never suspected that I was gay. But then I remembered that in high school we believed that we were funky dudes, we believed that going to Mickey Rats was the next best thing to going to California, and I had believed that the Turk could win an election with the campaign slogan "Don't be a yellow-belly; vote for Pete Petrocelli!" And in 1976 we all believed that we looked good in our high-school yearbook photographs.

Whenever I look at my high-school yearbook photograph, I see how ridiculous it looks today and I ask myself, *What was I thinking?* My thick mane of hair is hairsprayed into place as it sweeps across my forehead and completely conceals my ears. I have on a large pair of aviator-style eyeglasses that are much too big for my face and the large collar on my shirt pointed down at my white tie as if it was making fun of it. I used to think that the most ridiculous part of my high-school-yearbook photograph was my appearance but what seems more unbelievable than my hairstyle was that in that photograph I'm pretending to be straight. It has nostalgia value, but on me, heterosexuality looks more ridiculous than pukka shells and blue suede clogs. What *was* I thinking?

"Bob, I usually write a lot of crap like 'Have fun always,' 'Good luck in college,' 'How's your mother?' but for you I'll just say, stay friends and do whatever you feel like doing no matter how dumb and crazy you think it is" tells you that I was fortunate to have met a group of smart and thoughtful friends who supported and encouraged my most outlandish dreams.

War and Piece of Ass

Turtle Bay Resort, Costa Rica

I HAD to make a decision before I received my dog tags, a sartorial item that was *de rigueur* for the classic disco tea dance that was being held at one of the resort's swimming pools. Vaughn, a handsome dark-haired man in a green bathing suit who had inquired about my availability, handed out the dog tags to each classic disco dancer. He spoke in a flirtatious tone which suggested that at puberty there had been an unfortunate mishap in which his voice had become deeper while he'd become more shallow. "Hello, handsome, now what's your story? Are you single, married and unavailable, married and available, or . . . ?" Every word Vaughn uttered was inflected with a salacious accent as if he had learned English from parents who only spoke in sexual innuendos at home.

Vaughn's insincerity was obvious but his skill at flirting was such that I admired his knack for deception without ever feeling deceived. I enjoyed flirting with Vaughn but I understood that I didn't have a chance with him. From several scurrilous reports of his conduct I gathered that Vaughn's ass was like Harvard. Theoretically it was open to all Americans but in practice the admissions policy favored the rich and famous.

Vaughn smiled. "Look out. Bob's decided to break out the sexy shirts. These boys better be careful." I felt my face flush as I thought, *Am I that obvious?* I didn't want to wear clothing that announced "I'm sexy" in the same manner that clothing can announce that "I'm homeless." Today, I was shooting for "Hey, he's not bad"—the compliment that doesn't sound much better than it looks.

Having roused my uncertainty (now he'd woken the baby), Vaughn quickly added, "Not that you don't look good, because you do! But here, let me fix something. The tag is sticking out on your shirt." Vaughn tucked the shirt tag under the collar and said, "There. That's better."

No matter how hard I try, I'll always be an incompetent perfectionist. I always overlook the detail that separates the studs from the stooges. Enlisting into a strict world of self-imposed queer pressure, I regard every other gay man as a potential drill sergeant. And this would be fine if I had a fetish for boot camp but my obsession is more prosaic: fear that my uniform isn't going to pass inspection.

Alas, Vaughn's inquiry about my marital status was purely professional. It was part of his job as a member of the staff of Wilde Vacations, a travel company that had brought four hundred gay men to a resort in Costa Rica for one week. Now, in the real world, a person might actually have to spend valuable time determining another person's marital status by the clumsy old-fashioned method of making conversation. But please, with our busy schedules as gay men, who has time to make conversation? Therefore, as a customer service, Wilde Vacations devised a dog-tag system that allowed their clientele to arrange a rendezvous with the man of their dreams or the man of their passing fancy with a swiftness that makes streetwalkers seem poky.

If I was single, Vaughn would place a round green sticker on the reverse side of my dog tag. If I was in a relationship and considered myself unavailable, he would give me a round red sticker. And if I was willing to consider a proposition, but not necessarily willing to do more than that, he would slap a yellow sticker on my dog tag.

Of course the system of stop, go, and caution didn't actually guarantee that I would be causing any traffic jams. I amused myself by thinking if I flashed green, would the men keep on going? If I flashed yellow, would men accelerate to get past me? And if I flashed red, would I only attract guys who wanted me to change?

Thinking aloud, I said to Vaughn, "I could be green. Eh, maybe I should be a yellow . . ." My choice of color unintentionally revealed my cowardice about dating again after ten years with Tom. While waiting for Vaughn to make the decision for me, I availed myself of the opportunity to explain in unnecessary detail why my relationship had ended.

Being a genuinely kind man, he listened patiently. Everything about Vaughn was only skin-deep, but it was his superficiality that somehow made him vulnerable and easily touched. He failed to suggest that one possible reason why my boyfriend skedaddled could have been my habit of questioning the accuracy of my own scales whenever I had a decision to weigh. Before I could finish Volume One of *What He Did to Me,* Vaughn interrupted my confession. A line of men with equally complicated personal lives had formed behind me.

Like a nurse, Vaughn made a quick perusal of my injuries and determined that my recovery would be speeded by therapeutic exercise, and he recommended classic disco dancing. Vaughn said, "Listen, Bob, you're definitely not a red. He's the one who ended it—am I right?" I nodded yes. "Well, then, why should you be a yellow?" Without another word he placed a green sticker on my dog tag, slipped the chain over my head, and sent me out on my first reconnaissance mission in ten years with the command, "Now go dance. I'm ordering you to have a good time."

As the dog tag dangled around my neck, for the first time it occurred to me that the metaphor was real: I'm in a war. While heterosexuals fight the Battle of the Sexes, gay men and lesbians are fighting the Battle Between the Sex, and as most historians will attest, civil wars are always the most brutal of conflicts, pitting brother against brother and sister against sister. As I mustered my courage to proceed to the poolside bar near the dance floor, I realized that the Battle Between the Sex is fought by courageous one-man armies of unknown soldiers eager to introduce themselves and the worst defeat that can befall their troops is to be ignored. If all's fair in love and war, then lovers as well as soldiers should receive the Purple Heart for being wounded in battle, even if the injury is only a bruised ego.

Manhattan

Jeffrey suggested, "Bob, you need to get laid. And soon." Maybe he was right. That morning I had been reading the newspaper and caught myself staring at the crotch of the letter *M* in the word "Man." But I wasn't as sure as Jeffrey that getting laid was what I needed right now. As I grow older, getting hot and bothered becomes harder and harder to distinguish from anxiety. There are some days when having an orgasm would just add to my feelings of being overwhelmed. I wasn't averse to actually getting laid, but I definitely needed and wanted to feel that I *could* get laid.

I was staying with Jeffrey in his tiny apartment in Chelsea. Exercising his rights as an old friend, he dissected my sex life. Jeffrey advised, "You're not ready to start dating but you need to have some hot, meaningless sex after you break up with someone."

Jeffrey was being a Jewish mother and he made having an orgasm sound like his favorite home remedy for heartache. There were times when Jeffrey pushed sex on his friends like his own mother used to push food on him as a boy. Jeffrey encouraged me to go ahead and have that piece of ass in the same manner that his mother would insist that you have to try a slice of her crumb babka.

It's imperative for all gentile gay men to have at least one Jewish mother in their lives. An easily accomplished goal if you have any friends who are Jewish gay men. I happen to be blessed (it's a mitzvah!) with several Jewish mothers in my life—Jaffe, Glenn, Larry, and Jeffrey. Jewish gay men prove that maternal instincts aren't limited by gender. In fact, Jeffrey has such strong maternal instincts that he's the first man to ever be offered full membership in Hadassah. I also have several Jewish mothers in my life—Patty, Suzy, and Sharon—who happen to be lesbians, which is the enlightened version of the Jewish mother: they know that they make you feel guilty but they're more than willing to suggest the name of a wonderful therapist to deal with it.

Jeffrey was the go-ahead-honey-you-can-do-him voice of encouragement while Glenn, one of my West Coast yiddisha mamas was the worried head-shaking voice of caution whose encouragement is hard to distinguish from discouragement. Glenn is like the mother who has had misgivings about all the fairy tales with happy endings that she read to you as a child and now feels compelled to redress the situation by telling you bleak stories of disenchantment. After my breakup, Glenn counseled, "Don't feel that you have to rush things. It might be too soon. If it's too soon you could end up like my friend Garrett. He was on the rebound from his breakup and met a guy who he thought was the love of his life. The guy turned out to be a psycho who stole ten thousand dollars from him and slashed the tires on his car. You'll know when you're ready."

Glenn's faith in my ability to determine my preparedness was sweet but unfounded, because I have never felt ready for anything. I ascribe the source of this psychological quirk to the aftereffects of being a premature baby—a fact that has itself been a source of contention in my family, since my mother insists that she carried me for the full term of nine months. Despite her claims there's no doubt in my mind that I was born fifteen minutes early. I vaguely recall being rushed out the door before I was completely ready.

I told my friends that I was ready to start dating again

but I wasn't ready to feel that happy about it. Our first night together Jeffrey decided that we should go out for a drink to a bar called G. I thought this was the perfect name for a gay bar at the end of the twentieth century. It has the brevity of a commercial logo or brand name and it is also the sound of the wide-eyed wonder I still often experience in a gay bar: "Gee!" It also reveals a certain New York done-it attitude—we're so beyond the word "gay."

The bar G is a beautiful, slick space divided into two sections. The walls are paneled in light-colored wood and in the front of the bar sit several large all-purpose wooden cubes that can be used as tables, chairs, or, in a pinch, as pedestals. A large circular stainless-steel bar fills the back of the bar. In an alcove in the wall, a halogen pin spot illuminates a lavish flower arrangement. I was impressed. G looked like an expensive, well-designed one-bedroom apartment that a hundred male Manhattanites shared each night. And come to think of it, at most gay bars, there are always a few customers who do seem to live there.

Jeffrey ordered drinks and we scanned the crowd as if we were looking for an old friend in a new body. I must admit that when I had been single in New York I had rarely gone home with anyone from a gay bar. Yet I had some interesting encounters and loved comparing bar horror stories with my friends. (Someday I'd like to edit an anthology: *The Oxford Book of Gay-Bar Horror Stories.*) There's nothing more enjoyable than getting together with a group of gay men and swapping spine-tingling tales of scary come-ons.

The consensus among my friends is that I was the recipient of the nonpareil worst attempt at a pickup line.

When I still lived in Buffalo, I had only been going to the local gay bar for a few months when a man approached me and introduced himself as Lawrence. We talked and after a few minutes he said, "I live with my mother..." A tiny cuckoo popped out of my forehead and sounded the alarm: "Uh-oh." I still lived with my parents but I was attending college. He was in his mid to late thirties and my inflexible rule is that if you're older than Norman Bates in *Psycho* and still live with your mother, there's no chance we'll be showering together. Lawrence continued, "...so we can't go back to my place. But I work at a funeral home and I have a set of keys and they have a really nice lounge that we could use." It was tempting—I had always wanted to date a crypt keeper. I shuddered as I imagined that once he got me to the funeral home, he would suggest a ghoulish threesome. If I had been smart, as part of my long-range plans, I would have brought Lawrence home to meet my parents. The news that he was a mortician would have diverted attention from my perverted lifestyle since embalming is one of the few activities that most middle-class people find more repugnant than homosexuality. Then, after breaking up with Lawrence, any subsequent boyfriends I brought home would have been regarded by my parents as a vast improvement and welcomed with open arms.

I was insulted by Lawrence's offer. He barely knew me and it's not a compliment when a mortician wants you for your body. Did he really expect me to reply, "Yes, let's get out of here. Hey, do you want to make out in the backseat of the hearse beforehand?" I tried to imagine a romantic mortician: Lawrence lighting a Duraflame log in the crematorium in order to make the place look more cozy. I don't remember what I said to get away from him but I'm sure I let him down gently. "Lawrence, I'm flattered by your generous offer of a roll in the casket but I have a big day tomorrow and I hate to wake up screaming."

In G, I was only checking out the men who clearly didn't live with their mothers. I could pick them out because on a cool autumn night a mother would have insisted, "Honey, wear a jacket. That skimpy shirt won't keep you warm."

When my interest began to fade and I wondered, *Has an avant-garde theater director ever set a production of* Waiting for Godot *in a gay bar?* Jeffrey leaned into me and declared, "Bob, remember dating is like riding a bicycle. You never forget how to do it." No. It was more like riding a tricycle. It was something I was still capable of doing but I felt I had outgrown it and doing it now felt somewhat undignified and embarrassing.

Turtle Bay Resort, Costa Rica

I was sitting by the swimming pool trying to read my book but my concentration was disturbed by the sight of a parade of men in bathing suits. Part of the problem was my choice of book. I was reading another nonfiction account of rich white men who have climbed Mount Everest, flown around the world in a balloon, or sailed a yacht across the Pacific, because they want to achieve the same sense of accomplishment that average people can only attain by doing their own housework.

Pausing in the middle of a chapter, I was distracted by a poolside conversation. A guy was loudly bragging, "I was told that with my looks, I should go into modeling, and then I was told that with my voice, I should go into radio." An unbidden thought suggested, *Maybe they were just trying to get you to go. Period.*

The man sitting next to me asked in a low voice, "Do you think I should tell him that with his modesty, he should go into public relations?" I smiled broadly at his remark as he introduced himself.

Peter Luganero was in his late fifties and had a naturally fit physique, a throwback to an era when being in shape meant simply that your body was recognizably human and you weren't obese. Peter's deep tan suggested a barbaric form of sun worship where the faithful were slowly roasted alive as human sacrifices. His solar devotion was such that his body now cast a shadow that was paler than this skin. Hanging around Peter's neck and wrists were masses of heavy gold chains that made him look like a Houdini. For his next magic trick, I hoped he would try to escape from his own bad taste in jewelry. With only the slightest prompting Peter told me his life story.

Born and raised in Cleveland, Peter was a hairdresser who owned three Casa d'Eleganza Beauty Salons. From his description there was nothing remotely faggy about him being a hairdresser. As he put it: "I cut hair." He made hairdressing sound like a manly job and I got the impression that Peter crafted a spit curl like a metalworker forged a decorative spiral on a wrought-iron fence.

Without boasting, Peter revealed, "When I got out of the navy, my cousin Freddie talked me into cutting hair but I never expected to make a pile of dough doing it. Most of my customers were middle-aged ladies who grew up in Cleveland and lived there for their entire lives. You know, one husband, one job, and one hairstyle.

"My job was to find that one hairstyle. With a new customer, I would remove her doubts by cutting slowly, a clip here, a clip there, and once I found her hairstyle I never forgot how she liked it done, and when I was finished, she was usually a customer for life."

I knew the women he was talking about. They sounded exactly like my godmother, who for over fifty years wore the same hairstyle. Her hairdo had outlived two beauticians and she never wanted her hairdresser to suggest a new style. She wanted her hairdresser to be the curator of her hairdo. He was responsible for doing minor restoration work and preserving it unchanged for posterity as if it was a historical artifact.

While we talked Peter casually asked me questions about myself and I almost imagined that I could hear a pair of scissors clipping away. I confessed that my reason for coming to Costa Rica was the classic effort to kill two birds with one stone: I was curious to see the rain forest and I was ready to start dating again. If I could see a toucan and meet a man on one bus trip then so much the better. Peter said to me jokingly, "Well, Bob, if you're on a manhunt, you have to let me know if there's anything I can do to help."

I guess I was on a manhunt. But I was trying to be careful. I didn't want to be one of the reckless gunners who shoots at anything that moves. A manhunt is a scary analogy, because when you bring home a trophy, the only way to keep it is to have it stuffed and mounted. Too often my manhunting technique was to wait for something to happen. And a hunter can wait forever for the duck to introduce himself. In cartoons Bugs Bunny and Daffy always introduce themselves to Elmer Fudd but it's much more infrequent in real life.

So many of the metaphors for love involve hunting or war, whereas I would be happy if falling in love was more like gardening: I could just choose a boyfriend from a seed catalog and grow him. I think it would be a sign of progress if we moved beyond a hunting-based culture and developed boyfriend agriculture.

Puerto Vallarta, Mexico

Wilde Vacations had hired me again to perform in Puerto Vallarta and my friend Mark was my self-appointed guide for this week's manhunt. Mark is a stand-up comedian who has the ability to tease his own masculinity as if he's playing tag with it.

He's a mama's boy but his Oedipal complex is purely a business arrangement. He was attracted to his mother because she was a great source of material. One of the most popular characters in Mark's act is his mother, Mavis. He isn't doing drag, even though he dons a gray wig and a pair of outdated women's eyeglasses. Mark doesn't impersonate his mother, he *becomes* her, which for a gay man is either a gift or a curse, depending on whether he's on or off stage.

I've always thought that Mark should bill himself as "The Man of a Thousand Girlfriends." He has a vast repertoire of impressions at his command and spending time with him means that you're able to enjoy the company of his various voices. At the appropriate time, he can do a pitch-perfect Ruth Draper drawling, "I think she's perfectly dreadful. We have to get rid of her!" or he will leave a message on my answering machine as Suzanne Pleshette exclaiming in her smoker's voice, "Oh, Bob!" or he might utter his mother's flinty-sounding cry of despair, "I've *had* it!" There are countless others, and while it helps to know which actress he's doing, to Mark's credit, his voices are usually still funny even when I have no idea who he's doing or what old movie or TV show he's quoting from.

Mark's saving grace, though, is that he has a sense of

timing and a sense of proportion. He knows when to let one of his voices speak and when to keep them quiet and be himself. Mark is capable of a serious heart-to-heart conversation but he never allows a serious conversation to become solemn and will leaven it with a few perfectly timed asides from one of his girlfriends.

In Puerto Vallarta, Mark was in high spirits but he was frank about being subject to periods of depression. If I hadn't spoken to him in a while, when I asked what was going on in his life, he would occasionally mention the days or weeks when his personality went dark like a theater on a Monday. He was matter-of-fact about his melancholy, as if the masks of comedy and tragedy were the only two expressions that a performer was allowed to have.

It was possible to assume that Mark never experienced moments of sadness because he always wore clothing that made people smile. In recent years he had toned down his flamboyant dandyism, but when Mark first started performing, he wore theatrical clothing in his daily life that gave the impression that he was being fitted for costumes for several plays at once. I could sometimes imagine that he was doing the first act of *Cabaret* and then at intermission dashing to the theater across the street to perform the second act of *Streetcar*. I can remember Mark once showing up for dinner wearing a tight purple rodeo shirt and a pair of silver lamé capri pants with high-top red sneakers. (Correction: Mark has informed me, as if I was a dunce for confusing the two, that they weren't capri pants, they were *bolero* pants.) In a holdover from those days Mark still "hid" behind a huge black pair of women's sunglasses that shielded him from the glare of public scrutiny in a manner guaranteed to be even more of an attention getter. One time I made the mistake of commenting on Mark's sunglasses and he informed me, "They're not women's sunglasses! I think of them as more . . . Catherine Deneuve. They're a star's sunglasses!"

Mark was on the prowl for a man, and after looking around the room, he declared, "Tonight, you know what would make me happy? To be wrapped up in the big hairy arms of a bear." For a second I imagined Mark wearing a large furry man as a mink stole. On that night, I was surprised by his desire for a hairy man. It was a humid ninety degrees, and when I felt a trickle of sweat drip down my neck, I suggested, "Mark, it's too hot for a bear."

Mark laughed and gave me the compliment of slowly repeating what I had said. "It's—too—hot—for—a—bear."

I bought drinks for us—a mineral water for Mark, who had given up alcohol and drugs almost as if sobriety was one of the sacrifices that he had to make for his career. Unlike many twelve-steppers Mark looked back fondly on the hazy years, and when he reminisced he sounded almost wistful. "Oh, I used to love a good pot brownie. They're sweet and a little savory. And the buzz is so long lasting. And with brownies, I found that I never got the munchies as bad as I did when I smoked pot. So in the long run they actually were better for my figure."

Mark isn't fat now, but he had been fat as a boy and former tubbies always maintain a watchful vigil over their long-lost figures. They live in fear that the fatso they thought had been dead for years is going to show up asking to reclaim his life.

Tonight Mark decided that I needed a little pep talk. "Bob, now that you're single again," he whispered confidentially, "you might want to rethink your entire sexual life. This could be an opportunity to try something different. To explore new aspects of yourself."

I reacted skeptically. "Well, I have always had a secret ambition to be a leather daddy."

"Bob! I'm serious," Mark cried. "Anyway, I can't imagine *you* as leather daddy." Lowering his voice to the basso profundo of a porn star, he imitated me growling, "Yeah! I want you to read *all* the Sunday *New York Times.* Yeah! Read it *all*! From cover to cover. Yeah! That's right!" Dropping the impression, he concluded, "Bob, I think you'd be happier as a slave bottom."

"Really?" I replied as I played along. "I'm too bossy to be a slave bottom. And there's nothing worse than a bossy bottom. You can never please a bossy bottom."

Still, Mark had a point. Ending a long relationship is like ending one life and beginning another. The ability to start over again is a quintessential American belief which is one reason why we've named a city Phoenix, after the legendary bird that rises from its own ashes. I like to think that the American contribution to Eastern religions has been the idea of multiple incarnations within one lifetime. Americans, and gay men especially, believe why wait to die to live another life when you can do it all now. I was moving into my next incarnation, and I could choose a new life. I could come back as a drag queen, a leather-clad S&M master, a circuit party boy, a bear, or a suburban gay father if I so chose. Or I could be a slave bottom to my own destiny and remain a comedian.

I've met enough gay men to know that I could even combine several lives. In Las Vegas, I met a drag queen who was also a father raising a teenage son. They live in a large suburban-style house and lead a life in which Dad's job at night impersonating Barbra Streisand seems as regular as having a stockbroker Dad who spends his day pretending to be a financial whiz named Merrill Lynch. (Note: Meryl Lynch or Mary Money would make good drag names for gay Republicans.)

As I considered the possibilities, there were a few that I could immediately rule out. I'm not going to become a drag queen. I'm still working on my performance as a man and I'm not ready to tackle a second gender until I've completely mastered the first one.

Moving down the list of possibilities, I immediately crossed off S&M leather master. I'm probably a hopeless romantic but I'm fairly certain that "Ow! That hurts" are not the three little words I want to hear from a man.

Eliminating leather and drag from my prospective future was a relatively easy decision. Wearing a uniform all the time would make me feel like an employee of my own sex life. Working those late shifts at gay bars in drag or leather had about the same appeal to me as working at a fast-food restaurant that stays open until two A.M. I've noticed that people in uniforms, whether at gay bars or McDonald's, do not usually look as if they're enjoying themselves. I'm afraid it would become routine and I would spend my weekends at the Queen Mary or the Spike looking forward to my retirement to a little piano bar in Fort Lauderdale, where I would no longer have to wear my wig, beaded gown, and pumps or my black cap, studded vest, and boots, depending upon which "type" I had become.

West Hollywood

The first rule for waging the Battle Between the Sex is to be thoroughly prepared. Today I inspected my one-man army to determine my current level of readiness. Before taking a shower, I stood in front of the bathroom mirror and after giving my body an audit decided that the looking glass was half-empty. I was a blue Narcissus staring in transfixed horror at my perceived flaws—the love handles that dare not speak their name, the tiny scar on my stomach where a divot of skin cancer was removed, the small red bump on my chest that looks perpetually embarrassed. Gazing in the mirror, I looked for signs of sex appeal as if it was the symptom of an illness, only it was someone else's temperature I wanted to be able to raise.

Then I reinspected myself, double-checking everything, just to make sure I didn't miss something the first time. Looking again, I began to think that maybe the looking glass was half-full. There was no doubt that I looked better than I had eight months previously when I was in a relationship. It's human nature that once you have a boyfriend or girlfriend you relax and tend to think that since you're no longer single you can let yourself double in size. And while I had never let myself go, parts of me had started to wander. But finding myself single again, I had put myself through basic weight training and had shed unwanted flab like it was an albatross around my waist. And I thought my arms appeared to be a little thicker. Of course the pump was probably all in my head. I still wouldn't have dated myself, but my rejection wouldn't be brusque. I would be polite and smile before turning myself down.

Silverlake, California

If Beverly Hills is home to the stars, then the Silverlake area of Los Angeles should brand itself as home to the porn stars. (Now there's a business opportunity for someone: selling maps to the porn stars' homes.) Silverlake funky, artsy, and dirty and whenever I drive over there from West Hollywood I momentarily rouse the suburban sense of daring that comes from visiting a neighborhood that isn't truly bad but is slightly naughty. It's definitely not a slum; it's just untidy. Silverlake is an area that looks like it was the scene of a big party one night in 1934 and the bohemian residents are still sleeping in and haven't gotten around to cleaning up the place.

The party I was invited to was being held on a street south of Sunset that had been haphazardly gentrified. A beautifully restored Craftsman bungalow with a brand-new Volvo and a Range Rover in the driveway could be seen next to a shabby 1950s apartment building where all the Honda Civics parked in front were missing either a taillight or an antenna. It was a world where Switzerland lived next door to Guatemala in relative peace and harmony.

Victor, the host of the party, was the office manager of a gay pornographic film company. I had met him at Tampa's Gay Pride Celebration, where he was handling the appearance of three Bronco Studios porn stars. Victor was responsible for making sure that plenty of ancillary merchandise was available for sale to the porn stars' fans. They could pay twenty dollars to have a nonerotic Polaroid taken with their favorite star or buy autographed copies of their videos. And for the fan who can't get enough, one of the porn stars sold plastic replicas of his penis, mouth, and rectum. And I used to think that people who collected *Gone With the Wind* commemorative plates were weird. You really have to be a devoted fan to want to own a knockoff of your favorite star's asshole.

Victor generously insisted on giving me a pornographic refrigerator magnet and several videos. Videos that the porn stars had carefully selected for me after they disapproved of Victor's choices. "Bob, don't take that one. This one's my best video." When I flippantly inquired, "Victor, you don't happen to have any free sample assholes?" he answered, tongue-in-cheek, "Bob, those assholes cost money. We can't just be giving them away." I asked, "How do I know I'm getting a real porn star's genuine asshole and not some cheap imitation? Is his asshole copyrighted?" Victor smiled but didn't deem my question worthy of a reply. Pleased with myself, I then asked, "Victor, does your company have an asshole factory outlet? Where you sell assholes with slight imperfections at a substantial discount." Victor laughed and said, "I'm going to suggest that idea to my boss."

I immediately liked Victor even though his beard and tattoos made him look like a potentially dangerous gang member. Victor's right arm and shoulder were completely covered with an elaborate multicolored tattoo that included an angry portrait of the comic-book character the Green Lantern surrounded by intricately detailed decorative patterning. Sounding like the owner of a valuable art collection, Victor mentioned, "I have to keep my tattoos from the sun or else the colors will fade." When he spoke I observed that he had a small metal stud through his tongue which made it look like one of his fillings had just fallen out or that he was sucking on a breath mint and had forgotten to remove the foil wrapping.

Victor's fierce appearance belied his gentle and thoughtful nature. On the way back from Tampa, I overheard the flight attendant, a middle-aged woman, say to him, "You know you look kind of scary but you're actually very sweet." Her comment caused Victor's uninked flesh to redden, which only reinforced his charm.

Every Sunday during the summer Victor gave a pool party at his house in Silverlake and a week after we returned he called to invite me. I accepted his invitation, not knowing what to expect, but my new rule as a single man was that absolutely no invitations were going to be turned down. I'm rediscovering that searching for a boyfriend is like searching for extraterrestrial life. You know he's out there but to find him you have to be either extremely lucky and have him make First Contact, or be prepared to systematically investigate the entire universe. Silverlake was as good a place as any in my universe to start looking.

Victor lived in a completely unrestored Craftsman bungalow with two roommates. To get to the backyard we walked through the house, which had an interior that was somewhere between a house of horrors and a biker bar. My wide-eyed response to Victor's house was similar to my reaction to Pensacola, Florida. It's not a place where I would want to live but I'm glad that I saw it. Seeing that I was impressed, Victor asked, "Bob, do you want a tour?" You bet I did. The living room featured a display of horror and science-fiction action figures—most still in their boxes—and some mounted on the walls for our admiration. To set off the collection, the walls were painted such bilious colors as snot green and scab brown. In the dining room, the large table was painted black and then embellished with six large screaming faces. It was a decorative motif that brought back memories of many family dinners that I sat through as a child. Victor's bedroom was painted an intense strident fluorescent blue. With the lights turned off and the shades drawn, the throbbing color itself rubbed my eyes in disbelief.

Leaving the house, we passed through the Op Art orange-and-white-checkerboard-painted kitchen, a dizzying color combination that gave the blender vertigo. Then we exited to the backyard, where a built-in pool was surrounded by a brutally ugly cinderblock fence. The cinderblocks were painted dark green to soften their harsh appearance but it worked about as well as makeup on a crack whore.

Victor was a gracious host and offered me a can of beer or a soda. I grabbed a soda from a galvanized washtub filled with iced drinks, and as I looked around I observed that all the other guests were either tattooed or had one part of their body pierced. When I removed my shirt my pale unmarked skin made me feel like a blank canvas that had been mistakenly hung at the Museum of Modern Art. I realized then that tattoos and body piercing satisfy a huge need in contemporary life. If we can't all be artists, we can at least all be canvases.

As Victor introduced me to people, I tried to remember everyone's name by using their tattoos or piercings as mnemonic devices. Preston had a bloody figure of the crucified Jesus on his back with the slogan "Action Speaks Louder Than Words" in Gothic-style lettering. Mickey had a shaved head and "Daddy's Boy" tattooed above his ass with another tattoo of a threaded sewing needle unwound from a spool running up his arm. Rick had a huge silver knob on his chin, making his face seem like the lid to his head. I was tempted to lift it and check to see what was cooking inside. He also had a huge bloody dagger on his forearm and tattooed starbursts around his nipples. Dylan had a snake and a crescent moon on his chest, and a small 1950s-style spaceship on his left biceps. All Calvin had was a bolt pierced through his left nipple but he was unable to pull off the look and somehow on him it looked like he was the manager of a restaurant and his name tag had fallen off, leaving the pin that held it dangling in place.

Chet was pierced all over. From his appearance I guessed that he must have taken a lot of shrapnel in the Battle Between the Sex. Fortunately I was wearing sunglasses, which allowed me to stare. Gaping at him, I suspected that Chet had metal washers in every orifice. He had taken his piercings beyond bodily ornamentation. It was aggressively off-putting, a way to make people keep their distance, as if he was surrounding himself with a chain-link fence. Then again, that was my interpretation and Chet might have seen it as a way to keep out people who weren't going to take the time and trouble to find the gate in the fence and discover the wonders inside. Or maybe Chet was a bit of a dope and didn't know that he had overdone it.

It seems to me that Chet and Peter Luganero, the hairdresser from Cleveland who wore all the gold chains, have a lot in common. Tattoos and body piercings are butch brooches for men who want to adorn themselves but don't want to appear effeminate. If Liberace was just starting out today in Las Vegas, he would probably have gaudy tattoos and wear nipple rings—an unpleasant thought, because his nipple rings would be oversize eighteen-karat-gold pianos embedded with gems the size of quail's eggs.

Of course, two minutes after I sat down no one seemed scary in the least. Chet put on a pair of campy sunglasses with star-shaped lenses and it was impossible for him to remain threatening when he seriously lamented, "I can never find the right hat for myself." I started thinking of everyone as a group of boys who had tripped while running with sharp objects and had punctured themselves through every piece of loose flesh and in one case the tongue. And instead of recovering from their injuries, they grew to admire and appreciate the look.

I wasn't attracted to anyone at the party and I think it's fair to say that no one was interested in me, so consequently I relaxed and enjoyed myself. When I felt too hot I swam or floated on one of the many inflatable rafts in the pool. I actually worried when I saw Chet climbing aboard a raft because I thought a piece of his hardware might cause a blowout. Victor's dog Molly, a stout wire-haired mutt, came over and invited me to pet her by resting her head on my knee. As I scratched her head and her tail wagged in slow strokes, I tried to ascertain if she had nipple rings.

After swimming, I sipped a soft drink while I sat sprawled in a beach chair. Catching the eye of the man seated next to me, I introduced myself. His name was James. "What do you do?" I asked. James replied, "I have my own mail-order dildo business." In my head I exclaimed, *Really!?* and I searched in vain for recognition in James's eyes of how absurd his words sounded. Immediately intrigued, I asked, "How did you get started in that business?" He took a deep breath and like all proud entrepreneurs he embarked on the creation story of his business. "Well, to be honest, I've always been hard to fit. Every time I bought a dildo off the rack, it was either too big or too small or too flimsy. I'm a special size, deep but narrow. I'm a double-E wide—I know; impossible to find, right?—and I just couldn't get one that fit right.

"So one day, I thought, a dildo can't be that hard to make. It's just a lump of plastic, right? So I buy ten pounds of latex and think I'm going to make my own. Well, of course it's not as easy as it sounds. My first few batches burned. I'll bet my neighbors were thinking, 'What the hell is he cooking?' They probably never guessed a skinny nine-inch cock. Well, finally, I get the size right but I can't get the plastic to harden and who wants a soggy dildo, right? I felt like I was Thomas Edison. Only I was trying to invent a lightbulb I could shove up my ass. Well, finally I get everything right. I make a dildo that fits my ass like my own dick fits my balls.

"Well, one night I tell my friend Michael about my dildo and how happy I was with it. And to my surprise, he says that he's also hard to fit and he asks me if I would make him one. So I do and give it to him as a gift for his birthday. And he tells me that it's the best goddamn dildo he ever had up his ass. And he's tried them all. He could wear my dildo for hours and still feel comfortable without it riding up and pinching.

"Well, before you know it, pretty soon he's recommending my dildos to all his friends and they start to tell their friends and so on and so on. Well, what had started as a hobby turned into a career. In fact, now I have my whole family working for me. My mom handles our telephone orders and my dad runs shipping." The image of a sweet-looking gray-haired woman sitting behind a desk talking into a telephone popped up. "Sure, honey, we can send the Pile-Driver to you by overnight delivery. You'll have it first thing tomorrow morning. Oh, I know, I'm the exact same. When I buy something I don't want to wait three weeks to get it. I want to use it right away."

It was a classic tale of capitalism. James had found a need in the marketplace and filled it. Mistaking my interest in his business as the interest of a potential customer, he asked, "Would you like to receive our catalog?" I was entertained by his start-up story but I didn't really want to be put on his mailing list. I imagined James's unconditional guarantee. "Try one of my dildos for one month. If you're not completely satisfied, then return the dildo and receive a full refund. No questions asked." And I was curious if he put out a special Christmas catalog. I thought to myself, *Tattoos, nipple rings, dildos, and plastic buttholes. Who needs all this stuff?* To paraphrase Thoreau: Our sex lives are frittered away by detail. Simplify, simplify.

Victor interrupted our conversation, saving me from James's mailing list by asking, "Hey, if I fired up the grill, would you guys eat something?" We both gave him the go-ahead. Victor made the perfect meal for his guests. Shish kebabs.

Turtle Bay Resort, Costa Rica

My friend Dennis had been on the party circuit for so long that it wouldn't surprise me if he said, "I'll never forget my fifth birthday. The White Party. For weeks afterward it was the talk of the first grade. We had this DJ flown in from New York to spin for us when we played musical chairs . . . He was incredible! We never sat down for the entire night. And I drank so much Kool-Aid, I was still feeling the effects in the second grade."

I waited while Dennis ironed another shirt. We were going to the White Party but we weren't going to *the* White Party held annually in Miami. Our White Party was merely the biggest party of the week for the four hundred Wilde Vacationers in Costa Rica. Our group was about two-thirds couples and Dennis was one of the few muscled circuit party boys indulging in a bit of eco-tourism. I'm sure there would have been hundreds more if the tour promoters had the foresight to market the trip as the Green Party.

Waiting for Dennis to finish ironing his shirt, I sat in a chair biting my thumbnail looking like an unhappy cannibal who doesn't like what's being served. Dennis muttered to himself as he ironed. He's furious because he spilled iced tea on his favorite tight white tank top. After Dennis knocked over the glass, he started swearing and slammed a door hard enough to rattle and break an entire set of glasses. From watching Dennis's temper tantrum, I'm not sure there's much difference between 'roid rage and a hissy fit. All of Dennis's friends suspected that he was taking steroids. He denied it, but he was starting to look more overbuilt than Los Angeles.

I'd read a book that reported that in America's large cities supposedly half the gay men are taking steroids. And I presume the other half are taking antidepressants because they don't look like the guys on steroids.

Getting his posing trunks all in a bunch isn't Dennis's normal behavior. Most of the time he's a gargantuan pussycat, but travel doesn't bring out the best in him. I think when Dennis travels he misses the comforting purr of his blender as it mixes his protein powder. He began complaining as soon as we arrived in Costa Rica. I suspect that wherever Dennis travels he scrawls the same message on all of his postcards: *I wish you were here—to see how I'm being treated!*

Dennis has a habit of insinuating that every problem of his is as serious as global warming. He can misplace his sunglasses and suddenly it's an issue that affects every person on the planet. On this trip he's been more argumentative than usual. Our first night here, in an after-dinner discussion, Dennis forcefully defended circuit parties by arguing, "They're not sluts! They're just men who like to have sex." His reasoning ended the debate by causing everyone to laugh.

As we finally got ready to leave, we were joined by two of Dennis's friends. Initially I decided that Tommy and Mark were matching bookends who had never read a single book between them. I was suffering from one of my paranoid moments where I started to think of these three perfectly muscled gay men as the Intimidators. They looked like androids sent from the future to make my present a little more grim. I didn't consider that my thoughts were only revealing how I have been programmed.

I discreetly gave Tommy and Mark the once-over, two or three times. Gay men have a tendency to examine an attractive body almost as if, by some miracle, they might have to identify it later when it turns up in their beds. Having first learned to covertly observe men's bodies in the latitudes of Buffalo, I've developed the ability to spot a great physique through a parka. In the tropics, my powers of observation proved unnecessary. Mark wore a loosely draped white silk shirt that seemed to suggest that his splendid torso was just waiting to be unveiled, while Tommy's white shirt was more akin to a lamp shade; it wasn't meant to conceal his beauty but to soften the glare of his radiance.

Over the next few days, as I saw more of Tommy's wardrobe, I estimated that all of his shirts put together contained less fabric than one heterosexual man's beefy T-shirt. (No wonder circuit parties are popular. Travel is a breeze for these pumped-up men. They can simply fold shirts for a week, place them them in a business envelope, and mail them to their destinations.)

While we waited for Dennis to finish getting dressed, Mark glanced at his Rolex almost as if he was checking to make sure that he was still *au courant.* From turning the pages of only the most polished of glossy magazines, Mark and Tommy had become the arbiters of their own fashionable lives. They knew exactly what to wear, what to eat, what to drink, where to go, what to do, what to see, what to listen to, how to dance, and who to fuck. From their poised appearance I took for granted that uncertainty was as alien to Mark and Tommy's minds as fat was to their abdomens.

It turned out that I was the most superficial person in the room. All right, maybe not the *most* superficial person in the room. But I shouldn't have assumed so much about Tommy and Mark based on their appearance. Dennis, who was a nurse, told me that Mark was a pediatrician and Tommy worked as a social worker. I briefly fantasized about moving to Chicago and going on welfare just to have Tommy become my caseworker but dismissed the thought because I now regretted having judged these two muscle magazines by their covers. I had looked into their shininess and had found only my own nastiness reflected back.

I was completely won over by Tommy and Mark when they asked if I had any interest in seeing leatherback sea turtles nesting on a nearby beach. While most of the men on this trip were interested in doing at least one eco-tour, there were a few vacationers who had no interest in anything except lying in the sun and partying. The previous night I had been in a conversation with three men and had mentioned that it might be possible to see leatherback sea turtles nesting soon. In a burst of enthusiasm I confessed to wanting to witness the primordial urge of sea turtles to return to their birthplace. A look of disbelief crossed the faces of the three men almost as if I had announced a nighttime expedition to watch a woman give birth. Clearly, they didn't regard watching sea turtles laying their eggs as a once-in-a-lifetime experience. It was an evening wasted.

We left Dennis's room and headed down to the resort's dance pavilion. Overlooking the beach was a circular structure, a dance bunker, built out of reinforced concrete. When we arrived, the music was already playing. Tommy and Mark went to the bar to get drinks while Dennis and I stood near the dance floor.

We saw a lone dancer swaying to the beat. Watching him dance was as hypnotically entrancing as staring at a spiraling barber pole—which the dancer's body resembled as it rotated in a long twisting wiggle. A wiggle that began at his feet and oscillated up to his head. At the moment the first wiggle reached his hair and spun away, another wiggle would appear at his feet and begin its ascent. In front of his face, his hands slowly waved to each other. He seemed transfixed by the sight almost as if he was trying to applaud himself but was unable to bring his hands together.

Feeling frisky myself, I said to Dennis, "Look at that guy. I think dancing by yourself in public is like masturbating in public. It might give you intense pleasure but it usually repels other people." The solo dancer began to wave a laser pointer that shot a red beam in all directions. Getting into my own groove, I declared, "That's not good. You're in danger of coming across as a little too desperate if you need to carry your own spotlight to get some attention."

Dennis had listened to my disparagement of the uni-dancer with growing impatience and then, with the astringent candor of a friend, put an end to my mockery of him. "Bob, all you're really admitting is that you wouldn't ask yourself to dance because you'd be embarrassed to be seen with yourself. Why shouldn't he dance with himself? He's having a good time while you're standing here being bitchy."

Taken aback, I thought for a second and then I admitted it. "You're right."

"I know," Dennis replied, a trace of forgiveness creeping into his voice. "Bob, think about it. Who's more ridiculous? The guy who acts like a fool or the guy who's always afraid to make a fool of himself? At some point in your life you need to grow up and ask yourself to dance."

"You're right." Stung by his reasoning, I couldn't resist adding, "And so, even if you spill iced tea on your favorite white shirt and go nuts, you need to accept and embrace your own insanity."

Dennis gave me a big affectionate fuck-you smile and replied, "Exactly, bitch."

I had to agree with Dennis because of his irrefutable logic and succinct presentation of an idea that I had completely overlooked. I like to think that I choose my friends because they're smart and insightful but why do they always have to use their perceptiveness to reveal my stupidity?

I suddenly imagined the lone dancer turning toward me and shouting, "What are *you* giving me attitude for? Almost every night you stand on a stage in public and talk to yourself. I would rather be seen dancing by myself in public than talking to myself in public." Later on, I interpreted what Dennis had pointed out as meaning that while I've embraced being gay I'm still sometimes afraid of acting queer. And if I was going to find any happiness as a man, I had to learn that it's not only okay to be gay, that it's okay to be queer. Queer even in terms of the behavior and expectations of other gay men.

I was reminded that years ago when I first heard the chant used at ACT UP demonstrations, "We're here. We're queer. Get used to it," I thought, *That's brilliant. We've come up with a rallying cry that every person on Earth can identify with at some time or another.* For some reason, our rallying cry wasn't adopted by the masses, but for a minute it was a nice fantasy to entertain.

Tommy and Mark returned with bottles of water and a friend named Rick. When Tommy introduced Rick, he mentioned that Rick was a doctor, and then added that he was a surgeon. As soon as the word "doctor" came out of Tommy's mouth, Rick interrupted him with, "Hey, I don't want people to know I'm a doctor. I want them to think I'm a party boy!" He was kidding but I remember thinking only on the dance floor of a gay disco would a man apologize for being an accomplished surgeon.

As I sipped my water, other men began to join the uni-dancer on the dance floor. I had a nice buzz on because during our walk to the dance bunker we had smoked half a joint. My definition of a nice buzz being that I was still capable of conversation. The pot was mind-altering enough to make the surprisingly good lighting system as entrancing as a fireworks display, but I wasn't so wasted that I descended down a hole in my head to Wonderland.

Whenever I "party" these days, I know that getting drunk or spaced out on drugs is always a pyrrhic victory over unhappiness. The next day the triumph feels too costly. My definition of adulthood is when you stop taking drugs to get fucked up and start taking drugs to stop feeling fucked up. I might puff on a joint a few times a year but I usually prefer a tranquilizer or a cocktail over other mind-altering substances.

The round walls of the dance floor were open to the ocean, which allowed the strobe lights and lasers to flash out to sea. I imagined the dance bunker as a lighthouse, shining confusing beacons to disorient passing ships, causing them to flounder and belly up to a sandbar, where they'd spend the night getting wrecked against the pounding beat of the surf.

We were soon out on the dance floor squeezed in a throng of vibrating flesh. I'm a terrible dancer—even when I'm dancing with people, I appear to be dancing by myself—but that night I danced with wild abandon. All right, it was the domesticated wild abandon of a terrier taken off his leash. A terrier who would quickly resume civility upon hearing one sharp reprimand.

The evening was balmy and at times I danced with all four men, then at times with three men, two men, or just Dennis. Dancing with a large group of gay men can feel boyish and innocent and yet sexual too. We're *adults* jumping on our beds and we don't care if they break. As I danced, the dog tag I had worn all week bounced against my chest.

After dancing for an hour, I began to feel that I had danced enough but I refused to be the first party pooper to leave the dance floor. So then I found myself in the ridiculous position of dancing under peer pressure, hoping that someone I was dancing with would now ask me if I wanted to stop dancing. When this happens, I'm usually saved by the DJ playing a bad song that breaks the rhythm of the night, providing me with an alibi to gracefully retire from the dance floor. I danced for a few hours and then, around two in the morning, when the DJ played the disco version of the *Titanic* song, I excused myself and said good night to Dennis, Mark, and Tommy, who were still gyrating to the forelorn pennywhistle with a pulsing backbeat.

In my new life as a single man I'm not going to become a circuit party boy. It's all right. I know I don't have the body for it and I certainly don't have the desire or stamina to go out except once or twice a year. It's possible to party too much. I've met a few guys who have spent so much of their lives celebrating that the sparkle in their eyes is stale glitter from their glory days at Studio 54. I consoled myself by remembering the wisdom of my mother: "Bob, what do you expect? You can't have fun all the time!"

As I walked up the hill to my bungalow, I saw in the darkness hundreds of fireflies twinkling in the grass. A buggy reflection of the star-filled sky above. I could still hear the sounds of the *Titanic* song coming up from the dance floor and I had the strange and dreamy sensation that the fireflies were blinking on and off in sync with the music.

Boston, Massachusetts

My friend Robert once said that he could read people like a book. Maybe that's possible but it's a skill that I've never acquired. Or perhaps my experience in reading a book is different from my experience of reading a person. A book doesn't take offense when you ignore it for months, let alone a few hours. I've never had a book surprise me by telling that we were finished when I thought that the story still had a long way to go. If people were like books, you might like the beginning but then you would find out later that entire chapters were missing or the story keeps inexplicably changing genres. What started out as a romance novel suddenly became pornography, then became a comedy of manners, switched into a Victorian melodrama, deteriorated into a war novel, melted into a tearjerker, morphed into a how-to manual, survived as a case study, and, having beaten the odds, ended up as a self-help tome that you read like a magazine, scanning it and then tossing it aside.

Comparing people to books was an inescapable idea when I attended a three-day gay and lesbian writers' conference with the title "Pride and Prejudice." I thought the name of the conference was inappropriate given that prejudice wasn't going to be given equal shrift with pride. As far as I knew, none of the panels and seminars would be led by fundamentalist ministers and assorted antigay bigots. It was also misleading. What if a Jane Austen scholar mistakenly signed up for the weekend?

The conference was held in Boston and seeing intellectuals en masse reminds me of what my mother always said whenever she saw a picture of Einstein. Shaking her head at his messy hair and unkempt appearance, she would remark, "You can be too smart. I wouldn't want to be that smart." She implied that the possibility of being a genius was less important to her than keeping her hair nice. What scares me is that I sort of think that she had a good point. In some ways I am my mother's son. I would definitely pass on being able to paint like Salvador Dalí if I had to look like him too.

My mother's opinion of Einstein's hair occurred to me while I was talking to a well-respected writer of fiction named Charlie. I tried not to notice Charlie's greasy-looking hair and to ignore the thought that his comb probably had to grit its teeth on the rare occasions when he used it. Charlie was wearing a rumpled jacket, and as he spoke, I wondered, *How is it possible to wrinkle corduroy?*

I enjoyed talking to Charlie because he was a master of the short story, well, the very short story—gossipy anecdotes. He was relating a mishap that had occurred to a writer we both knew: "... William was trying to meet a man at his book reading. And when William signed his book, he wrote the name of his hotel and room number in the inscription. That's a little tacky. And when the object of William's affection read what he had written, he was not happy about it and refused to pay for the book. I don't know what was worse for William—the rejection or the loss of the sale." Charlie started chuckling at his own zinger. When he laughed hard he always started coughing, which made it seem like he was mildly allergic to humor.

Charlie was gay but a better definition of his sexual orientation was that he was a smoker, because I never saw him making out or even flirting with a guy but he was always sucking on a cigarette. Charlie smoked each cigarette with such aggressive determination you thought the cigarette had stopped breathing and he was trying to resuscitate it.

Changing the subject, Charlie announced, "By the way, I told Arthur that you'd meet him for coffee downstairs at seven." Charlie had set me up on a blind date. Well, almost a blind date—a *legally* blind date—with his friend Arthur. It wasn't completely blind because Charlie claimed that the year before I had met Arthur at "Sense and Sensibility" but I couldn't recall meeting him.

It's not always the case, but when I don't remember meeting a man who remembers meeting me, it's usually not a good sign. It's been my experience that when I meet a guy and think, *Yowza!* I can usually remember his name for decades. I feel certain that when I'm eighty-seven and on my deathbed, if someone asks me, "Who was the guy you had a crush on in the tenth grade?" I'd immediately blurt out, "Kirk Bradley!"

I met Arthur for coffee at seven o'clock and my first date in ten years didn't go well. Arthur was attractive but I didn't feel anything one way or the other when we met again. I believe that there should be some reaction when two potential lovers meet. Throughout our coffee date, I waited to see if any chemistry developed between us. An experiment that had all the scientific suspense of dissolving a teaspoon of sugar in my coffee and waiting to observe the reaction.

I soon felt that things were moving way too fast. On our first date, we were like an unhappily married couple who had nothing to talk about. We were rushing things. I like to wait awhile before becoming bored and dissatisfied with a relationship.

Arthur lived by the bore's motto: "You can change the subject, but you can't change my personality." Arthur was one of those bores who thinks that he has the gift of gab. He just didn't realize that it was a shitty gift. Arthur worked as a college history professor. I thought that sounded promising, as I had loved history in school. But Arthur wasn't interested in any of the historical events that I was fascinated by, such as the Lewis and Clark expedition. When I tried to show an interest in Arthur's specialty, the Middle Ages, by mentioning that I had read Barbara Tuchman's book about the fourteenth century, Arthur dismissed the book. "I skimmed it. It's a good *popular* history." Arthur made the word "popular" sound pejorative. He implied that being unpopular bestowed distinction, which was a belief that had probably gotten Arthur through high school, college, and graduate school. It didn't look promising for our future happiness together that on our first date we had thousands of years from which to choose and we couldn't agree upon a time.

We started and dropped subjects of conversation with the rapidity of a telephone operator giving directory assistance. And telephone operators have more meaningful conversations than Arthur and I were having.

As we talked, I decided that Arthur was a "know-it-almost." Generally, he knew what he was talking about, but he kept getting his facts slightly wrong. He talked about the writer J. P. Salinger instead of J. D. Salinger and near the end of the date we even had a little spat about the feeding habits of hummingbirds. Arthur lived in San Diego and so it was natural that we would discuss living in California. Arthur disparaged California and I might have joined him if he had acknowledged even one good thing about the place. By this time I had given up on Arthur and I mentioned that one of the things that I love about California is the hummingbirds. I figured I might as well bore him too.

He reacted unenthusiastically to the subject of hummingbirds, as if he had never even noticed one. But hummingbirds gave Arthur a whole new area of inexactitude to trumpet. Sounding like a bored professor, he said, "Hummingbirds live entirely on nectar."

I replied, "No. They eat insects too."

Arthur huffed. "I don't think so. I believe they get enough protein from the nectar."

I became sarcastic. "Arthur, I'm glad you don't teach natural history. Flower nectar's all sugar. Even kids who live on chocolate need to eat a burger every now and then." On that discordant note, Arthur and I quickly finished our coffees and got out of there.

When we first met I had told myself, if it doesn't work out maybe Arthur and I can be friends. It's the falsely optimistic hope that I use to comfort myself, almost as if friendship is the booby prize for a bad date. I had forgotten that in a friendship there has be some connection or attraction even if it's a nonsexual one. Arthur and I had spent an hour talking but we actually had nothing to say to each other. On our date two strangers had met and by the end of their encounter had felt even more removed from each other than they had been before they introduced themselves.

Lake Tahoe, California and Nevada

I've decided that Lake Tahoe is the best example of the American tendency to divide the world into good and bad since it's clearly marked by the State Line. The California side of Lake Tahoe is a touristy Bedford Falls with cozy 1950s-style motels with names like the Sit-a-Spell Motor

Lodge. But as soon as you cross the State Line, which is the name of an actual street dividing the two Tahoes, the Nevada side becomes a Bedford Falls gone bad. A Pottersville where ugly garish casinos with names like Dollar Bill's have flashing neon signs to alert the woozy, who are trying to save up for rehab, that no drink in the place costs more than a buck.

I was in Lake Tahoe to do stand-up for the Winterfest, a gay ski week. In two years this was the third gay ski week at which I'd performed. I'd done shows at Aspen's gay ski week and Whistler's gay ski week in British Columbia, and if I had known ahead of time that I was going to become the comedian of the slopes, I might have learned to ski. At first I had been worried that not skiing at a ski resort might be a social liability. But I soon discovered that if I dressed as a skier I would be treated as one. Sportswear allows everyone to become an athlete impersonator.

I wasn't in Lake Tahoe to ski but I was going to try to get a skier in my bed. I had decided that this week I was ready. On this trip I wasn't looking for a potential boyfriend or a long-term relationship, which made me think that since I wasn't looking for commitment, I would receive three proposals of marriage from guys who wanted to wait to have sex on our honeymoon.

I had been going to the gym for months and I was now ready to reveal the results of all my hard work. Going to the gym four times a week is like practicing the piano. After all that hard work, at some point you want to show yourself off by giving a recital. Putting myself on display was risky but I was hoping for the same reaction that people give at a piano recital by a twelve-year-old:

"To tell the truth, I didn't expect much, but he was better than I thought."

"Yes, he's really coming along."

"He still needs to work on a few things."

"I know. Some of the chords are still chunky. Especially in the midsection."

"Oh, I could overlook that. He's got to be almost forty."

"You're right. And it takes a lot of nerve to do what he's doing at his age."

In preparation for my recital, I had bought a tight-fitting black shirt at a store in West Hollywood. The shirt was made out of a stretchy material that would cling to me in the same manner that I wanted a man to, but I wished that it had come with a set of directions on how to wear it. I tried tucking it in normally but it pulled up in back and bloused out. Then I tried tucking it into my underwear but the underwear crept up, showing the waistband, letting everyone know that I had tucked my shirt into my underwear. What was I supposed to do? Tuck the shirt into my ass? If I was more of a handyman I would have thought of using duct tape. I finally tucked the shirt into my underwear and then just yanked the underwear lower. I checked myself in the mirror and then shrugged.

I was in the position of being able to introduce myself in one night to the four hundred men attending the ski week by performing for them. No wonder so many gay men are attracted to theater. It's the quickest way to introduce yourself to large groups of potential boyfriends. After an hour of me talking about myself, my audience would have the same reaction you do when someone corners you at a party. They would either like me and be enthralled or they would have had more than enough of me and vamoose.

Okay, I had a great show. Everyone laughed really hard at my jokes and no one laughed at my shirt, which stayed tucked in, and afterward I felt elated and looked forward to going out on a manhunt. Unfortunately, right after the show everyone returned to their rooms and went to bed. Without me. To my surprise, skiers, even gay skiers, go to ski areas to ski. They ski all day, go out to dinner, discover that they're exhausted, and go to bed early in order to ski all the next day. The skiers at Winterfest were mostly upper-middle-class-to-wealthy men and they maximized their recreational time with the same efficiency they show in their jobs. The gay skiers partied for one scheduled hour each day. And if you missed that hour you were out of luck. I was disappointed that everyone went to bed, but since the show had gone well, I didn't really care. Tomorrow would be my last opportunity to meet someone.

The next day was Saturday and it was going to be the last night of the gay ski week. If the gay skiers were going to party it would be tonight. I made plans to go to a cocktail party, a dinner, a dance, and later, the one gay bar in Lake Tahoe.

At the cocktail party, I met Kurt a few minutes after I had walked in the door. Kurt was about a foot shorter than me, with blond hair and a very handsome face. If he showed his smile in a toothpaste commercial, they would have to artificially tone down his teeth to make them look a more believable shade of white. He introduced himself and, having seen the show, was very complimentary about my performance. He was flirting with me.

While that thought raced around my head yelling

"Yee-ha!" I looked at Kurt more closely. He had on a thick blue ski sweater and baggy blue jeans that appeared to be completely filled out by his huge thighs. I was stunned by his obvious interest because the evening had started only thirty minutes before and to have found a man interested in me this quickly was beyond my range of experience. Even in my wildest sexual fantasies I have to talk to the guy for several hours and win him over before anything happens. By the way, I have to remember to find out what the astrological alignment of the stars was that weekend, because the next time it occurs, I'm buying a lottery ticket.

Kurt told me that he lived in the Bay Area and I noted with approval that he worked in the computer industry writing software. I always think that anyone who does something technical that I know nothing about has to be smart, when in reality all I've really learned is how ignorant I am. During a pause in our conversation Kurt declared, "It's a little hot in here." He reached down and pulled off his sweater. As he did, it became entangled with my line of vision and yanked my eyes out of my head. Underneath the sweater Kurt wore a body-hugging black-and-gray surfer's shirt that revealed a torso that got my attention as quickly as a kick in the balls. And in this instance it felt great. Suffice to say, buff-a-teria! Kurt had brains *and* brawn.

Feeling light-headed, I asked Kurt, "How often do you come up here to ski?"

He answered, "I come up here almost every weekend during the winter."

I said, "You must be a very good skier."

There was a moment's hesitation, more for politeness' sake. He didn't want to sound conceited. "Yeah, I am," he admitted as his cheeks flushed slightly.

I thought, *That's sexy*. I couldn't tell if the cause of my frisson of pleasure was the realization that such a jock liked me or if it was from meeting someone who was unabashedly competent at something. I've reached a point in my life where the ability to do anything well is a big turn-on. Well, almost. I can't see getting too turned on by an accountant saying, "Tell me your income, and in my head, I can figure out what you owe to the state of California to the nearest penny." I would be impressed but it wouldn't make me start panting with desire.

Kurt and I spent the entire night together. We went to the dinner and sat next to each other. We danced. We even went to the local gay bar and had a drink. There, Kurt announced an ability to read palms and offered to read mine. This was fine. I didn't want him to be too good to be true, and having a wacky belief in palmistry was not the worst flaw someone could have. I could accept his palm reading as long as he didn't start to wear a turban. I found it interesting that someone who worked in the computer industry also believed in reading palms, as if rather than making us more dryly rational, our technological advances were making the supernatural more available to human understanding. Kurt will probably develop software that allows you put your hand on the computer screen and the machine predicts your future.

We walked out into the hall, where there was more light, and Kurt took my right hand and examined it closely. As soon as he did this, I realized that it was merely a ruse to hold my hand in the socially acceptable fortune-telling manner. I couldn't believe that it hadn't occurred to me before. I was willing to play along but at this moment the only future that concerned me was the next few hours. Peering at my hand, Kurt pointed to a short line on my palm—I think it was a paper-cut scar—

and tracing it with his finger, he said this line meant that I was creative . . . I sort of knew that and so did he. A fortune-teller could attribute creativity to any gay man and he would think, *Yes! He's good.* The lack of major calluses on my hand and the fingernails bitten to the quick were a dead giveaway that I knew how to avoid manual labor and spent long hours imagining all sorts of bugbears and chimeras. Frankly he could have told me that I was destined to become a sheepherder and I would instantly have begun to wonder how many border collies I would need. While I liked having my hand held, Kurt could have easily skipped the mumbo jumbo by taking one look at my face and reading my mind. I would have been impressed when he stated the obvious: "You want me."

When we decided to leave the bar, Kurt talked a snowboarder dude into giving us a ride in his pickup truck. After being dropped off, we began to walk toward the condos and I wasn't sure what was going to happen next. Earlier in the evening Kurt had mentioned that he didn't like sleeping with guys on the first date. As a rule I didn't either, but I had deliberately planned on ditching that rule this week.

It was a bitterly cold night, and while I spoke calmly with Kurt about when he was leaving the next day, the little puffs of steam escaping from my mouth seemed to embarrassingly betray how I felt on the inside.

As we walked I thought, *He's probably going to go back to his room. I think we passed his room. No, he's coming back with me to my room. We're inside my building. He's coming to my room. I'm unlocking the door. He's coming inside.* Because I'm nervous, before I turn around, I try to light the gas fireplace. I can't get it to ignite. Kurt bent down and pressed the little switch, holding it longer than I did, and the gas jet whooshed into flames.

We took off our coats and faced each other. Big smiles. We kissed awkwardly because of the difference in our heights, but I made a little adjustment, bending, making it easier for us get a better seal on our liplock. This didn't even fluster me for a second. He was a great kisser. Then he took off his clothes. With his shirt and pants off he looked like a pumped-up gay action figure, Ski-Man, and I couldn't wait to test his kung fu grip.

Since I'm not writing this book under my porn-writing pseudonym, Bob Smith, if you need to imagine what happened next, I'll allow this much: in bed I enjoy staying at a reasonable point between vanilla sex and more hard-core activities. Going to either extreme is not for me. I find the fetish of a bed covered with sickeningly cute stuffed animals almost as repulsive as bestiality. Suffice to say, sex with Kurt was better than what I imagined, let alone what you can imagine.

Kurt stayed the night. Afterward, we both immediately fell asleep, but around three in the morning, I woke up with a painful charley horse in my right leg. For the rest of the night I had shooting pains in my legs and hips and I couldn't get comfortable again. It was almost as if I had released the tension from one part of my body by transferring it to another. As I lay awake I remembered that when I had first started dating Tom I had trouble sleeping through the night with him too. At times he would cuddle up with me but I couldn't fall asleep with his arms entwined around me. When I told Tom about this it became a source of misunderstanding, and to my regret, we sometimes fought about it.

We often refer to any sexual encounter as "sleeping with someone" but the two are very different experiences. Intimacy isn't just about being able to have sex with another man; for me one of the most challenging parts of being in bed with a man is being able to fall asleep with him. Then, the really interesting part begins. Once I learn how to sleep with another guy how do I keep the relationship from nodding off?

I have a new strategy for my next relationship. Every day I'm going to pretend that my boyfriend has taken an accidental overdose of sleeping pills. And I'm going to tell myself that, at all costs, I have to keep him alert or else I'm going to lose him.

Turtle Bay Resort, Costa Rica

My last morning in Costa Rica, I was sitting by the pool drinking iced tea and reading *The Diaries of Dawn Powell* when a man walked by wearing two nipple rings and a ring though his navel. Suddenly I realized that my knight in shining armor should be able to take off his chrome at the end of the day. Then it dawned on me. *That's my type.* Yes, of course I want a guy to be attractive, but most of all I want someone who would think my joke about the knight was funny, or better yet, someone who would make me laugh by making such a comment to me first.

I removed my dog tags this morning. I don't want to feel as if I am always fighting the Battle Between the Sex and that every other gay man is the enemy. I know that there really are enemies out there, but statistically I think only a few truly evil queens are allotted for each generation. I'm talking about evil queens on the scale of Roy Cohn or J. Edgar Hoover. I prefer to imagine that in all the sexual wars, everyone is a potential ally.

Yesterday I woke up early and took a walk on the rainforest trail of the resort and I heard a bird calling *tsk-tsk, tsk-tsk* repeatedly. There were many different birds calling that morning but this particular bird stood out because it sounded so familiar to me. *Am I that one note?* I wondered. *He sounds like he disapproves of everything.* But the more I listened, I began to realize that despite his carping tone, he wasn't really judging the forest. In fact, I'd bet that he's probably pretty happy.

Acknowledgments

I want to thank my family for their unwavering support over the years, even when they wondered if I had gone too far: my brothers, Jim and Greg, my sister, Carol, and, my brother-in-law, Mark.

My friends have been instrumental in helping me complete this book. I want to thank Jaffe Cohen, David Koch, and especially Elvira Kurt and Jason Ross for their invaluable and astute suggestions. I also want to thank Suzy Berger, Richard Kramer, and William Lucas Walker for their advice and encouragement. Glenn Rosenblum became my technical expert in all matters theatrical and always had the answer or knew where to find it. I also want to thank Larry Hymes, Judy Gold, Mark Davis, Sharon Callahan, and Tom Lasley.

My managers, Bob Read and Ross Mark, and my agent, Jim Stein, were, as usual, always supportive and indispensable. I want to thank my publisher and editor, Rob Weisbach, to whom I am grateful for three things: his friendship, critical insight, and incredible patience.

Finally, the most important thank-you goes to my mother.

About the Type

This book was set in Walbaum, which takes its name from the original designer, Justus Erich Walbaum, who engraved and cast the first Walbaum typeface circa 1804. Type historians have called Walbaum one of the most important vehicles of typographic expression in the German language during the nineteenth century. It was very popular for setting poetry. Walbaum is a modern typeface with high contrast between thick and thin strokes and is effective for body text and headlines in books and journals.

WE THINK THE WORLD OF YOU
BOOKSTORE